To Rich
The wise man read it twice
God Bless
John Kotselas

Socrates
In New York

by John Kotselas

Athena Publishing
2340 University Avenue
San Diego, California 92104
Toll Free: 1-888-473-3503

On the Internet:
Email: kotselas@athena-publishing.com

First Printing March 1998

© Copyright 1997 John Kotselas. All Rights Reserved.
No part of this publication may be reproduced in any
form or by any means without the prior written
consent of the copyright owner and publisher.

Library of Congress Catalog Number 97-78173
ISBN 0-9662316-9-4
Printed in the United States of America

To my wife Donna

No quantity nor quality of words will suffice. They all pale in comparison to your virtue. Nothing would have been possible without you.

Contents

Acknowledgments vii

Preface ix

Chapter 1
Wake Up New York! 1

Chapter 2
The Artificial Artist 21

Chapter 3
The Two Horses 43

Chapter 4
Justice 65

Chapter 5
Freedom 87

Chapter 6
Illusion 121

Chapter 7
Love 145

Chapter 8
The Veil 169

Chapter 9
The Modern Philosopher 195

Chapter 10
Divine Love 209

Chapter 11
Divine Justice 231

Chapter 12
The Natural Artist 253

Notes 291

Acknowledgments

Although it is primarily the ideas or writings of Socrates, Plato, and Aristotle that are responsible for producing this book, I am grateful and indebted to the following people for making it possible: my philosophy professors, in particular Dr. Casey and Dr. Sweeney, whose rhetorical questions and ideas are occasionally used in this book; professor of astrophysics, Dr. Scapattichi, for spending many days listening to the first eight chapters, while the manuscript was in its infancy; Dr. Issa Khalil, professor of theology, for his support and friendship.

For the physical production of this book, typesetting and production assistance, Mr. Donald Rasky; cover illustrator, Kathryn Gates; the editorial group: editors Scott Palmer; Glenda Palmer; assistant editor Lynnete Heitman; proofreaders Thomas Kirby and Eric McClure. I am indebted to my wife Donna for taking over our restaurant business these last five years while I finished my graduate studies and spent most of my time writing both of my books; and my mother Evlabia for filling in during times of need and distress.

In this book, Socrates dialogues with three New Yorkers: a physicist, a professor of philosophy, and a theologian. By sheer coincidence, the three characters painted on the cover of this book speaking with Socrates, are my friends: Don Fredericks, who is a physicist, Jim TerBest who is a professor of philosophy, and myself, masters in theology. I would like to thank both Mr. Fredericks and Mr. TerBest for allowing me use of their likenesses on the cover. I would also like to thank Chris Gobich for allowing me to use his striking resemblance to Socrates.

In particular, I would like to thank the philosophical group who met regularly at the Olympic Cafe, "The Foot of the Acropolis." Many of you, consisting of both men and women, young and old, scholars and lay people, atheists and theists, remained past 1 or 2 A.M., long after the restaurant would close at 10 P.M. Our long, and many times heated debates are partly responsible for producing this book. Thank you all.

Preface

It is a timeless statement and universal testimony, that "Life is a mystery." The average person spends somewhere between sixty to eighty years curiously living within life's mystical borders of birth and death. Others die prematurely, as young children, intensifying the riddle. Within life's mysterious existence appear the philosophers, the sages, who commit their life to unraveling the puzzle of life. The fact that humankind is able to ponder its own existence, to ask philosophical questions, elevates and separates us from the animal kingdom. The fact that philosophers exercise this ability elevates them from the rest of humanity.

It has been stated that philosophy is the mother of all science. Unfortunately, modern scientific discoveries and technological advances have not offered answers to most of life's dilemmas. For the most part, science has failed both in asking the questions and in continuing the quest. Thus, we must look to the ancient sages such as Socrates. If one believes that the teachings of Socrates are not applicable to life today, it only reveals the possibility that such individuals have yet to ponder the issues. They have failed to identify that the teachings of Socrates, ancient as they may be, are still being taught in our colleges and universities throughout, even in these modern times. This book will not only attempt to introduce the modern reader to some of life's timeless questions, but possibly offer conclusive answers.

It should be noted that Socrates did not write anything, but his pupil, Plato, wrote down the dialogues which

Socrates held with others. Thus, when one hears the term "Plato's philosophy" throughout this book, it more accurately describes the philosophy of Socrates.

For myself, it all started with a game; a mental exercise. Having been born in Greece, but living in America as a young boy, I would pretend to visit ancient Greece and hold dialogues with Socrates, his pupil Plato, and other Greek philosophers. I would teach these philosophers (who lived around 400 B.C.) about scientific discoveries and modern 20th-century technology. I would explain the operations of the internal combustion engine, the physical laws which enable an airplane to fly, the workings of electricity, etc. It has been stated that unless one is able to effectively explain something, one has not understood it themselves. By attempting to explain to the ancient philosophers modern scientific and technological advancements, I was able to better grasp these advancements myself.

Things began to change, however, when I attempted to understand the environment that produced the thinking of Socrates, Plato, and Aristotle, in their ancient surroundings. Instead of teaching them modern-day discoveries, they began teaching me timeless and universal issues. Instead of transporting modern information to these people, I began to transport wisdom and insight from these philosophers to my modern-day friends. Both groups of friends, those with college degrees and those who lacked a formal education, found it interesting and intellectually stimulating to hear what these ancients had to say.

So sophisticated was the thinking of these philosophers that *A History of Philosophy* describes Plato's philosophy as being "highly intellectualist, caviar for the multitude." It is the goal of this book to simplify, and offer Plato's philosophy, not as caviar, but bread for the masses. After all, at issue here is the most important concept of our reality; our own existence.

1

Wake Up New York!

Without philosophy, we would be little above the animals.

—Voltaire [1]

Newscaster: We now turn from our "Wake Up New York" studios to reporter Ron Jensen who is at the entrance steps of a downtown New York museum. Good morning, Ron.

Ron: Good morning to everyone at the studio. Good morning to all our viewers in New York. This is Ron Jensen. You must be wondering what I am doing in front of the museum here at eight thirty in the morning for today's "Wake Up New York" show. As our viewers of "Wake Up New York" remember, a few weeks ago we did a segment on what we perceived to be a beggar walking the streets of New York. He was dressed in sandals and a toga similar to the ones worn in ancient Rome and Greece. The people initially called him a beggar not because he was begging for food or money, but due to the fact that he was begging for answers. Well, as all New Yorkers know now, for the last three days this individual has entered the museum and stayed there from the time it opened until closing time. This man is more than a city-wide curiosity. For some, he is an obsession.

We were informed that he will be coming again this morning by invitation of the curator of the museum. Since we were unable to interview this answer-seeking beggar on our last segment, we are hoping to conduct an interview with him prior to his entering the museum this morning. His name, according to our sources, is Socrates. We will now return to our studios for the rest of this morning's news and traffic update. But we will stay here to keep you posted. For 'Wake Up New York,' this is Ron Jensen.

Professor: Pardon me, could you please move the cameras. They are blocking the door and we need to enter the museum.

Ron: Excuse me, sir, we are with the morning television show 'Wake Up New York.' My name is Ron Jensen. I believe the museum is closed. It opens at nine and it is now a little after eight thirty.

Professor: Yes, we are aware that it is closed. But my friend the Curator has invited me to meet him prior to the opening of the museum. He tells me he has a special guest to introduce to me.

Ron: Socrates?

Professor: That is what he calls himself.

Ron: We are hoping to interview this man. What do you know about him?

Professor: Only what I saw on T.V. Everyone in New York seems to have heard of him. Two of my philosophy students heard him speak at the museum yesterday and have informed me of this man. They say he talks about ancient Athens and Greece as if he lived there. Both students were astounded by this man's wisdom, and in their own words were "embarrassed" to call themselves 'students of philosophy.'

Ron: You teach philosophy, I take it?

Professor: I teach philosophy at the university.

Ron: And your two friends accompanying you?

Professor: To my left is Dr. Lattison, who is a professor of mathematics and physics at the university. My name is Thomas. To my right is my neighbor, Philo.

Ron: My pleasure, gentlemen. Your friend, the distinguished scientist Dr. Lattison, has held interviews in our studios on many previous occasions. Now concerning this man Socrates, professor Thomas, what else do you know about him?

Professor: Socrates the ancient philosopher, or the man visiting the museum?

Ron: Both.

Professor: The only other thing I know concerning the man in the museum is the impact he has been having upon people. As it was reported in the news last night, two police officers went to remove him from the museum the first day he appeared there, only to meet with great protest by the people in the museum toward the police officers. After Socrates spent a few hours in discussion with the officers, one of them, who was regarded as one of the best officers in the department, quit his job. The other officer returned to the department and confessed to his superiors that for the last five years he has been taking bribes.

Ron: Our reporters have attempted to interview these officers but both officers have declined. What can you tell us about the ancient philosopher Socrates?

Professor: He lived between 400 and 500 B.C. His physical stamina equaled his mental vigor. When he was a soldier, he walked barefoot in the freezing mountain snow, indifferent to the cold, while other soldiers were bundled up and huddled around the fire. But he was able to challenge people's beliefs to arrive at truth and motivate them intellectually. He sought justice and equality for all, including such issues as women's rights, of which he was an early champion. In fact, T. Z. Lavine, a contemporary author, describes the positions of Plato and Socrates on sexual equality as follows:

Plato stands out in the history of Western philosophy as the first supporter (along with Socrates) of the intellectual equality of the sexes. Book V of the Republic has been hailed by the contemporary women's movement for its defense of the equality of the sexes. [2]

Simply by asking questions he forced people to look deep within to know the self before they attempt to know anything else. If one does not know the self, of course, how can one know anything? Today's system of education and process of teaching would be perceived by Socrates as similar to filling a vessel with information. One only knows what one is taught. On the contrary, he believed that the truth was within each person and Socrates attempted by rhetorical questions to draw it out of them. He believed that reason was within each person and by reason one would arrive at truth. But he would usually draw out people's ignorance, biases, and prejudices.

Ron: But does his philosophy really concern humanity today?

Professor: Well, would a doctor treat a patient from the directions of a hundred-year-old medical book?

Ron: I should hope not.

Professor: Neither would a chemistry or biology professor teach from *a 50-year-old* book?

Ron: Undoubtedly.

Professor: Books for technicians, such as books for structural engineers, have become outdated in only twenty years as one can witness twenty-year-old bridges being retrofitted to become earthquake-resistant. Books on computer engineering become obsolete within a few years. But, contrary to these other studies which belong to technicians, the refinement of the mind which is the wisdom of philosophers takes time, and experience, as fine wine is aged. This is why Socrates and Aristotle in ancient Greece demanded at least forty years of life's experience and cultivation of the mind to be a requirement in order to illuminate the one that will strive to become a seasoned philosopher. In the last 2,400 years, since the days of Socrates, the timeless questions of philosophy have remained the same and are still valid. This is why these ancient books on philosophy are not outdated but alive, vibrant and still being read, even today.

Ron: But what could this man who lived 2,400 years ago teach us today? In particular, what will a modern day journalist, such as myself, achieve by walking into the museum later today and having a discussion with this man?

Professor: Let's suppose you did talk to him and he asked you "Tell me what it is that you know?" Socrates teaches that philosophy is in pursuit of knowledge that is absolute, true, and unchanging, and not mere beliefs and opinions.

Ron: Certainly I could share some knowledge that I have acquired during my life.

Professor: Such as two-plus-two equals four?

Ron: Yes, we could start from there.

Professor: And how about your mother, you certainly do know that she is indeed your mother, is she not?

Ron: Of course.

Professor: But how do you know? Do you know that she is your mother directly as you know that two plus two equals four?

Ron: C'mon what sort of question is this?

Professor: Really, if Socrates asked you, how do you know that your mother is your mother? How will you answer him? Would you say by the fact that she treated you as a son? That her attitude toward you was similar to other mothers toward their children, because she called you "my boy?" Do you not see that you have no direct knowledge, but the only knowledge you really have is that you must rely on someone else's knowledge? In this case you are relying on your mother's direct knowledge that you are her son.

Ron: I have not been given any reason to believe otherwise.

Professor: Well, what if your mother informed you tomorrow that you were adopted? Then your knowledge that she was your mother will have been shattered and is wrong, which means that it was only an opinion all along. For this, indeed, has occurred to many adopted children, has it not? Discerning between knowledge and opinion, with verifiable results such as two plus two equals four, is the task of the philosophers.

Ron: But if philosophy takes us to such extremes to remove all opinions and beliefs in order to understand reality, then what are absolute knowledge and truth besides arithmetic?

Professor: Well, that is the study of philosophy. Many people today believe that philosophy is everyone's beliefs and opinions, while in fact philosophy is just the opposite. For philosophy is the inquiry and analysis of one's beliefs. Once someone's beliefs are challenged and proven wrong then that individual must modify those opinions to accept the truth as the evidence demands. But how many people desire to have their beliefs confronted? Everyone will go to their own Church, Temple, Mosque, Synagogue, or friends house, where the Pastor, Priest, Cleric, Guru, or friend will confirm their opinions and substantiate their belief system.

Philosophy does not pat people on the back or falsify people's beliefs pretending to be knowledge, but confronts, and dares to challenge them. One of the disciplines of philosophical studies is logic. Philosophers look for inconsistencies in formal and informal fallacies to validate or invalidate arguments. Similar to a math problem that is either true or false most people are unaware that philosophers are able to transform any statement or argument into an algebraic equation and uncover formal fallacies as one would with a math problem. For an argument to be valid it must pass the philosopher's scrutiny of formal and informal fallacies. Otherwise, it is invalid and a false argument.

Ron: How about the "Socratic Method" that we constantly hear about in the university that attorneys attempt to emulate. What exactly is it?

Professor: It was a method which Socrates invented. He would propose a question such as "what is freedom?" The respondent would state that he knows that freedom is such and such. Then Socrates, would begin his cross-examination by asking this individual questions concerning that which he proposed to know. Then Socrates solely by means of questions, would force the individual to identify and admit what he really did not know. Usually Socrates would expose prejudices, biases, opinions, ignorance, and lack of knowledge of which his opponent was unaware. Hence his opponent did not know that he did not know, but only thought that he knew.

Ron: And how will you avoid such an intellectual trap?

Professor: Primarily because I agree with Socrates concerning the ignorance of humanity. Where we disagree is that Socrates believes in God and in a human soul, but I myself am skeptical concerning both of these beliefs. Other than that we generally agree on most issues. But I am concerned for my scientist friend, Dr. Lattison, for he is looking forward to trapping Socrates using his scientific knowledge.

Ron: Do you really believe the questions of Socrates who lived 2,400 years ago will, indeed, reveal much ignorance in a modern person?

Professor: Suppose you were to enter the museum and Socrates asked you, "Do you agree that freedom is the opposite of bondage and force?" How would you reply?

Ron: I would say, "Yes, bondage is the opposite of freedom."

Professor: Then he would ask, "What is freedom, and how do you know you are free?"

Ron: I would respond that I am free to choose as I please, free to vote my conscience for a leader, free to change jobs if I decide, etc. Being free to choose is the opposite of having something imposed upon you without a choice.

Professor: And if Socrates asked you, "Were you given a choice and the freedom to choose to be here alive on planet earth? Is there any person alive upon this planet that was given the choice to be here?" How would you respond? Was it your preference, decision and freedom of choice to be here living upon this planet?

Ron: I am not aware that I was given a choice.

Professor: Then Socrates will state, "Since you had no choice, and no choice is the opposite of freedom, then you have been forced to be here, living on planet earth. What makes you so certain, then, that you are free to choose while you live when the evidence seems to indicate that you were not free to choose to live?"

Ron: Oh boy!

Professor: There was an eighteenth-century philosopher named Kierkegaard who modeled himself as a disciple of Socrates.

He states...

Listen to the cry of a woman in labor at the hour of giving birth. Look at the dying man's struggle at his last extremity–then tell me whether something that begins and ends thus could be intended for enjoyment.[3]

So how would you answer Socrates if he asks you, why? Why does humanity naturally desire pleasure and oppose pain, while the nature of life reveals the opposite, which is to begin and end in pain. Why is it that nature has reserved most of its destructive diseases and ailments for the elderly?

Ron: But why such pessimism? Why not look at the positive side? Look at a mother caressing the child and the love that the mother shares with her newborn baby.

Professor: Philosophers must look at everything possible and obtain knowledge from the positive as well as negative; the good on an equal basis to the bad, pain as well as pleasure. But since Kierkegaard desired to look at the negative, must we not also look at the negative along with him and wonder why? Why is it that between painful birth and death some people turn to drugs and alcohol, while others become incarcerated? Is it to induce more pain between their birth and death, and prove Kierkegaard correct? Or is it to escape the pain which in turn multiplies the pain?

Ron: But when does philosophy become implemented, pragmatic, and useful in our daily lives? Or are we to assume that philosophers simply recline and contemplate a theoretical and indifferent world?

Professor: It will surprise you to know that the spirit of Greek philosophy is still alive and abides within us in our modern civilizations, including the United States. As you probably know, Socrates did not write anything for he claimed to know nothing, since he only asked questions. His pupil, Plato, wrote down most of the debates that Socrates held. Plato's pupil was Aristotle and Aristotelian ethics have even been recommended for implementation in our school systems today by William Bennett, former Secretary of Education.[4] Other prominent persons of our age have also either borrowed heavily from Socratic and Platonic ideology or recommended it to the masses. Freud, the famous psychiatrist, borrowed much from Socrates and Plato, including the idea of the id, ego, and super ego of the psyche.[5] Dr. Martin Luther King writing in his "Letter from Birmingham City Jail" also suggests that we need to become like Socrates.

King says...

Just as Socrates felt that it was necessary to create a tension in the mind so that individuals could rise from the bondage of myths and half-truths to the unfettered realm of creative analysis and objective appraisal, we must see the need of having nonviolent gadflies to create the kind of tension in society that will help men rise from the dark depths of prejudice and racism to the majestic heights of understanding and brotherhood.[6]

The Stoic philosophers originated in Greece around 300 B.C., about 100 years after the death of Socrates. They gave directions on how to liberate the mind even during the worst physical turmoil. They held Socrates as their honored hero. The stoic philosopher Epictetus was a slave who wrote a book called *Enchiridion* that was deemed worthy to be carried to the battle field as the manual of the mighty Roman soldiers. One might ask what such an ancient book could offer a modern day person or even a modern day soldier? Which is precisely what a young soldier named James Stockdale asked himself after receiving Epictetus' book from Philip Rhinelander, a former dean of the School of Humanities and Sciences at Stanford. As it turns out, Stockdale spent eight years in bondage as a Vietnam prisoner of war. After he was released, he credited Epictetus and his 2,000-year-old stoic book to have comforted his state of mind, keeping him sane while in the bondage of solitary confinement.[7] This is the same James Stockdale that was a 1992 Vice Presidential candidate.

Ron: I didn't know that, and I doubt most Americans are aware of it.

Professor: Many modern people today like to impress others by flaunting their sophisticated tastes, with the belief that they are sophisticated people. But many fail to realize that even the word "sophisticated" itself comes from a group of philosophers in ancient Greece in 400 B.C. called the Sophists. Many of Plato's dialogues describe Socrates debating with this group of philosophers, who were known, not necessarily for their sophisticated tastes, but for their sophisticated intellect. How sophisticated are we today when we lack knowledge of the highest and most sophisticated of intellectual endeavors to which the human mind has ever aspired and which are known to have come out of ancient Greece?

It was the pursuit of reason and knowledge by the Greeks that developed into the scientific innovations and understanding which we possess today. Science, art, democracy, theater, medicine, philosophy, logic, among other branches of study, are owed to the refined and sophisticated minds of these ancient people. Socratic philosophy and its vibrant teachings which we call Platonic philosophy continues to surround us and permeate our thoughts today. Socrates' philosophy is not only for the college professor and Washington diplomat, but can also be seen in our art, literature, even our television shows.

Ron: Television shows?

Professor: Indeed! Socrates stated that humans are composed of body and soul. He described the allegory of a dualistic existence concerning two horses pulling a chariot, which Freud borrowed and utilized in his psychiatry. The erratic horse on the left pulling the chariot, according to Socrates, symbolized the body revealing passions and physical desires. The steady horse on the right pulling the chariot symbolized reason that listens to the charioteer, which is identified as the soul. Reason should guide the chariot of life and not the bodily passions identified as the left horse.

Ron: But how does Socrates' dualistic allegory correspond to today's television shows?

Professor: Gene Rodenberry, creator of the television series "Star Trek," admitted, after being pressed by a professor of philosophy at the university of Nebraska, that Rodenberry did indeed utilize this Socratic philosophy for his "Star Trek" series. The character Spock was the rational one relying on reason alone and lacking emotions and passions. He was the horse on the right.

McCoy losing himself in his passions and emotions lacking reason is identified as the left horse representing the passion of the senses. While captain Kirk was the charioteer, the soul of the spaceship, that kept both reason and passion in balance and thus kept the Starship Enterprise upon a straight course. Many times when Captain Kirk was absent the reasoning of Spock and passions of McCoy would battle and bicker with each other as many of us battle daily between our bodily passions and reasonable thoughts.

Ron: But was it not the case that it was not the ideas of Socrates that propelled him to fame, but his death?

Professor: It was both. Contrary to modern philosophers who write one thing yet live in opposition to what they believe and write, Socrates preached, practiced, lived and died for his convictions.

Ron: But if he claimed to know nothing, how then did he arrive at such powerful convictions?

Professor: The oracle of Delphi in a religious ceremony had announced that Socrates was the wisest man in Athens. Most Athenians had accepted that he was 'the wisest' indeed. The cynic philosopher, Antisthenis, has been said to have walked five miles every day to hear Socrates speak. But Socrates did not accept the fact that he was the wisest, as was commonly accepted, for he really believed that he knew nothing. "I went to the politician," Socrates states, "but found out that he pretended to know, but in reality did not know, and also was unaware that he was unaware of what he did not know." Likewise he went to the artist, poet, etc. These were men who studied nature, knowledge and reality and "They all thought they knew, but in reality they did not know; and what is worse did not know that they did not know." Then Socrates responded that "I know that I do not know, and since I know that I do not know then I must be the wisest by knowing the truth of my ignorance."

Ron: He must have upset people by revealing their ignorance.

Professor: On a daily basis. Many ancient Greeks that were not philosophers held the mythological gods as truth. Consequently Socrates challenged their beliefs for he perceived the nature and characters of the mythological gods as deviating, changing form, matter, and opinions, behaving unjustly, and even lying, which must be contrary to the nature and behavior of the true God. According to Socrates, if there is any real knowledge, only the divine is real, unchanging, and true.

This is contrary to human knowledge, which for the most part is ignorance, opinions, and beliefs, and is prone to change and continuous modification. His wisdom upset the Athenians so much that they charged Socrates with impiety and corrupting the minds of the youth. His penalty was death. However, they offered him release from prison and relief from condemnation of death by paying a small financial penalty to save his life, but he refused, since he was not guilty of anything. The Athenians did not want to make a martyr out of him. He had already uprooted the foundations of Athens. Making him a martyr would defeat the Athenian cause against him. The Athenians, therefore, had practically left the door open for him to escape from prison, tempting him to compromise his principles. They had even imprisoned him during the highest of holy months, thus allowing Socrates more than a month to contemplate his escape.

As Plato writes, his pupils pleaded with him to leave and go to a Greek island and continue to live in peace. But Socrates believed that every human by nature has a moral obligation which is to behave justly. He therefore preferred to drink the poison with which the state judged him, instead of breaking the laws of the state by escaping.

For he believed that each individual has a binding contract to abide by the laws of the state, and every individual is naturally obligated to fulfill this task. He also believed that God is just and that everyone is cast in the image of God and should behave justly. Justice was to die. Injustice was to escape.

Ron: Since Socrates took the poison and died, who is this man walking around New York calling himself Socrates? You do not really believe this is Socrates reincarnated, do you? Do you believe in reincarnation?

Professor: No, I do not, and neither does my colleague here, Dr. Lattison. Even my neighbor, Philo, who I think is somewhat religious, rejects reincarnation.

Ron: Then who is this man Socrates?

Professor: The only thing I know is what I saw on the television news, and the information I received from two of my philosophy students.

Ron: I notice that Dr. Lattison and your neighbor, Philo, each carry books with them into the museum.

Professor: Yes. Dr. Lattison is most interested in finding out who this man is, and how he has turned New York upside down these last few months, and especially, these last three days. He is carrying a couple of books on Plato's dialogues, which describe the debates of Socrates. He received a crash course in Platonic philosophy last night with me, in preparation for our meeting with this man today. My neighbor, Philo, is an author and carries his own book which was recently published.

Ron: May I ask what Philo is writing about?

Professor: I am not sure. Although we are neighbors, this is the first time we have been out together. I know he's been working on his book for seven years. It's about ancient Greek mythology, focusing on all of the virgin born sons of god and resurrected saviors that predate Christianity.

Ron: Virgin-born resurrected saviors predating Christianity? I thought Christ held title to this claim.

Professor: That is what most people think, but history and archaeology have revealed dozens of mythological religious saviors predating Christ. Joseph Campbell is one of many scholars who has written extensively on this subject. Philo grew up in Greece and believes if this is indeed Socrates, then Socrates will be able to identify with Philo's book. After all, his book describes many mythological saviors. Socrates rejected these figures which were objects of worship in ancient Greece. Now you must excuse me. The museum opens in five minutes and we would like to be first to meet this man and avoid the lines and confusion.

Ron: Socrates is inside already?

Professor: He is like a magnet that attracts the intellect. In ancient Greece as I stated, some pupils walked five miles a day to hear Socrates speak. The museum's curator has had Socrates to himself by inviting him to come in at seven o'clock this morning.

Ron: Then as an interviewer who thrives upon asking questions, allow me one last question. For I would like to know if you, a modern day philosopher, could ask one, and only one, question of this ancient man Socrates; what would that question be?

Professor: Well, I have not given any particular question special thought. But it might be concerning his last words which he stated as he was dying.

Ron: We have knowledge of his last words, and details of his death?

Professor: Plato wrote many books including the *Apology* which describes the trial of Socrates and another book called *Phaedo* which reveals Socrates' last hours.

Ron: Then it seems that friends of his were present in prison?

Professor: Over a dozen were there during his death. They including his pupils Crito, Apolodorus, and Phaedo, for which the book was named. Here, allow me to borrow one of Dr. Lattison's books. It would be better if both Philo and Dr. Lattison were aware of the facts of Socrates' death prior to meeting this man. We pick up a few hours after Socrates had sent his wailing wife and three children away from the prison in order to philosophize up to the point of his noble death.

We begin to read as Plato writes in the dialogues . . .

Then raising the cup to his lips and showing not the least distaste, undisturbed and silent, he drank the hemlock. Most of us had, till then, been more or less able to restrain our sorrow, but when we saw him drinking and then that he had drunk it all, we could not hold our tears any longer. For myself, despite my efforts, I found that the tears were flowing down my cheeks; so I covered my face in my cloak and wept for my misfortune. Not for his misfortune but for my own, to think that I am parting with such a friend. Crito found himself unable to restrain his tears had gotten up and walked about as I followed. Apollodorus even before him had been weeping ceaselessly, and then he burst out crying aloud, and distressed us so much that he made everyone present break down, except Socrates himself. "What is this bizarre outcry, strange fellows?" Socrates said. "That was my main reason for sending the women away, in order that they might not misbehave in this way; I have heard it is better to die in silence. Please be quiet and be brave." When we heard his words we felt ashamed, and refrained our tears. Socrates walked about, until as he said his legs felt heavy and that they began to fail. Then he lay down on his back as the fellow who administered the hemlock directed him to; and after a while this man who had given the poison felt him. Examining his feet and his legs, and then when the man pressed his foot hard he asked if he felt it; and Socrates replied "No." After that the man did the same to his shins; and then, he showed us that he was cold and stiff. He continued to feel him, and said that when the poison reaches his heart, then he would be gone. The region among the groin was now becoming numb and rigid, then Socrates uttered his last words: "Crito we owe a cock to Asklepious; please pay it. Do not neglect it." "The debt shall be paid, Socrates," said Crito. "Is there anything else?" Socrates did not reply to this question, but after a minute or two he made a movement, and his eyes became fixed. Seeing this, Crito closed his eyes and lips. Such was the end of our friend; the best man of our time, in our opinion, that we had ever come to know, and in general the wisest, and the most just. [8]

Ron: Wow! A real heroic death! An unjust society condemned an innocent man for revealing their ignorance. But what is it about his last words that interests you as a philosopher?

Professor: Before he closed his eyes he stated that "We owe a cock to Asklepious."

Ron: Who is Asklepious?

Professor: If you look in your mythology books you will see that Asklepious was a mythological son of god, raised from the dead, virgin-born savior.[9] Why, I wonder did Socrates four hundred years before Christ, identify with this myth when he spent so much of his time rejecting the Greek myths?

Ron: But now I am beginning to wonder, how did the whole nation of Greece succumb to Christianity, since many mythological sons of god, virgin born, resurrected saviors, predated Christianity? Was it ignorance of the lay people or brilliance of the philosophers?

Professor: I'm afraid I do not know. Maybe Philo here with his many years of research and the fact that he was raised in Greece would be more qualified to answer this question. I see the curator is opening the door. You must excuse me.

Ron: Our *"Wake Up New York"* morning show is concluding in our studios right now at nine o'clock. Our producers will be upset that we missed Socrates once again. Maybe you would like to come to the studio of *"Wake Up New York"* tomorrow morning for an interview, concerning your discussions with Socrates?

Professor: We'll see.

It is one of the great paradoxes of history that the birth of "modern" philosophy should coincide with the death of its first practitioner . . . by the execution of his [Plato's] great teacher, Socrates, in 399 B.C. This tragic event marked the end of what is perhaps the most intense period of intellectual creativity the world has ever known.
—Erich Segal [10]

Indeed Plato emulated Socrates's maieutic method which incites the listener to independent thinking and therefore does not draw any conclusions, but leaves a sting. This is an excellent parody of the modern method of learning by rote, which brings out everything at once, the sooner the better, a method that does not arouse any independent mental activity, but only causes the student to repeat by rote.
—Soren Kierkegaard [11]

2

The Artificial Artist

Life on this earth is not only without rational significance, but also apparently unintentional. The cosmic laws seem to have been set going for some purpose quite unrelated to human existence. Man is thus a sort of accident by-product, as the sparks are an accidental by-product of the horseshoe a blacksmith fashions on his anvil. The sparks are far more brilliant than the horseshoe, but all the same they remain essentially meaningless.
—Bertrand Russell [1]

Socrates: I presume you are the professor of philosophy, a friend of the curator.

Dr. Lattison: No. My name is Lattison. I am a friend of professor Thomas, and this is Philo, neighbor of professor Thomas, whom I have had the privilege of meeting today for the first time. I teach mathematics and physics. I believe you are Socrates.

Socrates: So they call me. Tell me, I have been observing the object on this pedestal and cannot figure out what it is, or what purpose it has.

Dr. Lattison: What do you see?

Socrates: All that I see is a square piece of metal twisted and bent over a round metal tube!

Dr. Lattison: This is called modern art, Socrates. Unlike you ancient Greeks who carved human sentiment, tragedy, hope, love, and death in graceful art from inanimate stone, our modern art is very abstract. The art you ancients left us is still to be appreciated as exemplifying your ideal of rational thought and human endeavor which has left an incredible mark on civilization.

Socrates: And how, may I ask, is modern rationality communicated in this abstract modern art of yours?

Dr. Lattison: Science, Socrates. Our scientific discoveries have progressed far beyond our art as proof of our rational minds.

Socrates: Tell me, oh modern man, does not the modern day scientist hold the belief that all information entering our conscious mind comes through our sensual organs of sight, smell, touch, hearing, and taste? I mean, is it not your modern science which states that if you cannot experience it with the senses, you cannot know of its existence?

Dr. Lattison: True, our basis of knowledge has not changed since ancient days. Our five senses continue to figure strongly in our learning process. However, development in technology by modern science has so enhanced our senses that our knowledge has increased beyond your wildest imaginings! We can see better because our sight can be enhanced by technology which you ancients never had. We can also hear better by the use of modern radar and other radio devices. Our five senses that provide us with information have been enhanced by scientific advancements which allow us to examine a far star or galaxy via the telescope and examine the microcosmic bacteria through a microscope.

We therefore introduce more knowledge and information through the senses which allow us to possess more information than you ancient Greeks ever had. Ancient Greeks taught us for more than 2,000 years. It has been said that it took 2,000 years and by technological advancements due to modern science that we finally smashed the Greeks in the last 150 years.

Socrates: Correct me if I am wrong; you are saying that through science modern man is able to understand and comprehend the physical universe around us, and when something of material substance crosses our path, it is witnessed and understood by the senses due to technological advancements of modern science?

Dr. Lattison: Yes, that is correct.

Socrates: Then, it would seem that everything that possesses matter in our three-dimensional universe of length, width, and height has been studied and comprehended by modern science?

Dr. Lattison: Correct.

Socrates: Therefore everything that is matter in our three-dimensional universe, including the smallest atom, is divisible by modern science?

Dr. Lattison: Everything, Socrates. Even our smallest atom has been divided and studied.

Socrates: Even the air, which is invisible to the naked eye, but is experienced as the wind when running or riding a horse–has modern man through science divided this also?

Dr. Lattison: Yes, even the air itself, Socrates.

Socrates: Then modern science must have given names for everything, including the smallest atom?

Dr. Lattison: Everything, ancient philosopher; there is nothing left made of matter which has not been given a name.

Socrates: And God almighty? Was he found in your scientific endeavors?

Dr. Lattison: Not quite. The idea of God in the modern world is as abstract as our modern art. Everyone who wants to believe in God must reach beyond our world of matter and laws of physics. For those who want to believe, God exists beyond our world of understanding and its three dimensions. But do we not agree, Socrates, that all information comes through the five senses? The information of God is therefore missing; consequently science has yet to find anything which sounds, looks, tastes, feels or smells like God! If God existed in the physical world then science would have made such a discovery. Then scientifically all of us would agree that there is a God.

Since there is no such proof, then it follows that anyone who chooses to believe in God almighty must therefore go beyond the world of the known physical universe which is comprehended by all. Those who choose to believe in God must not only go beyond the physical universe but also enter the realm of the unknown, of the nonexistent. This is why there are so many different beliefs concerning God. All of these diverse religions can hardly agree on most issues concerning the divine, if there is such a being.

It is the five senses which all modern people still have in common. This is why we use the term "common sense." The fact is, that everyone who believes in God must reach beyond the world of common sense, or the five senses which we have in common. That everyone does not comprehend God through the five common senses reveals the fact that there is no common God for all.

Socrates: Therefore modern day scientists conclude that there is no God?

Dr. Lattison: Not exactly. What science proves is that there is matter in our universe, and since most of the religions claim God possesses no matter, how could he be known to anyone and unanimously agreed by everyone? "Nothing" equally possesses no matter, therefore "nothing" and "God" possess an equal amount of matter. God is not a tangible item, a physical being, in any particular place. He does not exist in our three-dimensional universe.

Imagine Socrates, that the same God who gave us our five senses with which we experience, explore, and understand the world in which he placed us, has left us ignorant of his existence by eluding our known world of the senses. A very contradictory statement, further verified by the many contradictory religions of our world.

Socrates: Most fascinating, modern man. It seems today's technology has developed modern science to an art. Tell me more concerning your discoveries as they relate to physical truths concerning the known universe.

Dr. Lattison: We have discovered 92 elements which are the basic building blocks of our universe. The atomic theory which you ancient Greeks postulated, has been verified and dissected. In fact, we have added a few of our own. There are seventeen man-made elements for a total of 109.

Socrates: What you are telling me is that the discoveries and calculations of science have in reality determined that the 92 elements form the building blocks of the entire universe?

Dr. Lattison: Yes.

Socrates: Therefore, if we take a rock to its smallest particle, to the atomic level, you modern chemists and physicist know precisely which of the 92 atoms the rock is made of?

Dr. Lattison: Correct, Socrates.

Socrates: And water? I suppose you have discovered the atomic composition of water?

Dr. Lattison: Two hydrogens, one oxygen.

Socrates: Then it seems that all physical things are made up of a combination of 92 elements. This includes air or water or rock on earth or any planet; literally everything in the composition of the universe, correct?

Dr. Lattison: Your understanding is correct.

Socrates: But I do wonder. These atoms that make up the physical universe which you scientists study, do they possess life or are they lifeless atoms?

Dr. Lattison: Atoms are all lifeless, Socrates. Gold, for example, is one of the 92 elements and is, as you know, lifeless. In fact, none of the other atoms or combination of atoms reveals any life. They are but lifeless matter.

Socrates: And my physical body? Surely modern science has divided the human body to the smallest atom since it possesses matter, does it not?

Dr. Lattison: It does, yes.

Socrates: Therefore, since all of the various and diverse atoms that make up my body are lifeless matter, I wonder, modern man, how do these lifeless atoms organize themselves and give me life? Which combination of lifeless atoms produces consciousness? By what right can I, possessing this body full of lifeless atoms, produce thought? In particular, the thought that I am conscious, and the thought that I am alive?

Dr. Lattison: Ah, there you have discerned the mystery which science with all its powers has yet to unravel! Even the science journal "Discovery," after interviewing experts in this field of consciousness and life, acknowledges "What is consciousness?"[2] and "How did life start?"[3] to be two of the "ten great unanswered questions of science."[4] We scientists suppose it is something in the brain which we still do not fully know.

Socrates: And of what does my brain consist? Has modern science not divided up the brain also?

Dr. Lattison: Physically it has. We found that the brain is made up of 500 billion neurons as an approximate figure. Anytime you move, your neurons behave similarly to an electrical circuit. They fire in sequence connecting one neuron to another which will cause you to move, walk, talk, etc. Different combinations of neurons firing in sequence will cause different movement in the body.

Socrates: Fascinating. Suppose I am standing in front of my clothes closet deciding whether to put on the dark coat which hangs on the right, or the light coat which hangs on the left. If I choose to wear the coat on the right, a circuit of neurons in sequence will trigger in order to move my right hand to the right side of the closet.

Dr. Lattison: That is correct.

Socrates: If, however, I choose the coat on the left side, then a different circuit of neurons will trigger in sequence which will make my left hand move to the left.

Dr. Lattison: Yes.

Socrates: If I have understood you correctly up to this point, all of the 500 billion neurons in my brain are composed of some unique combination of the 92 lifeless atoms.

Dr. Lattison: You are correct.

Socrates: There is one point on which I still desire to be enlightened by modern science. Primarily, while I was idly standing in front of my closet undecided as to which coat to wear, where was this decision made to reach to the left or to the right? Who decided whether neurons to the left or neurons to the right will trigger? In particular, what I would like to know is who triggered and made this conscious decision in my universe of thoughts, a lifeless atom, a group of lifeless atoms, a master neuron or an immaterial conscious being?

Dr. Lattison: I am afraid, Socrates, that science has not yet found an answer to this question.

Socrates: Allow me to continue, modern man. While I am sitting on my couch, thinking to myself, are modern scientists able to see my thoughts, or hear them? Can you feel, smell, or taste them through any of the five senses?

Dr. Lattison: No, we cannot.

Socrates: May I conclude that modern science does not know what thought is because thought does not possess matter in our known universe and thought has the ability to be undetected by the senses of the scientist?

Dr. Lattison: My fields of study are mathematics and physics, partly regarding the study of the 92 atoms. I can assure you we are not that advanced as yet to describe what thought is.

Socrates: Then tell me, if a man who has died due to the fact that his heart ceased to beat a couple of hours ago, if we bring him to your lab, do you possess the knowledge and technology to replace his heart?

Dr. Lattison: Yes as a matter of fact we do, however....

Socrates: Then he shall live again, will he not?

Dr. Lattison: No, no he will not.

Socrates: But you as a scientist find yourself with a human body, kidneys, brain, veins, all of the physical components present which a human needs to function. Certainly with such advanced technology a modern-day scientist can bring him to life can he not?

Dr. Lattison: He cannot.

Socrates: In that case could you please tell me exactly what it is that is missing from this lifeless person? What has been omitted from the body that was formerly there and alive within the body which is now gone? Certainly modern science and its sophisticated equipment can tell us what is missing can it not?

Dr. Lattison: Just because you describe that something has been omitted, it does not prove that something has been omitted for certain. Be it a soul or whatever you want to call it.

Socrates: But you do agree, modern man, that the substance of life force which is missing from the dead person is the substance which he was? And that same substance which he was when he was alive is the substance which you and I are at present, being alive. And that substance which he was is the substance which we do not know. Therefore, the substance of life which you and I are is unknown. Not even modern science knows the internal universe and substance of living humans. Without that substance of life of which we are and which is that which we do not know, the body disintegrates. Hence body cannot exist without that substance of life and that substance of life is the immaterial, immeasurable soul.

Dr. Lattison: These are questions which modern students of philosophy still wrestle with, Socrates, just as in your day. Thoughts, mind, metaphysics, my particular fields of physics and mathematics are limited in this area. We have recently established a science which attempts to look within the brain called cognitive science. But to what extent they can measure the mental process of the brain, I'm not sure.

Socrates: But my thoughts which belong only to me in my own subjective private universe cannot be divided, studied or observed in the objective and public universe by your modern equipment.

Dr. Lattison: They cannot.

Socrates: And since my thoughts cannot be divided and do not posses matter they cannot exist according to modern science?

Dr. Lattison: If you're implying that thoughts cannot be measured, divided, observed and studied by modern equipment, then you are correct.

Socrates: Although my thoughts cannot be studied and observed by your modern equipment, you as a scientist agree that I have thoughts?

Dr. Lattison: I agree, but the study of human thoughts in today's world is done by scholars of cognitive science, human behavior and psychology. I believe psychology was a branch of philosophy in ancient Greece, was it not?

Socrates: It was, but why bother with psychology, which looks at the individual and patterns of behavior, while neglecting the individuals connection with truth, reality, and the cosmos as a whole? You and I, as philosopher and scientist, should be able to measure some aspects of the internal landscape, the private universe, if you will, of the mind where thoughts originate.

Dr. Lattison: As I have already stated, we have no means of measuring and observing the thoughts of the mind even with the sophisticated equipment of modern science.

Socrates: I can hardly believe my ears! What you are telling me is that the mind of modern man, which has progressed to the level of observing, cataloguing, and calculating the known universe to the smallest atom is still incapable of measuring, or observing, or dissecting itself? The mind which does the studying cannot be studied, the mind which does the measuring cannot be measured, the mind which does the observing cannot be observed?

Dr. Lattison: A paradox, it is. Even when we operate on someone's brain, be it alive or dead, we cannot extricate their ideas, thoughts, or memory.

Socrates: So if the universe and substance of thoughts and ideas, possessing no observable matter, cannot be measured or studied, but do exist, how can you state with any conviction that the thoughts, substance, and mind of God do not exist? Can we not allow that the thoughts and mind of God exist if we cannot truly know the substance of mind and thoughts of mere human beings?

Dr. Lattison: We scientists need proof of substance that is measurable, visible, and divisible. Science is not guesswork.

Socrates: Since modern science is unable to examine the immaterial world of metaphysical ideas, could it not be that the essence of the mind can be measured, to a certain extent, by the philosopher?

Dr. Lattison: What exactly do you mean?

Socrates: Observe this statue here on my right, or the wrist watch on your arm, the shoe on your foot, the door, the lamp; what do they all have in common?

Dr. Lattison: They all possess matter. They have form and occupy space in our three-dimensional universe. They are all visible and divisible.

Socrates: I say that what they all have in common is that all of these were first ideas in the mind of man. It was in the private universe of thoughts and ideas that these forms took shape. Although we cannot see or hear or measure the thoughts and ideas of man the thinker, we can measure a certain aspect of the world of thoughts in everything the artistic nature produces, which surround us in the physical universe. Therefore the shape of a building, a chair, or a shoe is a product of man the thinker, and was first produced in the private universe of thoughts. These ideas of mind and thought can now be measured and observed in the public universe of matter by the five senses. You will agree that the artist or designer knew conceptually the precise form your watch or shoe was to have before fashioning it in the physical universe?

Dr. Lattison: Yes.

Socrates: How about the remaining half of the physical universe which we observe, the things that possess shape, form, and matter, whose ideas and thoughts are responsible for the other half of the visible public universe?

Dr. Lattison: Are you referring to living things, Socrates?

Socrates: Very fitting, modern man. If one cannot measure or observe the personal thoughts of man except when revealed by their tangible artistic achievements of tables and chairs produced in the physical world, how can you possibly guarantee yourself that the thought and mind of God was not responsible for producing the plant, the animal, the tree, and human being alike? Does there not seem to be a coexistence in the public universe of God the thinker which became God the doer? Is it not evidenced by his art-form which is all living things? This includes man, the thinker, who becomes man the doer, in man's artificial art which is contrived and lifeless.

Dr. Lattison: I do agree that the physical universe does, indeed, possess the artistic nature of man, found in the tables, chairs, and in all of humanity's lifeless art, but how does it follow that I must accept that the forms and shapes of the living things were produced by the mind of God?

Socrates: We both agree, scientist, that the lifeless art in this chair which is in our physical universe was first, indeed, a shape, and thought, in the mind of a man. Then we must also agree that thought, alone, was not enough to produce this chair; that first the artist thought the chair, and second willed it, and the chair came to be. Therefore the essence of thought along with the essence of will fashioned and manufactured the chair, which we both experience before us.

Dr. Lattison: Certainly. I agree with that statement.

Socrates: Do you not see then, that the mind of God thought of the tree and then the will of God made the tree, just as the mind of man thought of the chair and the will of man made the chair? Since there is, indeed, a coexistence in our physical universe between nature in the living things and the thoughts and will of man in the lifeless things, would you not say that the thoughts, mind, and will of God must have a being and does exist as surely as the mind and will of man has a being and also exists? Either nature has no thoughts and no will, or a higher creativity must have bequeathed to humankind the attributes of thought and the attributes of will which has enabled man to think, will, and produce. Therefore, mind produces mind, thought produces thought, will produces will.

Dr. Lattison: You have not shown me any proof, nor any empirical evidence which by the senses would describe the external universe, that the mind of God thought and willed the living things.

Socrates: Is it not usually the case that a more cultivated and sophisticated civilization has a tendency to produce more refined minds in its people? A more refined mind will usually in turn produce more refined art. The first and most ancient civilizations upon this planet were producing static, unyielding, and rigid representations of living things within their statues. As civilizations became more sophisticated and capable of generating more refined minds, sculptors began to display more grace, balance, refinement, and vitality in their art. Since, however, the mind of a human is not yet so refined as to produce living art, how then can we reject and deny out of hand the existence of the most excellent, refined, and sophisticated mind which produces animated, living, breathing art? Now you must agree that this chair, the table, the building, and all of man's lifeless art exist by thought and will of the human mind. You must also agree that the same human mind is able to reflect upon its own creation.

Dr. Lattison: The human mind can certainly observe that which it has created.

Socrates: Therefore, if the human mind exists, and is able to reflect upon that which it has created, then you are implying that the mind of man that creates only imitation art exists, and observes its creation, while the

Natural Artist, the more refined mind, which created living things, does not exist and, indeed, cannot reflect upon its creation. If the superior mind of the Natural Artist does not exist, as you believe, then do you believe that the inferior mind of the artist, which creates artifice and an imitation of life, does exist? How is it possible for the inferior mind to ever pass judgment upon the life-giving superior mind of the Natural Artist and conclude that it does not exist? Does not the artificial artist borrow from the cow of the Natural Artist to produce the leather shoe? Does not the artificial artist borrow from the tree of the Natural Artist to produce a wooden chair? Therefore, would you not say that the artificial artist must have also borrowed his creativity, and will to produce, from the Natural Artist?

Dr. Lattison: If you are implying, Socrates, the analogy that one knows that a table or chair is first conceived in the mind, and that one also knows that by sheer ability, by will, one can produce a table and a chair in the physical universe, I agree with you. I disagree that an omnipotent entity called God knows that he knows that he conceived the elephant, lion, giraffe, trees, vegetables, etc. And also knows that he knows that only by his will were the living things produced. I cannot accept that the mind of God was responsible for creating the living things.

Socrates: There must be some good reason why you believe that the mind of man who has created artificial art exists but the natural mind of God was not responsible for creating the living things in our physical universe. Human minds with all of their scientific knowledge have yet to produce any living species, have they?

Dr. Lattison: Not yet, but we are getting close... yet this does not mean that I must accept your belief that the mind of God is the great artist of nature; neither do I accept your philosophy that there is a soul which survives death and is not of material elements in some form.

Scientists have discovered by D.N.A. tests that humans are 95% similar to creatures such as gorillas. All natural living species were gradually created by natural selection and evolution. Unless, of course, I am to believe in theistic evolution, which states that God originally implemented a plan which naturally evolved into each species which we recognize today.

Socrates: Then you would also believe that the mind also evolved from a common animal ancestor such as the gorilla into the homosapien we know today as man, which makes me wonder. When you state that a human is 95% similar to a gorilla, you must be referring to the external universe; the physical composition of the gorilla. Simply by looking at a gorilla one can deduce that he has certain human-like physical characteristics. I do not, however, think you can be implying that the internal universe or mind of a gorilla is 95% human-like. I doubt that you can show me a gorilla that can draw a line 95% straight compared to a human that is able draw a 100% straight line.

Dr. Lattison: Of course not.

Socrates: If the gorilla truly is 95% human-like, I do not suppose a full-grown gorilla is able to formulate language, speak, and communicate 95% human-like? Neither has the gorilla ever created a chair to sit on nor a table on which to eat? Or do we surmise that the gorilla has understood freedom of choice 95% when compared to humans and has chosen not to build a table and chair?

Dr. Lattison: Absolutely not.

Socrates: Neither do we see a 95% coexistence in the physical universe between the thought, will, and creative art of man and the thought, will, and creative art of a gorilla. We do, however, see a relationship in the coexistence between the flowers and trees of the Natural

Artist and the tables and chairs of man the artificial artist.

Dr. Lattison: No, we do not see a relationship in the external universe of a gorilla and of man.

Socrates: Since the gorilla's thought and will resulting in production and creativity is much closer to 0% compared to the internal thoughts and will produced externally by humans, how is it that you are willing to so closely associate the human creative mind which has produced 100% of the inanimate art in the physical universe to the mind of a gorilla which has not thought, not willed and not produced anything originating in the gorilla's thoughts, in the physical universe? At the same time, when you choose to connect, relate, and identify the physical makeup of humans with the physical makeup of a gorilla, you disassociate yourself with the mind and will of the Natural Artist whose thinking and willing process coexists with the mind and will of man the artificial artist, in the physical universe.

If we look at the external universe and study the physical attributes of a gorilla as compared to humans, we, indeed notice, that they are almost identical. But if we look in the internal universe of the mind, thoughts, and will, and measure the thoughts of humans in the physical universe of creative effort, then the artificial artist has indeed vastly more in common with the mind, thoughts, and will of the Natural Artist who also creates, thinks, wills, and lives.

Do you really suppose a gorilla without thought gave humans their thinking process, a gorilla without ability and will to produce gave humans the will and ability to produce? Modern scientist, if your belief were true, then you realize it would mean no mind, thought, or will is to be found behind the living things. But your considered judgment is that nothing but a collision of lifeless atoms, a freak accident, without aim and purpose, is behind all of nature, life, and reality.

Dr. Lattison: If I do judge, I only judge by the facts, and evidence that I have. Consequently, I have no verifiable information that the mind of the Natural Artist exists.

Socrates: The inferior mind of the gorilla cannot pass judgment on the mind and will of humans and their creation, whether lifeless or not. Likewise, the inferior mind of man truly cannot pass judgment that the superior mind and will of God is not behind the abundance of the living art surrounding us. Especially considering the fact that the artificial artist has always borrowed, will continue to borrow, and whose existence relies on the Natural Artist. It follows then, would you not agree, that the nonproductive inferior mind of a gorilla cannot study and judge the superior mind of humans who have the capability to think, will, and produce. How is it, then, that the inferior minds of humans presume to judge the superior mind of the Natural Artist? But the superior mind can, and indeed is, capable of judging the inferior mind.

Dr. Lattison: Since the inferior mind cannot study and judge the superior mind but the superior mind does study and judge the inferior mind, then you must be implying, Socrates, that when you perceive God as the Natural Artist, not only do you perceive a being who has thoughts, and a will, but a being that also possesses justice, due to the fact that he is capable of judging?

Socrates: Would you say that it is preferable to live with the refined mind of an individual that abides with justice or with the uncultivated mind of the brute who breaks the laws of the state on a regular basis?

Dr. Lattison: To abide with the refined mind of the just man would be preferable.

Socrates: Since the refined mind of the just man, then, is capable of behaving in a more just way, what could be more refined than the mind that is capable of producing living art? That perfected and refined mind then must not only possess justice, but possess the ideal and perfected essence of justice. Hence, justice should be but one of the many attributes of the Natural Artist. For in such a refined mind it would be more natural to be just than unjust.

Dr. Lattison: Socrates, if God has thoughts and a will, as you claim, then the greatest will of God should be to reveal himself to us, his creation. His will to reveal himself by general revelation of trees, flowers, animals and humans is not conclusive and seems very ambiguous. Suppose someone named George thought of a chair in his mind and by his will he produced that chair in the physical world. As I observe George's chair, it tells me very little about the character and personality or identity of George, other than the fact that George willed to make a chair for his own pleasure and relaxation which is a good for himself.

If God made every living thing, then why is God's natural art saturated with bloody red tooth and red claw scrambling for survival? Why would the Natural Artist's creation be permeated with pain and misery resulting in death for every one of his living creatures? Was this God's will for the good of himself, as the chair was the will for the good of George? And if God is judge then how does God justify himself of his will to produce a moaning, groaning, and painful reality which ends in death?

Science postulates in the 'big bang,' Socrates, that everything came out of this ball of energy or matter, including time, space, energy, matter, and all living things. Darwin described evolution and the idea that species evolved until they gradually produced the conscious mind of humans.

Socrates: Therefore, your modern day judgment is that mind did not exist prior to the mind of man and thought did not exist prior to the thought of man. Yet, for those who know that they cannot judge, and also know that they do not know, see as feasible and probable that it was a superior mind that produced the mind of man. Indeed it was the unique thought of God that produced the thinking man and it was the extraordinary creation of God that produced the creative force in man. Hence, both the natural mind of God and the inferior mind of man display their artistic ability to create together in the canvas which we call earth. Our discussion is not about creation versus evolution, Dr. Lattison. The issue here is one of design versus accident.

Dr. Lattison: For those who want to believe, that remains as their belief, Socrates, since it cannot be proven. I and most of my scientific colleagues, believe that all of the living things were acts of nature gradually becoming more complex and specialized for billions of years without mind, without plan.

Socrates: Why does modern man insist on studying the evolution of the physical body, such as the physical makeup of a gorilla, instead of studying the natural substance of the mind? It seems that modern man has neglected the study of the uniqueness of the mind but is compulsively obsessed with studying this recyclable physical substance called the body. For the most part, your physical body, as well as everyone else's, has been but reusable substance, blowing around planet earth being reused for all of these years. Or are we to assume that your physical body is something special, unique that belongs only to yourself?

Dr. Lattison: No! We are all composed of matter that has been recycled.

Socrates: But the composition of this substance which is part of these 92 elements that make up the human body, reveals a unique illumination, a living spark of consciousness within. One belief is that a life-giving agent implemented this unique illuminating characteristic within humankind. The opposite belief is that nature, which created all of the living things, is unaware of its own life, creativity, and ability to produce, since there is no mind behind nature, while the mind of man which created the inferior lifeless objects of tables and chairs is conscious and aware of its own creation.

In this case artificial art such as a dead, lifeless chair is produced by design of a mind, and what is spirited, living, animated art is produced by no design at all but by accident. Since we cannot verify with absolute knowledge one way or another, if you were a gambling man would you not bet that mind produces mind, thought produces thought and life produces life? Or that nothing but accident produces thoughts, hydrogen produces consciousness, energy produces life and matter produces mind? Is this, indeed, the judgment against the Natural Artist by the artificial producing mind of modern day physicists such as yourself? Or would you say not all physicists share your view?

In the case of living systems, nobody would deny that an organism is a collection of atoms. The mistake is to suppose that it is nothing but a collection of atoms.
—*Dr. Davies*
Professor of Physics [5]

It has been a long, slow process, but we are finally realizing that within each of us there is a spiritual as well as a material aspect.
—*Dr. Gerald L. Schroeder* [6]
Physicist

3

The Two Horses

Whenever soul and body are together, the nature of the body bids it be servient and ruled over, while the soul's nature bids it rule and dominate. Here again, which of the two do you think is like the divine, and which is like the mortal? –or don't you think that it is the nature of the divine to rule and to lead, and of the mortal to be ruled over and to serve?

—*Socrates* [1]

Socrates: Tell me, Professor Thomas, what is the requirement for an individual to become a teacher of philosophy in today's world?

Professor: Personally, I spent over 12 years of philosophical studies in college. I received my Doctorate 3 years ago at the age of 32 and have been teaching philosophy these last 2 years at the university.

Socrates: So where does modern philosophy stand today? Have the modern philosophers all-together denounced the existence of God, as Dr. Lattison, the scientist has done?

Professor: The concept of "God" puzzles me. If there is a God, where did God come from? And if God made everything, then who made God? Although I am not closed to this prospect, I have not been provided substantial evidence to believe in God. I am an agnostic.

Socrates: Humans think in images, do they not? If I say mountain, we do not spell out the word in our mind, but remove all other objects that are not associated with a mountain and envision a high, elevated peak. Maybe your imagined mountain is full of pine trees and wildlife, while the peak of my mountain is barren and covered with snow. In either case, if I could see your idea of the imagined mountain I would identify it as a mountain, as you would also identify mine. But when I mentioned God, I am curious to know, as to what was removed from your imagination and what had remained in your concept of God?

Professor: When the word "God" became introduced, everything in my known universe was removed from my imagination, and I was left with nothing. Excluding a possible question mark, I was left with absolutely nothing. But I am curious to know, if I could have seen inside your mind when the word God became introduced, what image would I have seen in the mind of Socrates?

Socrates: You would see divine attributes, such as the nature of justice. As the mountain is associated with pine trees and snow-capped peaks, God is associated with, and would be one with, justice.

Professor: But what is the nature of this divine justice that I may identify it in your mind as easily and readily as I could identify your snow capped mountain?

Socrates: Herein is my search for truth, professor Thomas. For I cannot tell you what ideal justice is; I am only in pursuit of identifying it. But you seem to be an expert in this field, for you have made the statement that justice is not!

Professor: How did you ever come up with this conclusion? When did I make such a statement?

Socrates: If God is not, then justice is not. When you asked "Where did God come from?," if you could have examined my mind, as you desire, you would have seen "Where did justice come from?" When you asked "Who made God?" you would have seen, "Who made justice?" And since I believe that the nature of God, the Natural Artist, is justice and mercy combined, then when you stated "I do not believe in God," you really said you do not believe that there exists a unity of justice and mercy. Thus, anyone who states, "There is no God," is really stating that there is no justice, there is no mercy, no Natural Artist. This would be justice in its ideal state of being, of course. Now, how, may I ask, did you arrive at this conclusion?

Professor: As I stated, I am an agnostic; I have not drawn an absolute conclusion either way. I simply have not been given sufficient evidence to justifiably believe that there exists a universal wholeness harmoniously united in one, that is ideal justice. I have not been given reasons to believe that all of the injustice that takes place upon this planet is subject to judgement by one, universal mode of justice.

Socrates: And where do you stand, today, young lad? Is there a soul that possesses no matter, which is found within the body, and survives death? Or is the consciousness that is found within the body one with the body, which is only a mechanism that ceases to exist when the body dies?

Professor: As a modern English poet asked, "What is matter? Never mind. What is mind? Doesn't matter." You see, Socrates, this question continues to haunt modern day man, as it always has. And it has been haunting me ever since I began to seriously study philosophy.

Socrates: You must be leaning toward some conclusion.

Professor: You stated in your arguments to the ancient Greeks, that a child and a dog that were born into the same household on the same day possess identical sense organs. They are both able to see, touch, hear, smell, and taste. The child therefore does not possess any more sensual organs to comprehend the external universe than the dog does. But what does the child have within that the dog does not? What gives the child the ability to learn, talk, do arithmetic, build buildings, and to seek for and to attempt to communicate with God? Is there a soul within humans, which a dog and other animals do not have? I'm afraid we still do not know the answer.

Socrates: Let's not forget, young man, that the dog is able to smell better, and hear better than humans, describing an even greater dilemma as to why an animal is unable to be human like. Now it puzzles me that if the human body is only mechanical, full of lifeless matter, it would be similar to a mechanical automobile. This makes me wonder why a doctor cannot make the body function again once it has been identified as inactive and dead, as a mechanic is able to make an inactive automobile function again.

Professor: Why indeed, Socrates? Regardless of what today's mechanic does to the car, the car will not move, operate, turn left or right once the driver is removed from inside the shell of the car. The moment the driver walks away, the car becomes nonfunctional and inactive. Likewise, when the soul that is the driving force within the body is removed, then you will have the inactive shell of the human body, as you have the inactive shell of the car.

Socrates: Then you agree that an immaterial soul exists within each living person, which is that breath of life?

Professor: I'm not sure, Dr. Lattison described the picture of 'the big bang' theory, that it all started with only energy and primarily hydrogen gas. Your philosophy, on the other hand, states that there is a mind and thought behind it all. The only thing that I know for sure, is that either the mind and life source of a cosmic being was the cause that gave me my mind and by design is the source of life, or, hydrogen gas and energy somehow accidentally produced the mind and life of human beings.

Socrates: But don't you think it is more feasible for mind to produce mind, life to produce life, as opposed to an accident; that hydrogen gas is capable of producing mind and life?

Professor: If there exists the greater mind of a divine agent, as your philosophy implies, Socrates, then it's very probable that there is a soul within each one of us. But if there is no God, as Dr. Lattison believes, then it's probable that there is no soul.

Socrates: If there is a soul within the body, lad, then there exist two separate and independent substances; one of physical body and one of immaterial soul, fused together within the body. This dualism would be similar to that of the driver inside the car that continues to exist when the driver walks away from the inactive shell of the car.

Professor: But in order to accept that a soul exists, we need proof that there are indeed two separate actualities, and substances which separate at death, one material and lifeless and the other immaterial and living.

Socrates: According to Dr. Lattison, the external universe, where our physical bodies are located, has been dissected and studied to the smallest atom.

Professor: Indeed it has.

Socrates: I wonder. Suppose a dozen people see a car traveling at a fast rate of speed. They hear it screeching to a halt when it crashes into another car. Then a man emerges from one car, pulls out a gun, and begins to fire at the other driver. You agree when such a scene takes place in the physical, external universe, it is in the universe which is common and shared alike by both drivers and the dozen witnesses.

Professor: Of course.

Socrates: And the scientist has the capability to accurately measure the weight and speed of the cars, the sound waves which they emitted, the weight and velocity of the bullet, and all other external activities.

Professor: Indeed the scientist can.

Socrates: But of the dozen witnesses and the two drivers in this scenario, who is to measure the internal universe where fear developed, where hope, prayers, panic, wishes, and other mental activities took place? Are there not two independent universes of existence; one public and external possessing lifeless matter which can be studied, therefore measurable, and the other universe of immaterial, conscious mind which is not measurable or observable?

Professor: For thousands of years, Socrates, humans have pondered this question, but still no one has the definitive answer of two opposing universes: one external and one internal.

Socrates: But if there are two opposite universes, one of body and one of soul, they would possess two different realities, heading in two different directions.

Professor: What do you mean?

Socrates: Imagine a chariot being pulled by two horses, one on the left and one on the right. The horse on the right is very rhythmic. It runs at a perfect pace in synchronous motion. Contrary to the smooth, flowing horse on the right, the horse on the left runs very erratically and is uncontrollable; sometimes it runs fast, while at other times it runs more slowly. Many times it just stops to eat or begins to buck. Obviously, this irrational horse frustrates the rhythmic horse on the right, and frustrates the charioteer even more. Now, if you are the chariot driver, would you not wish for the rhythmic horse on the right to overpower the frustrating horse on the left so they both can pace in synchronous motion? Then your chariot would flow smoothly upon a fine and straight course.

Professor: I certainly would.

Socrates: What if the motion of your chariot was dominated by the irrational bucking horse on the left? You definitely would have a difficult time moving along the street in a gentle straight line.

Professor: Definitely.

Socrates: We consider the smooth flowing horse on the right, young man, as the mind, the rational mind; the soul within the human body. The irrational horse on the left is the body itself, or the bodily desires. Each of these are separate entities; the rhythmic, rational mind exemplified by the right horse and the irrational horse on the left, which displays the bodily desires. Each of these horses dictate everyone's daily behavior and lifestyle as in the allegory of the chariot.

For example, the horse on the right, or the rational mind, says, "I should not drink anymore. I am becoming an alcoholic." But the irrational horse of bodily desires overpowers the rational mind and continues to drink anyway, causing the charioteer or life of the alcoholic frustration and pain.

The rational mind says, "I should not commit adultery since I might produce illegitimate children or bring a sexually transmitted disease into my house and infect my wife. I might possibly even pass this disease onto my children." But the bodily desires of the horse on the left overpowers the horse on the right and commits adultery anyway.

How many times does the overweight person's rational mind say "I should not eat this much?" But the bodily desires overpower the rational mind and compulsively eats anyway. How about the drug addict? Certainly the rational mind knows better. But again, the bodily desires overpower the rational mind.

This is why the philosopher does not live to please the senses, or bodily desires. Instead, the philosopher has shifted away from the life of passion and toward the life of the rational mind. Thus, the philosopher's chariot of life is pulled more by the horse on the right, the horse of reason, than by the horse on the left. The mind of a true philosopher must always overpower and suppress the bodily desires. Only then, when we all become philosophers, might we understand the purpose of our existence and our destiny upon planet earth.

Professor: Socrates, so far you have been easy to follow, but just now you lost me. What does controlling our sensual desires have to do with understanding the purpose of life?

Socrates: When you eat soup, modern man, do you use a fork or a spoon?

Professor: A spoon, of course.

Socrates: When you want to cut a piece of paper or cloth, do you use scissors or a fork?

Professor: I use scissors.

Socrates: Do you not see that everything we develop has arrived at a purpose and serves a perfected function for its existence? As you know, we call this refined state of being the teleological purpose. But the mind, which is overpowered by the bodily desires, is far from reaching such an existence of teleological purpose, or perfected state of being. The mind should be controlled by philosophical ethics and should overpower the sensual bodily desires. Therefore, when all humans become philosophers striving toward the rational mind, only then might we understand what is the perfect state of mind and perfect state of being. In this way, we accomplish our mission and fulfill the purpose of life.

Professor: What you are saying, Socrates, is that if we humans are governed by the irrational bodily desires, we can never know what our purpose of life is, since we are bowing to desires and passions, fooling around with each other's spouses, wasting our time being alcoholics, drug addicts, cheaters, liars, or drug peddlers. Am I right?

Socrates: Do you agree, modern man, that a spoon does something better than anything else could do in its scooping up soup to feed the human mouth?

Professor: It does.

Socrates: And a fork, it pierces a piece of meat to feed us better than anything else, does it not? A knife or scissors also serves their own perfected state, having been developed to possess a teleological purpose.

Professor: It seems everything made by man possesses a teleological purpose and serves its refined state of being, whether being scissors, fork, screwdriver, etc.

Socrates: Now, when you listen to music, do you use your ear or your eye?

Professor: The ear, of course.

Socrates: And does the eye not also have its purpose and teleological existence, which means in its refined state of being the eye can perform its function better then the ear or nose? The ear and nose have their own mission, or purpose in life as their teleological design, do they not?

Professor: They do. This would seem to indicate that not only what is man-made serves its teleology, or refined state of being, but everything made by nature seems to serve its teleology as well. But if God is behind nature and is the one who gave us the eye and the ear, you would think that the highest teleological purpose for the ear to fulfill would be to hear its maker, and the most refined state of being for the eye would be to see God. But as Dr. Lattison has stated, not all of the eyes in our world can universally agree that they see and identify God, and neither have all of the ears universally heard God!

Socrates: Indeed they have not, but as long as the five senses are overpowered by sensual pleasures and bodily desires of the horse on the left, then our pleasure-seeking attitude defeats the purpose of the ear and the eye which are seeking for God. But while the ear and the eye and the other senses communicate directly to the soul within, the soul of a philosopher has the ability to subdue and to overpower the sensual desires. This means that the senses of a philosopher are used as avenues of teaching the soul and not merely suppressing the soul to pleasure-seeking adventures dictated by the body. But I do wonder about the soul, or the mind, which governs the body. What is the purpose of the soul or mind which is found within humans? Does that not have a teleological mission, a refined state of being, a design, or purpose in life?

Professor: It should, but how can we humans arrive at such a perfected state of being where we can truly say this is our teleological purpose, our refined state of being or existence in life? And if one were to arrive at such perfection, by what means and whose judgement can that perfect being know that they are indeed perfect?

Socrates: Modern man, as you stated, as long as humans are murderers, rapists, thieves, liars, and pleasure-seekers, they will never find themselves understanding their purpose and mission in life. As long as the bodily desires control and dictate human behavior, then it is the same as the crazy horse on the left controlling the chariot of life. But when reason overpowers the bodily desires, then we come in contact with the true essence of the soul, which was implanted in us by the soul of the divine agent.

Professor: Such wise words you proclaimed to the Athenians 2,400 years ago, Socrates. How do you suppose we, today, measure on your spectrum of left horse and right horse? Are we striving toward the rational mind? Will we soon be able to understand our purpose and teleological mission in life? Have we progressed at all?

Socrates: I am afraid I am not in the position to judge, modern man. Only the one who is and is found at such a perfected state of being is capable of making such a decision. But since you inquire regarding a location along the spectrum of the irrational foolish left side and the rational mind on the right, tell me this. I have been told a staggering fact: more than 100 million people have been killed due to war and other forms of human violence in this century alone. [2] I take this as being true?

Professor: Very grim, but true indeed.

Socrates: It has also come to my attention that in the last 10 years alone, more than one million people have died at the hands of their fellows, again due to war and other such violence. With such horrifying statistics, where do you place modern day man? Was this our mission in life? Has humanity served its function by murdering 100 million people? After humankind has been refining its scientific technology all of these years, where is our state of refinement and perfection for the soul? Is human behavior striving toward the right horse of rational thinking or marching toward the left horse of irrational behavior?

Professor: Those are pretty sad statistics Socrates; they seem to automatically place us far along the path of the crazy horse on the left! Certainly our mission in life, and teleological purpose, was not to kill 100 million people in the last century, but that is precisely what we have done. It seems on the scale of teleology, a true philosopher views modern society as repulsive, ailing, and evil on the scale of refinement, equating our irrationality as eating soup with a fork or brushing one's hair with a toothbrush!

Socrates: When your teleology has the result of 100 million people murdered, it is worse than that, lad.

Professor: But how can we possibly know if some individuals, today at least, are heading in the right direction? There must be a measuring tool by which philosophers can explain to us whether we at least are heading toward the rational mind of the right horse and away from the evil left.

Socrates: There are some measuring devices which philosophers are able to utilize, young man. Your life is your chariot driven by the irrational horse on the left and simultaneously the righteous horse on the right. From now on we will call the left side unrighteous or unjust and the right side righteous or just. While you are moving along the road of life upon your chariot, you agree that this same road of life is used by all of the other humans as well, riding their own chariots of life?

Professor: Certainly, Socrates, we are all riding and sharing this same road which we call life.

Socrates: You also agree that this same road of life which you are using is simultaneously used by everyone else, and their life or chariot is also continuously being pulled by the left side of injustice and the right side of justice?

Professor: Everyone's life is seduced, enticed, and tempted by the greedy and lustful desires on the left; but everyone should go through the struggles and temptations of life deciding if they are behaving justly or unjustly, focusing on the rational on the right and thus avoiding the irrational on the left.

Socrates: I suppose, being a philosopher yourself lad, you must be more in control of the mind striving toward the rational right of the spectrum; therefore sensual pleasures and bodily desires do not mean much to you. But you agree that another chariot or someone else's life which is controlled by the irrational crazy left side comes crashing into your chariot of life. Let's say a drunk driver who killed your child in a car accident, a rapist who raped your wife, or a thief who broke into your house. You do agree that it is inevitable that along the road of existence your chariot of life and reality is shared with people found in the extreme left side of irrationality and injustice?

Professor: Agreed. There are people out there, Socrates, that rape women and kill people and literally have no conscience of doing anything wrong. Their rational and just right side is completely erased. These people are obviously guided and driven by the irrational horse on the left.

Socrates: Now, lad, in order to be certain these irrational people are kept in check we have produced laws as deterrents to their crimes. This is the purpose for laws is it not?

Professor: Certainly. Laws are to protect society from the unjust.

Socrates: Now, if all of humanity became philosophers and were moving together toward the rational and just side, will we need more laws or less laws?

Professor: If everyone was a friend to everyone, and if every man behaved justly to their fellow man and focused on good and righteous behavior, we would not need any laws. Life would be so rhythmic the right horse would run perfectly with the left horse, mind and body would be one, and then and only then, we might be able to find our teleological purpose in life. But if our chariot of life is being pulled by bodily desires we would need more laws to keep a rebellious and unjust civilization in check.

Socrates: And society today, modern man, where is society located and headed today? The unjust left or the righteous right?

Professor: If we consider the factual number of more than 100 million people murdered in this century, and more than one million people murdered the last decade primarily due to war, without even mentioning the many local murders and crimes, it looks pretty bad for us. If we measure injustice by how many laws we are producing as opposed to righteousness and justice by how many laws we are omitting, we are definitely striving toward the left, witnessed by the fact that we are producing more laws daily. Even in these days of scientific enlightenment we pay lawmakers to produce new laws daily. They have produced 200,000 federal laws as of 1990 while there were about 30,000 laws thirty five years ago.

Your ancient philosophy of refined state of being and teleology is very contradictory to modern philosophers and some new religions who teach that humans are masters of their own destiny. Some even claim that humans are masters of the universe. They believe, since humans are the only known self-conscious beings in the universe, that humans have the potential to be gods themselves. I personally am not sure if there is a God, but these new philosophers instruct that man is not intrinsically evil but naturally good, and that humans can attain divine status.

Socrates: Young man, suppose you tell me if there is even one nation upon planet earth which has no police force.

Professor: Every nation has a police force, Socrates.

Socrates: Then suppose you name one nation in today's world that does not have laws.

Professor: Every nation has laws. In fact, every police force in every nation is utilized to enforce its own laws.

Socrates: In that case, I propose that we advise these modern philosophers and new religions to remove all of the police departments. Then let's simultaneously remove all of the laws that keep the people chained to law and righteousness. Remove all of your laws here in New York and elsewhere beginning tomorrow morning modern man; no law and no penalty for tax evasion, no law for rape, no law for murder, no law for someone stealing your property, your car, your home. There would be no law against extortion, kidnaping for ransom, no law for drug peddlers, no law....

Professor: I get your message, Socrates; chaos, total chaos, nothing short of anarchy.

Socrates: This is not my message, young lad; you have just glanced into the true nature of humanity. This is reality without laws. Only by the laws are we given some order and civility and are pulled a little toward the reality of justice and the divine right. Without laws, modern man, your teleological purpose and destiny in life are far to the chaotic left, toward complete injustice.

Professor: But Socrates, not everyone is responsible for the murder of the 100 million people! Not everyone is responsible for breaking the laws and making it necessary for adding new laws. Which means that there must be people that are just and good in our civilization.

Socrates: Let's hope there are, modern man, but where might you locate one individual who has never broken a law of the state, much less the moral law? For if there exists such a being, then only that individual is capable of judging where each one of us truly belongs between the spectrum of evil to the left and righteousness to the right. In other words, at the end of the left we find complete injustice, murderers, and people incarcerated on death row, do we not?

Professor: We do.

Socrates: In this case, young man, what is found at the end of the right side of the spectrum opposing such injustice?

Professor: Complete justice and righteousness; someone who is truly free. Someone who abides with complete righteousness and therefore not bound by any laws. This would be the condition of the divine, of God himself. This is the direction of teleology and refined state of being which the philosophers are attempting to attain.

Socrates: In this case, young man, if only the righteousness of God is found at the end of the right spectrum, which no human has attained, then only God in his righteousness, being at the end of the spectrum, can see the whole spectrum and dictate and measure where each one of us is located along the spectrum of justice and injustice. Therefore, only God possesses ultimate justice and only God is judge of all. Now what else do you suppose we might find at the right end of the justice spectrum?

Professor: As all other humans, I find myself somewhere between the scale of injustice to the left and justice to the right. Therefore I can only speculate whether there is such a perfect being whose righteousness is beyond the scale of justice. But if there is, we should find the personality of perfection, the character of righteousness, and the complete nature of God and all of his attributes. We should find not a material body, susceptible to bodily desires, but only mind, wisdom, and freedom, divorced of matter; therefore not bound by gravity or time. Only spirit in its purest form transcending time, gravity, and the physical laws of causality. Above all, we should find ultimate justice and the judge of all.

Socrates: Then we can safely conclude that in order for God to be judge of all, it necessitates the existence of the two elements which are required for justice.

Professor: And what might these two elements be?

Socrates: When one walks into a doctor's clinic, does one not find the doctor, who has the knowledge of medicine, and is licensed to practice the medical arts? The patient therefore becomes the second element which belongs in the doctor's clinic in order for the doctor to practice medicine, since without an existing patient there need not be a doctor.

Professor: Indeed, there must be both elements of knowledge of medicine and the existence of patients who need care in order for a doctor to exist.

Socrates: It follows then that if we go to a court of law we will see a judge who possesses knowledge of the law will we not? But there must also exist lawbreakers in order to have a judge. Which means that the law and the lawbreaker must exist in order to have a judge. Therefore the judge possesses knowledge of the law and only a judge can pronounce justice on a lawbreaker.

Professor: Indeed, this means since humankind, without laws, would find itself located on the far left side of the spectrum of injustice and God is to be found, judge of all, at the end of the right spectrum, then there is a sizeable gap between the injustice of man on one side and the justice of God on the other. By our human laws we are given discipline, and are pulled somewhat to the reality of abiding in a judicial manner. One could then say that by existence of our laws we are pulled toward the existence of God on the right. It follows that God must possess laws in order to draw us toward his justice, which would automatically make him judge and lawgiver.

Socrates: And if God is judge and God does possess laws, what is missing from completing this picture, young lad?

Professor: A lawbreaker.

Socrates: A lawbreaker indeed, and who would you say the lawbreaker might be?

Professor: Every human being. Everyone is found on the spectrum of justice and is imperfect, regardless of how far left or how far right the lawbreakers would find themselves. Your philosophy fits especially well with the major religions of the world, which state that humanity is deprived and separated from the divine presence of God, who is holy and thus cannot abide with our sinful nature.

Socrates: Therefore all of us are lawbreakers and sinners young lad! This seems to suggest that the consciousness of God and his moral law would be judiciously present in the mind and soul of all of us. It is this consciousness of divinity which sets us apart from the animals and forces us to make daily choices between human injustice and divine justice. We must allow our soul to dictate the morality of right and wrong and suppress the enticement of bodily desires which keep us in polar opposition, by seducing us with the belief "if it feels good it is just; if it is pleasing to the body it is righteous." Only our soul can identify with the soul of the just that is and is eternal, unchanging, and without decay. While surrendering to passion and bodily desires, we become drawn toward injustice and are riveted to the left horse of deception. A true philosopher masters the bodily passions and does not surrender to them.

Professor: If our true nature without laws, Socrates, is all the way to the left and only by the laws can we live a life of virtue so that we may be pulled a little to the right toward God, then God, being at the end of the right spectrum, must possess laws. His divine laws are given in order to make humanity aware and conscious of right and wrong. In this way only might we understand the nature of God, and who he is. But I wonder. You said to Dr. Lattison that God, the Natural Artist, the creative force of nature, who is responsible for the design of the trees, the animals, and plants, gave humanity his divine, creative mental ability. Therefore, there is a coexistence in our universe, of God the Natural Artist and man the artificial artist, who produces tables and chairs.

But now what you are saying is that the mind of God is also judge, and possesses divine laws. Therefore God the Natural Artist is also God the Natural Lawgiver, who gave humanity his special creation and the ability to also produce laws. Laws, therefore, come from the mind of God to the mind of man. Since humankind, the artificial artist, produces artificial art, then humankind should also produce artificial laws. You must be stating, therefore, that virtue, and the moral law within each one of us, is superior and more divine than the laws of the state, which were created by the artificial artist. Do you agree that I have correctly assessed your statements?

Socrates: In answer, allow me to ask you if one should lie to a friend, or better stated, one does not go to prison for lying in today's society?

Professor: Unless they lie in a court of law, generally no, they do not.

Socrates: Therefore, to lie is not against the laws of the state but to lie is contrary to the moral law. Since we do have moral obligations and there is a universal moral requirement generally found in human consciousness, then it is reasonable for a universal lawgiver to exist, is it not?

Professor: But how can I know for certain that this moral law within all of us is implemented by a divine lawgiver? Excluding Immanuel Kant and some others, many philosophers today do not believe that a moral law originates and leads to a lawgiver of divine status.

Socrates: Since conscience does not make the laws that it describes, it follows that the soul and mind of God must have implemented this moral law by design within the mind and soul of all of us. The alternative, lad, is to believe that somehow those 92 lifeless atoms had the potential to, and accidentally did produce, an unavoidable, universal moral witness within the human consciousness. In this case you must also agree with Dr. Lattison, although unknown to him, somehow these same 92 lifeless atoms which produced a moral law, were also able to produce consciousness and more miraculously, somehow they were able to count the existence of themselves to be 92 lifeless atoms. The choice is yours to make. Living justly and abiding by the laws of the state is not enough to produce virtue. One must rely on the moral law as well.

We know and approve the better course, but follow the worse.
                                              —*Ovid*[3]

All our lauded technological progress... is like the axe in the hand of the pathological criminal
                                              —*Albert Einstein*[4]

4

Justice

Every skill and every inquiry, and similarly, every action and choice of action, is thought to have some good as its object. This is why the good has been rightly defined as the object of all endeavour[1] ...[F]or if good, as a common predicate, actually is a single thing or something separate by itself, it is clear that it could not be an object of human action or aspiration. But it is something of that kind that we are seeking.[2]

—Aristotle

Socrates: Where does modern philosophy stand as it concerns accident or design in our universe, professor Thomas? Was it simply an accident that caused the 92 lifeless atoms to produce the nature of justice or is there an immaterial soul that craves justice which exists within the body? If there is a soul, is not the soul capable of rationally arriving at the knowledge of a just God who is at the end of the spectrum of justice.

Professor: I'm afraid I must agree with Dr. Lattison. The burden of proving there is a mind or soul within the body is for the one who makes the statement that a soul exists. The burden of proof is not for those who claim something does not exist, but for those who claim that it does exist. For example, I could state that thousands of feet below the surface and deep within the earth exists living people with markets, towns and villages. With such a statement, the burden of proof is on me to prove that such a place does indeed exist. It is not for the one who argues that such a place does not exist to prove that it does not exist. Likewise, those who believe that a mind or soul exists within the body which possesses no matter must satisfactorily prove that it does exist. This is why science does not deal with the issue of whether or not there is a soul which survives death.

Socrates: But you, as a philosopher, must have pondered if such a thing as a soul exists. Since this is one of the studies of philosophy, you must be familiar with the opposing view.

Professor: The opposing view held by Dr. Lattison is that there is no mind or soul but only matter. But he has the problem of explaining another question. If there exists only matter, which make up the building blocks of the 92 lifeless atoms, then how is it possible for matter to comprehend matter without mind or soul? He is faced with the fact that we are indeed able to comprehend matter. How is it possible for matter to measure matter without mind, as we are capable of measuring matter? How can matter, being composed of 92 lifeless atoms, thirst for the concept of justice? How is it possible for matter to communicate with matter as one human body made of only matter communicates to another human body made of matter?

Socrates: In either case, young lad, it seems there is no absolute answer.

Professor: This dichotomy has not changed since the ancient Greek philosophers. History teaches that certain philosophers, who lived in 400 BC, believed that there existed only matter. And, unknown to them, somehow matter comprehends matter. The opposing view, known today as mind-body dualism, that yourself, Plato, and certain other philosophers believed was that it is the mind within each body which possesses no matter and survives death. It has been some 2,400 years since this debate began; and even with the advancement of modern day science, we still do not know if the body is composed of only matter or if there exists a soul within the body that has no matter.

Even the influential thinkers of today disagree with each other on this issue. Nobel prize winner and discoverer of DNA, Dr. Francis Crick, sets forth the proposition that there exists only matter and no soul. [3] In contrast to Dr. Crick, the book *Theories of the Mind* reveals that neurobiologist, Sir John Eccles, also a Nobel Prize winner, is known for being a mind-body dualist. [4] Many ask the question, "If there was a living being who gave us our mind, what evidence do I have that the mind of the living being continues to exist today?" As you see, nothing has changed. Although you express some fascination, Socrates, you do not seem to be very impressed with our modern-day technological advancements and scientific discoveries.

Socrates: Have things truly changed since the ancient Greeks? Or do you suppose man's ability to conquer and control the physical environment by scientific advancements allows modern man to claim competence in conquering the self and mastery of the inner spiritual universe. Scientific advancements have, indeed, made impressive progress concerning secondary evils. However, to my eyes nothing has changed in 2,400 years, when we compare the primary evils.

Professor: And what might these evils be?

Socrates: Secondary evil is that which originates from without. These evils usually select us without any choice on our part. They are the evils and pains of nature in the form of disasters and diseases. The primary evils, on the other hand, are the evils that originate and develop from within man's desire, and are usually by choice. Evils and pains of morality manifest themselves in the form of murder, rape, child molestation, etc. In ancient Greece we battled against the secondary evils of disease and illness produced by nature with medicine, while the primary illnesses and diseases of human nature we battled with the laws of the state. The impressive progress you have made by scientific discoveries and technology can only do battle against the secondary evils of nature which fight the bodily ailments. Unfortunately, mastering the external universe by way of science and medicine cannot help in any way with the evils of human nature that originate and develop within. The evils of choice can only be controlled by philosophical ethics. Otherwise, these evils of choice will be fought by enforcement of the law.

Professor: If humankind had listened to the ancient philosophers and continued the legacy of virtue and ethics in pursuit of truth, then we today, two thousand years later, should only be battling the secondary sickness and disease of nature with medicine. We should have wiped out the primary evils and disorder of human nature completely. Diseases and infirmities of nature multiply and produce new strains constantly, forcing doctors to produce new vaccines and medicines on a regular basis. Likewise, humans continue to produce and multiply new strains of illegal and disorderly conduct constantly, forcing lawmakers to produce new laws on a regular basis. "The unexamined life is not worth living," which you stated to the ancient Athenians years ago applies in today's world more than ever.

Socrates: This great country of yours with its many colleges and universities must indeed produce philosophers who delve into the private universe within and who examine their own behavior and actions in the external world.

Professor: Our universities today focus on engineering, business, computers, marketing, and finance. People today do not generally study philosophy and reflect within themselves. The attempt is not often made to ethically unify man's internal universe with the internal universe of their fellow man, much less unifying the internal with the external universe that holds it all together. Since philosophy helps the student to think rationally, most of my students will apply their philosophical studies toward a law degree. The word philosophia or "lover of wisdom" has lost its meaning today. Most people do not study philosophy for the sake and love of wisdom.

Socrates: And how does one describe the word "philosophia" in today's world?

Professor: As I understand it from you ancient Greeks, "philo" means lover and "sophia" means wisdom. Therefore, a philosopher is a "lover of wisdom." Wisdom is that which follows on the heels of knowledge and information. Wisdom is the infrastructure which molds and brings knowledge together. For example, in 1929, the Stock Market crashed in America. Many people lost their fortunes overnight. Thousands died of starvation, and many others committed suicide during this time of financial collapse. Some people desperately needed a doctor, yet doctors were without work in need of patients. Likewise on one side people starved in need of food, while on the other side farmers produced food that spoiled. The information and the location of the food was knowledge, and so were the starving people. The information and location of the doctors was also knowledge and so were the sick patients. But the infrastructure that unites the supply with the demand was broken. That infrastructure is wisdom, the bringing together and integrating of knowledge and information. As a result of that infamous event in our nation's history, economists developed the wisdom of various financial buffers in order to avoid this scenario of total collapse from ever threatening our economy again.

We, today, have a tendency to honor the wisdom of the artificial artists. We esteem the wisdom of the artist who is able to gather a few different colors and produce beauty to the eye in a painting. We idolize the musician who is able to arrange notes and pitches of sound and produces beauty to the ear. We pay handsomely for the wisdom of the one who is able to arrange different ingredients and tantalize our taste buds in our expensive restaurants. The philosopher, however, does not chase after sensual desires, and pollute the senses through the arts and the pleasures of man, the artificial artist. But the philosopher uses the senses to teach the mind and soul in pursuit of understanding and identifying with the Natural Artist. Therefore, as you stated to the ancient Greeks; "Unlike the other arts that please the senses, philosophy is the greatest art of all, for it is art to the mind."

Socrates: Therefore, lad, wisdom seems to be located within the human mind, which is able to connect and integrate knowledge and information.

Professor: Indeed it is. An encyclopedia or a library has more information and knowledge than any human can possibly have, but it is the wisdom of the human mind which enters the library and is able to gather information together and make wise sense out of it.

Socrates: Since wisdom does indeed follow on the heels of knowledge and information as we ancients believed, it does make me wonder. Modern man possesses more knowledge and information than ever, which means that modern man should also possess more wisdom today than ever. And if modern man is truly wise, then humanity should be wise enough to remove the laws which battle with the primary evils of human nature and only do battle with the secondary diseases and evils of nature. How can modern man possess so much scientific information and knowledge in today's world, while at the same time lack so much wisdom?

Professor: In today's world, and primarily in this country, we are driven to master the external universe which reveals physical truths. We are not driven to master the self. Scientists today possess so much information concerning the external universe that nobody dares question them. Consequently, if one questions the scientist concerning the internal universe of thoughts, ideas, ethics, etc., which science does not deal with, that individual will usually only be scorned by the scientific community. The scientist's main argument against philosophy is that science reveals descriptive, external truths, while philosophy and religions reveal prescriptive truths.

In other words, the scientist's descriptive truths of the external universe describe something that is; they describe what it is, how big its mass is, how much its density and weight are, how fast it moves, how it changes its physical properties, etc. Contrary to this descriptive knowledge, which is pure science, philosophy, they claim, prescribes how things ought to be. You ought to behave like this and not behave like that, you ought to say this and ought not to say that. Anyone therefore, especially religions, that attempts to describe God cannot scientifically accomplish such a task. Religions are only prescribing what God would be like, if indeed there exists such a being. In fact, your own teaching of a divine agent, or a God possessing justice, did not describe something that is at the end of the spectrum of justice, but only something that ought to be there. Therefore, Socrates, you are prescribing something that ought to be there, not describing something that definitely is there. Many scientists view religious people as mystics and superstitious. At the same time however, scientists do not know much concerning philosophical inquiry and their timeless questions. Scientists, therefore, only know information of physical and descriptive truths, and are usually ignorant concerning divine, philosophical, and prescriptive truths.

Socrates: In this case, lad, as long as one is abiding by the laws of the state, then one is behaving righteously and living a virtuous life. Moral laws do not apply any longer in this society since moral laws are prescriptive and not descriptive, since they indeed prescribe how we ought to behave and do not describe what something is.

Professor: All you have to do is turn on the television, Socrates, to taste or sense a lack of morality. Your prescriptive morals will be verified as inapplicable by many in today's society. The average child will witness 15-20,000 murders on television before turning 18 years of age.

Socrates: Why a television, lad, and not a court of law where justice is served? In this age of scientific discoveries and descriptive truths, when a modern person goes into a court of law where truth and justice are the main concerns, does the witness swear to God or to science that he or she will tell the truth?

Professor: To God, of course.

Socrates: As I was told, if I understand correctly, your Declaration of Independence defines itself as "one nation under God, with liberty and justice for all." Again I am wondering, why, in this scientific age of enlightenment, do you state "one nation under God" and not "with one nation under science," if science seems to possess all of the answers?

Professor: Science cannot describe, nor give us justice. We agreed if there is a God at the right side of the spectrum who possesses justice, then God and justice are one. If therefore, science gives us justice, which is one with God, then science would have also given us God. But, we, today, even with so much scientific information and technology, are still far to the left on the spectrum of justice and guided by the left horse of bodily desires and injustice. I must admit, although science does not give us justice, it has liberated and freed us from ignorance. Scientists have discovered and taught us much about our physical world. Science has freed us from many superstitious doctrines. Science has also given us freedom from the secondary evils of nature by producing medicine to battle disease. It has also freed us to travel to the other side of the world in a matter of hours. Now we are able to ship megatons of food and goods from one part of the world to the other. Many philosophers today study the branch of philosophy which we call "philosophy of science." This is my field of expertise. We critically examine, evaluate, and scrutinize the latest scientific advancements, pursuing truth in a philosophical manner.

Socrates: It seems science has freed humanity, to a certain extent, and has also produced a certain amount of good for humankind.

Professor: A certain amount, yes.

Socrates: But this thing which we call good, which science to some extent has indeed provided for humankind. What is it? In other words, where would a scientist find this thing which we call good? Can a scientist weigh or divide good by a descriptive knowledge of the external universe?

Professor: If you are asking if good is a tangible thing possessing matter which the scientist can study, then such a thing does not exist. Such a concept does not exist in the scientists' descriptive dictionary. Good is not a tangible thing. Therefore, it is not a person, place, or thing made of matter.

Socrates: But how can we know if something is truly good if the descriptive knowledge of a scientist cannot reveal what good truly is?

Professor: If you were to ask the majority of the people today what good is, they would probably respond "If it feels good, sounds good, looks good, and tastes good, it must be good." But I, as a philosopher would say, "we cannot trust the senses due to the fact that what feels good to me might not feel good to you, what sounds or looks good to me, might not sound and look good to you."

Socrates: Therefore, you agree lad, that the same sense organs that teach the scientist concerning the external universe for descriptive truths are capable of deceiving us and can give us a distorted message concerning the concept of good. The senses reveal good as a relative term, which changes from person to person, while the concept of the ideal form of good should be eternally constant and undeviating.

Professor: I agree with you here, Socrates; we cannot rely on the senses, which offer and produce only a relative good. Which means, only by reason might we come to comprehend the ideal form of good. In other words, observe someone who is having a cavity filled in a tooth. The physical pain does not describe a feeling of good, but reason describes that ultimately this physical pain is for a greater good. Since we must yield to reason, then reason dictates that if something or someone's action does good for everyone else, then it must be good, regardless what the passion or the senses describe to us. As you ancient philosophers taught, for every single action man takes, the end result is for some form of good. Whether one is having a tooth pulled or does not enjoy one's work, such actions are indeed for the good of a livelihood and a bank account, which will indeed allow such a one to buy some form of good as a result.

Socrates: If every action which a human takes possesses an ultimate end for the form of good, then good is something that is always being pursued, and is something that is very desirable. Even you, yourself, defined good as to be identified as something that does good. Which requires the question, "If good is desirable, and every action we humans make is for some form of good, then which horse will you call the good horse, the horse on the left of bodily desires or the horse of reason on the right?"

Professor: We agreed earlier that good cannot be clearly understood by the senses and their pleasure-seeking desires which belong with the horse on the left. But good can be better identified by the rational mind of reason; therefore good belongs with the rational horse on the right.

Socrates: Since the horse on the right was the horse that possessed justice, and now you also identify good with the horse on the right, this means that good must be synonymous with justice. Since good and justice are to be found at the right side of the spectrum, then good justice is at the right and bad justice or injustice is to be found at the left side of the spectrum.

Since the murderers, rapists, and incarcerated are unjust and belong to the left of the spectrum, this reveals that we should all despise this side, and desire good which opposes evil, and in particular desire good justice opposed to bad justice.

Professor: Certainly!

Socrates: And if God is located at the end of the spectrum on the right along with justice, and God and justice are one, and we just concluded that good is also located along with justice on the right of the spectrum, then justice and good are one. Therefore, God, justice, and good must be one.

Professor: They should.

Socrates: Since we identify injustice to the left and justice to the right, and we locate bad and evil to the left and good on the right, then, which side would you say produces pain?

Professor: Since the murderers, rapists, and thieves are on the left, then it is obvious that on the left would also be the location of pain.

Socrates: This would mean that while injustice and evil produce pain on the left, justice and good should produce and offer pleasure on the right. Now, I ask you, lad, would you prefer to live in a society that produces injustice, evil, and pain or in a society which offers justice, good, and pleasure?

Professor: I believe most desire that which is good and that which is pleasure, and avoid that which is evil and causes pain.

Socrates: This means that there is indeed definite pleasure found in a society which offers good justice as opposed to a society which offers bad and painful injustice.

Professor: I'm following you.

Socrates: Since justice is found on the right side of the spectrum where God would also be, as we stated earlier, then God and justice must be one and the same. Since good is also located on the right side of the spectrum along with justice, then good must also reside with God. Therefore, good, God, and justice must be one. And since pleasure is also located along the right side of the spectrum, then pleasure must also be one with God. Therefore, justice, good, and pleasure are attributes of God and one with God.

Professor: That is, if there is a just God, who is found at the end of the right spectrum. If so, then granted, good and pleasure must be identified with God and be one with God.

Socrates: In this case lad, one will only find pleasure and happiness when one is good and just, and one will find most pleasure only when one knows God, who is the ultimate and ideal pleasure, justice, and good. Now lad, since most desire justice and oppose injustice, and desire good and despise bad, and since we prefer pleasure to pain, then we must conclude that our world must be full of justice, with an overabundance of good and a most pleasurable place to live in!

Professor: Not quite, Socrates. Unfortunately, the world is full of injustice, evil, pain, and misery, even in this age of scientific enlightenment.

Socrates: Then something obviously seems to be wrong with humanity, modern man. We wish, hope, and desire to live and exist toward the reality on the right, but the fact is our actions have pinned us down toward the reality of the left.

Professor: Most historical philosophers spanning the globe from yourself, and Plato and other Greek philosophers, Buddha, Lao–Tsu, Confucius and others, agree something indeed was wrong with humanity, which continues to be wrong, even today. The major religions of Judaism, Christianity, Hinduism, Buddhism, and Islam all agree: something indeed is wrong with all of us, and there exists a definite separation between the divine being with his nature of ideal justice and humanity with their nature of evil and injustice. Only some modern pop philosophy and some modern religions have elevated humans as masters of the universe with the claim, "if it feels good it must be of God."

Socrates: Let's disregard these new religions lad, while we figure out our true nature and uncover our problem of painful and unjust reality.

Professor: And how will we do that?

Socrates: Let's compare both the irrational left horse and the rational right horse, which pull our chariot of life daily. Pleasures and good for the senses are usually attained from the bodily irrational side on the left. But pleasure and good for the mind and soul is usually attained by reason on the right.

Professor: As a rationalist, I tend to agree to a certain extent.

Socrates: If good and pleasure are located on the right and are attributes of God, who is one with good and pleasure, then is it ever possible for such divine attributes to be found and attained on the left?

Professor: On the left is the location of injustice, pain, and evil. How can someone attain good and pleasure, which are attributes of God, and are both found united on the right?

Socrates: This is the problem, lad. This is at the root of evil, the sensual desires of distorted good and distorted pleasure. This is the force that pins humanity all the way to the left, separated from God on the right. Any human action which offers good and pleasure must also possess the essence of justice, since all three attributes of good, pleasure and justice are one with God. Therefore, if indeed the human action that offers good and pleasure also possesses the essence of justice, then that action also possesses the essence of God. If however any human action offers good and pleasure but does not possess the essence of justice, then that action cannot possess the essence of God. Since God is justice, God cannot be separated from justice.

Professor: Then you are stating that when one attains pleasure and good unjustly, they are not attaining pleasure and good from God on the right. They are attaining a distorted pleasure and a false good from the left, the side which offers pain, evil, and injustice.

Socrates: Let's take a drug addict for example. The addict might find a form of good and pleasure by using drugs. But since good and pleasure are attributes of God, who is on the right, then we can reason that the drug addict's good and pleasure is a distorted good and a false pleasure which was attained on the left. The reason it was attained on the left is because drug use is illegal and unjust. And without justice, the drug user's actions which produced good and pleasure are without God.

Professor: I follow you, Socrates. While the drug addict believes that there is good and pleasure in an unjust action, such an unjust action could cause pain and misery for others. This drug use could cause pain for the addict's family. The addict might be neglecting to feed and care for a child or a family to pay for drugs. And much injustice and many murders may occur in order for the illegal drugs to arrive at their final destination. And one may also ask, did the addict rob to pay for the drugs as addicts many times do?

Socrates: You see lad, good and pleasure attained on the left without justice is a distorted entity. We can see that on the left side one man's pleasure is another man's pain, one man's good is another man's evil.

Professor: But I wonder, wise one, about a married person who finds good and pleasure in an adulterous affair. Good and pleasure are attributes of God. There is no law of the state that declares the adulterer unjust, so the adulterer can indeed claim good and pleasure, which are of God, while not behaving unjustly. Therefore, I ask, is such a person receiving both good and pleasure from the attributes of God on the right, or is such a person receiving perceived good and pleasure from the distorted side on the left as did the drug addict?

Socrates: Remember lad, on the right side with God we identified justice, good and pleasure united as one, but don't forget, we also identified God as the Natural

Lawgiver. Which means that the adulterer might not be behaving unjustly by the laws of the state, but such a person is behaving unjustly toward a spouse, children, and even the adulterous partner by the laws of morality or the moral law. This means the action of adultery which produced good and pleasure to the senses is only an illusion of good and pleasure which the adulterer attains on the left side of injustice, which is the opposite of God who is just. Hence, only God justifies good, which means that all three attributes of good, pleasure, and justice must be present in order for someone's action to be true, authentic, and suitable to please God.

Then you see, the choices of the drug addict and adulterer have the properties of good and pleasure which are attributes of God. However, since their choices and behavior are unjust, which is the opposite of God, this means that their concept of good and pleasure is a greedy delusion of good and pleasure and opposes God who is just.

Professor: Although I am skeptical concerning the existence of God, it does follow that good, pleasure, and justice united, must be components of God, if there is a God. The concept of God eludes humanity and is most difficult to fully grasp and comprehend. Likewise God's attributes of good, pleasure, and justice united, are equally as elusive and as difficult to fully comprehend.

Socrates: We can add to something that is bad to make it better, can we not? Bland or bad tasting food becomes better by adding spices. Bad health becomes better health by adding medicine. What do you suppose we can add to good that is on the left, and therefore a distorted good, to make it better?

Professor: Justice, of course.

Socrates: When one adds the essence of justice one adds the essence of the divine. But at the right end of the spectrum, the final, ultimate, and ideal good is self-sufficient, and does not need anything added to its natural environment. It is in a perfect state of being.

On the contrary, the bad and distorted good on the left is actually mistaken in considering itself good. The good on the right conforms to the standard of justice, while the distorted good on the left falls short of the standard of justice. But since both the ideal good on the right and the distorted good on the left are judged by the standard of justice, then the good which possesses this standard is the true and ideal good, the ideal being, and ideal God. Once one removes justice from the good on the right, then one has produced the spoiled good of the left. Badness and evil on the left, therefore, are only spoiled goodness. Money, power, safety, and, in particular, pleasures are goods we are in pursuit of; when we attain these goods by unjust means, then only spoiled goods and unjustified pleasures are produced.

The beauty of the Natural Artist is evident in the fragrance of a rose or in the taste of fruit. Once the essence of the rose or taste of the fruit has decayed then we only possess a spoiled rose and a spoiled fruit. Likewise, once the beauty of justice is removed from the good which belongs with the Natural Artist on the right, we will have an unjust, decayed, and spoiled good on the left.

Do you see, young man? We desire and strive toward the right of the spectrum of justice to become more like God. For we know that the better we become, the more God-like we will be. We, by reason, truly desire to know the goodness of God, and produce just actions similar to God, but as long as the sensual pleasures describe good and pleasure but lack justice, we will continue to move away from God's pleasures, justice and goodness. Therefore, truth and God will continue to remain obscure in our world of illusion. Unless we use our bodies justly for the good to please God and do not use our bodies only to please ourselves and the senses, we will never know God. Unless the adulterer realizes that the spoiled good and selfish pleasure may cause a spouse pain and misery and endanger his whole family with a sexually transmitted disease, the adulterer will never strive toward God. Unless the just horse on the right, or the mind, overpowers the horse on the left and the bodily desires, we will never know God.

Professor: Is there a universal justice, Socrates? The minorities and some women in this country might not think so, for many times we have shown that justice is biased, catering to the ones in power. Even in our judicial system, I assure you that we have found people innocent that were guilty many times over. Many times this is due to the fact that one of the twelve jurors would not agree on a guilty verdict. Hence we cannot, and do not, possess a perfect, universal, and equal judicial system. Therefore, how is it possible for us to recognize and identify this foreign, yet desirable, attribute of ideal justice, since all of humanity resides along the left side of the spectrum of injustice? Even science attempts to justify itself in the good, pleasures, and knowledge that it provides for humanity. But since good and justice are of God, then even science cannot define what justice and good truly are.

Socrates: As we stated earlier, lad, science does not give us ideal justice. By all means, do not fool yourself into believing that science brings us the ideal good. For if science produced the ideals of justice and good combined, it would indeed describe God. But science is only knowledge of the external universe. How we use that knowledge defines our actions and behavior as just or unjust. One hundred million people have been murdered because of the misuse or even abuse of scientific technology.

Professor: I must agree that in this last century of ours the fact that 100 million people were murdered can be attributed primarily to scientifically advanced countries, using atomic bombs, chemical warfare or other technological advancements.

Socrates: In this case, lad, science is only neutral, since it can be used to produce either good or evil results.

Professor: How can one know, for certain, whether one's actions are truly just and offer justified pleasure, not only for the self, but also for one's fellow man, and for all of humanity as a whole? How can one identify this fine line in which someone's act has the potential to cause pleasure for all originating on the right, or causes pain to another human which would originate on the left?

Socrates: As I have stated in my dialogues...

How strange would appear to be this thing that men call pleasure! and how curiously it is related to what is thought to be the opposite, pain! The two will never be found together in a man, and yet if you seek the one and obtain it, you are almost bound always to get the other as well.[5]

Professor: Someone such as yourself, Socrates, when given the opportunity to escape from prison and continue the pleasures of living the good philosophical life, instead chose the penalty of the state which was death. As you have explained, living the pleasures of life without justice would be living a spoiled good, so you opted not to escape and behave unjustly but remained in prison in order to drink the poison and die for the sake of truth. You must believe then, as your actions proved, that to die with the truth of justice is to die with the essence of the divine, whereas to continue to live without justice is to live the life of a spoiled and rotten "good." Since I believe you are capable of answering, I ask, therefore, "What is this true and ideal essence of justice? Is it so desirable that dying with it is preferable to living without it?"

Socrates: Can you remember a time when injustice was done to you, lad?

Professor: Indeed I can.

Socrates: If you can, that implies that you have some understanding of the concept of justice. And if I were to inquire of the rest of the people in the museum, whether they remember a time when injustice was done to them, I am certain they will all answer "yes" immediately. This illustrates that we are experts in identifying with the concept of injustice, which is found on the left. But if I inquired of you, and all of the people here, if they remember some other person's actions having produced actual justice for them, how will they respond? I am not so sure they would all unanimously say "yes."

Professor: In this case, Socrates, we can only identify and describe what injustice is, while justice at the right remains veiled and obscured. What is the ideal essence of justice?

Socrates: Then you can understand, lad that...,

The result of the whole discussion has been that I know nothing at all. For I know not what justice is.[6]

Professor: Therefore, Socrates, your idea of a greater justice, or ideal justice, transcends our existence, which is beyond human reason and remains only as a hope. This, then, produces reason for my disbelief in the existence of a divine being who is ideal justice and ideal good, that is found at the right end of the spectrum of justice. The reason is, that which is, indeed, the ideal good, and is self aware of its goodness on the right, would wish to communicate its ideal goodness and not withhold such an ideal attribute from communication to us on the left; because an uncommunicated good is an unknown good. An unknown good is an unrealized and unidentified good. Therefore, an uncommunicated, unknown, and unidentified good is less good than a communicated, known, and realized good, which would be the more ideal good. Either the ideal good communicated itself, or it did not. If it did not, it does not exist. In conclusion, I am forced to agree with Dr. Lattison and his descriptive truths, which are contrary to religions that claim that God describes his goodness and justice. The fact is, religions themselves only prescribe what they want God to describe. For if God made himself descriptive, then we could all describe God. Only God can fully describe his goodness and justice, if he does, indeed, exist. If he does not descriptively communicate himself, then God is a lesser, uncommunicated and spoiled good, an unrealized truth that does not exist in its ideal form.

Socrates: With all of man's scientific advancements, and mastership of the external universe, 2,400 years later, I continue to discern that nothing has truly changed. As pertains to the knowledge, truth, and reality concerning the mind of God, I continue to find that I know not what justice is.

As an epicure snatches a taste of every dish which is successively brought to table, he not having allowed himself time to enjoy the one before, so have I have gone from one subject to another without having discovered what I sought at first, the nature of justice.
—*Socrates*[7]

And how could there exist a 'common good'! The expression is a self-contradiction: what can be common has ever but little value.
—*Nietzsche*[8]

Freedom

One who conquers himself is greater than another who conquers a thousand times a thousand men on the battlefield. Be victorious over yourself and not over others. When you attain victory over yourself, not even the gods can turn it into defeat.
—Buddha [1]

Socrates: The scientist describes the physical universe, which is occupied by matter in the large bodies of the sun, moon, stars, and planets that are in continuous motion. The scientist also describes the smallest objects of the subatomic level, occupying space, along with their qualities of mass, and electric charge. Is it true that not only the matter in the large bodies, but even matter at the subatomic particle level there is continuous motion, signifying change, as they are governed to behave and abide by the forces of gravity?

Professor: We have uncovered more laws than the laws of gravity, but indeed all matter submits to these laws of physics. This means that physical change is imposed upon all matter as your ancient philosophy has always described.

Socrates: These physical laws that impose force and change on matter also impose their regulations upon the human body, which is composed of these 92 atoms and therefore consists of matter.

Professor: Indeed, even the physical body of humans is bound by the laws of physics, which forces and produces continuous change upon our physical body, even after death. As we know, the dead body does slowly decay as the laws of physics dictate.

Socrates: Since the human brain also consists of matter, this raises the question, "Cannot the laws of physics which move and produce change upon all matter also move someone's neurons in the brain, forcing that individual to helplessly behave a certain way?" For example, when an individual is idly standing in front of a closet, undecided between the coat on the left or the coat on the right, it could be possible for the laws of gravity to impose their force upon the matter which make up the brain and propel the electrical circuit in the brain to move the hand to the right or coerce the electrical circuit to move the individual's hand to the left.

Professor: Yes, there is that possibility that the laws of physics acting upon matter could dictate our behavior.

Socrates: Since all of the movements and actions of the human body are preceded by different circuits of neurons which originate in the brain and dictate the body's actions, I do wonder. A person is standing in front of a jeweler undecided whether to buy a certain necklace. If that person chooses to purchase the necklace, certain neurons, or a particular circuit of neurons, in the brain will trigger, causing the hand to reach into a pocket, grab some money and pay for the merchandise. The scientist, or, in particular, the physicist studies such electrical circuitry.

Professor: Indeed, the physicist is the expert in such matters.

Socrates: While the undecided person is contemplating purchasing the necklace and notices the jeweler being distracted by another customer in the shop. Suddenly a completely different circuit of neurons begin to fire in the brain, forcing the hand to reach for, grab, and to steal one of the diamond rings. Is it possible for lifeless neurons which are incapable of knowing right and wrong, justice and injustice, to have been forced by the laws of physics to fire this particular circuit of neurons to cause the hand to steal the diamond? Or did that person's invisible universe of thoughts make the wrong choice of triggering a circuit of neurons, causing a wrong and unjust choice. But if that person did freely choose, then where is this choice of freedom located?

Professor: The topic of freedom has tormented philosophers since the ancient Greeks, and still continues to haunt modern philosophers today. Its effect continues to baffle the fields of law, neurology, politics, and criminal psychiatry! Concerning freedom and responsibility, if the scientific view is correct, that every action has a cause including all human actions, then in a mechanical universe, the laws of physics could cause, dictate, and determine everyone's actions every time.

Socrates: In this case lad, the one that stole the diamond ring would not be guilty of wrongdoing since the physical laws dictated the individual to raise a hand and to place the ring in a pocket. If everything in the universe, including our brains, consists of matter forced in motion by the laws of physics, then the physical laws forced the circuitry in the individual's brain to move and put the hand in motion, which means we are nothing more than pawns in a universe of cause and effect. Nobody's actions then deserve praise or blame for anything they do; since the physical laws determine every action for everyone at all times.

Professor: As a philosopher is in agony concerning the question of forced behavior upon humans induced by the laws of physics, jurors in a court of law are equally tormented by forced behavior which society induces upon certain people. A child born in the ghetto, for example, is raised with the behavior which society has imposed upon him. Is the child's behavior conditioned by the surroundings in the ghetto? To what extent is the child's freedom limited, due to an environment which in many ways encourages violent behavior? Although our society tends to sympathize with such subjects who were conditioned to behave a certain way due to their environmental situations, our judicial system usually passes judgment as if free will is the cause of any crime or unjust behavior. It is deemed cause for punishment.

Socrates: If we are indeed free, then how do you suppose the invisible and nonphysical thoughts trigger physical neurons to behave any particular way which the invisible universe of the individual decides? What and where is this invisible substance which is of mind that can reach into the physical world of atoms, push around electrons, nerves, and brain cells? Does mind disregard the physical laws of cause and effect and reach from the nonphysical universe of thoughts into the physical world of matter and rearrange physical objects that would have been otherwise arranged if mind did not exist?

Let's observe someone leisurely dining at home, shall we? On the table we find food, salt, pepper, water, etc. which are located in our physical objective universe. The individual's thoughts, ideas, etc., are in a personal, subjective, and private universe. The individual begins to eat the food consisting of matter, and their sense of taste signals the brain that the food needs salt. In the universe of thoughts the individual decides to reach into the physical universe for the salt and adds some to the food. The physical sensation of salt then informs the individual that the food has become too salty, and from the private universe of thoughts the individual decides to reach into the physical world, grasp, and drink a cup of water.

The individual then notices a glass of wine, suspends the water impulse, modifies his or her thoughts and decides in the private universe to reach for and drink the wine instead. How does this interaction of physical substance on the table, visible to all who are present, interact with the invisible mind of the individual which is visible to no one? How does the invisible mind interact with the physical matter on the table? Better yet, how does mind, which is not physical and does not occupy space, trigger neurons and cause action to be taken by the body and interact with physical matter in general? Does the invisible mind defy the physical laws and act upon matter freely, or did the physical substances of salt, water, etc., determine the individual's actions?

Professor: How indeed, Socrates? The most important and most fundamental question concerning our existence and we will do anything to detach ourselves from this question! The chemist will describe the chemical makeup of the sugar, wine, and everything else on the table. The physicist will describe the motions of electrons, neutrons, and the energy potentiality of the same physical substance. The biologist will describe the cause and effect of the physical substance, such as the wine, upon the individual's liver. While the psychologist will observe the individual's behavior, as to why he or she drank the wine as opposed to the water. But the philosopher's task is not only to understand the external universe of physical substance, and the external behavior of the individual which follows from the physical substance. Philosophy is the discipline which attempts to understand the interaction between the two; the process between matter and mind. Concerning the philosopher's task of understanding free will vs. determinism, which states that everyone's actions are determined by the laws of physics, modern science has indeed produced tremendous revelations assisting this study of philosophy in recent years.

Three hundred years ago Sir Isaac Newton made some important discoveries which we call Newtonian Physics or classical mechanics. Classical mechanics describes the particles of the universe in an absolute position which follow a mechanical cause-and-effect pattern for all matter. This revelation, revealed to many philosophers, such as Friederich Nietzsche that all of reality, which includes human nature, is nothing more than robots in a universe of cause and effect. Accordingly, all of reality is bound by the deterministic laws of physics. These were the hard determinists which believed there was no freedom for humankind, whatsoever.

Then, in this century, the discoveries of Heisenberg, Neils Bohr, and other physicists produced quantum mechanics, which is a brand new revelation concerning the workings of the universe in which we live. Quantum mechanics describes the subatomic level of atoms, neutrons and electrons including the composition of the brain, to reveal a universe of uncertainty, and not 100% mechanical. This new revelation assures us that nobody can simultaneously determine both the position and motion of a particle, and has consequently produced what physicists call "the uncertainty principle." This means that effects can take place without a known cause, which in turn have many modern philosophers believing that freedom is available from the deterministic laws of physics.

Socrates: Then it seems that most people here in the museum should be grateful to this uncertainty principle for liberating their minds from the laws of physics and determinism. But how many people do you suppose will respond to me if I inquire of them concerning the philosopher's understanding of this subatomic level of quantum mechanics and the uncertainty principle that has allowed them the possibility of free will?

Professor: Not many understand the revelations of quantum mechanics.

Socrates: Then I assume that when people insist on their freedom, they must be referring to political freedom.

Professor: Democracy and political freedom, which have their origins in ancient Greece, continue to be cherished in our country. In fact our Declaration of Independence is almost a replica of the declaration of independence by the statesman Pericles in ancient Athens. We are grateful to you ancient philosophers for originating and implementing political liberty, freedom to vote, freedom of speech, freedom of choice, etc.

Socrates: We can conclude, then, that the liberated mind would belong to an individual living in a state that allows the self to freely choose and decide as one's mind wishes; free to act as one pleases. Therefore, freedom is only available where there is no coercion of external force, such as the laws of physics. Freedom must also be without the intimidation, restraint, and coercion by any of the governmental agencies within the state toward the individual.

Professor: Human liberty would require freedom from the deterministic laws of physics upon the mind, and would also require freedom from force which the state can produce.

Socrates: The question of human freedom, however, does suggest the following question. Let's observe a human being that lives in a particular state with a particular divine law. This law implies that every time that human being decides to make a wrong choice which would be an unjust act, a divine agent would intercede in the individual's brain producing a right and just choice. Likewise, any time anyone living in such a society was to choose wrongfully, this divine agent would intercede, causing everyone to do the correct, righteous, and justified deed every time. In such a scenario, do you suppose this divine agent would extend from the natural and righteous good on the right or the distorted and unjust good on the left?

Professor: If the outcome was always a just deed, then obviously this divine interference would indeed come from the good that is identified with justice on the right.

Socrates: And if we were to inquire of everyone in the museum, if they would prefer to live in a society where a divine agent interceded to make sure everyone made the right choice, or to live in a society where people are free to make the wrong choice and do evil, in which society do you suppose the people would prefer to live?

Professor: As we would dread for the mechanical laws of physics to dictate our behavior and would also not desire for the state to force and coerce our free will, likewise we can do without this scenario of divine intervention upon our judgment which would be another case of force and restraint against our freedom. For this is one of the questions which we ask of all philosophy students: "Do you prefer to live in a society which is free to commit evil, or to live in a society that is forced to always make the right choice and do good?" Speaking from experience, most of my students, as most people will agree, say they would prefer to live in a society where one is free to do evil as opposed to living in a society where they are forced to do good.

Socrates: In this case, lad, you are implying that the justified good and ultimate freedom on the right should not interfere with the freedom of human desires to cause evil. For to interfere with our freedom to choose restrains us.

Professor: As I said, most would prefer to live in freedom as opposed to living with force, even if freedom entitles us to choose evil.

Socrates: Am I correct in assuming that you believe an individual is more free who is living in a society surrounded with evil, pain and injustice, while another individual is less free living in a society where there is no evil, no pain, and no injustice? This is indeed your perception of freedom young man.

Professor: I can only judge by the experience of myself and my fellow man. We have no way of knowing how it would be to live in a civilization that did only good, for no human has ever experienced such an existence. We can generally agree that since birth we have been conditioned to believe that to be free is to be allowed freedom of choice, including, of course, the choice to do evil.

Socrates: There is the possibility that your concept of freedom and understanding of force could simply be an illusion.

Professor: Explain.

Socrates: You are not free to contaminate all of the water supply of New York City and poison to death eight million people in a single day, are you?

Professor: I should say not.

Socrates: Neither are you free to harness all of the oxygen supply of New York and suffocate all New Yorkers.

Professor: Not by any means.

Socrates: If you had been granted such liberty, only then could you have cried foul and coercion once that freedom was removed from you. But you do not cry foul against this freedom having been removed from you because it was never within your power to suffocate millions of people. One does not cry foul against some evil which they are incapable of ever having the potential to commit. Likewise, in such a divine existence, one simply would not even consider murdering or raping someone while continuing to abide in freedom.

Professor: I don't believe people should murder or rape, but that they should be free to choose not to murder and free to choose not to rape.

Socrates: We identified injustice and pain on the left while its opposites of justice and pleasure we identified on the right. Do you not think therefore that a society that begins to produce less injustice and less pain is moving from left to right and is becoming more free? More freedom in this case offers freedom from injustice, evil, and pain. And if such a society relieves itself of all of its injustice and all of its evil and pain, then we can say that this society has arrived at the right or ideal location which includes the universally desired justice, good, pleasure, and freedom. This would indeed be the location where the divine resides, would it not?

Professor: Indeed it would, Socrates. But only if less injustice and less pain was the outcome of the people's free choice to move toward the right, for that would be the ultimate freedom, as opposed to having the right side of good being forced upon them. For freedom is difficult to identify when force is present, and that would include the force of good.

Socrates: Then you must agree that as long as humans are producing more laws, and causing more injustice and more pain, they become more enslaved to evil and less free; hence, your understanding of freedom would be but an illusion, an illusion of attempting to describe freedom while being in bondage to painful and unjust behavior.

Professor: We want to be free to do evil and we want to be free to do good. Free to strive to the left, if we so desire, and free to strive to the right.

Socrates: Human beings generally prefer the freedom to do evil as opposed to being forced to do good. This implies that God is not forced to intervene every time an unjust act is done. But God must also be free to intervene, or not to intervene, as he chooses, within his own freedom, while respecting our freedom of choice.

Professor: God should be free indeed, free to do as he wishes. But many, including our modern day process theologians, raise the inevitable questions, "Where was God during the Jewish Holocaust?...How could God—if there is a God—let such a horrendous event occur?"[2] If he is truly free, why does God not exercise his freedom to stop evil, Socrates?

Socrates: Your question of why God allows evil reminds me of a story concerning a very successful businessman. Throughout his business career this man always managed to make the appropriate and virtuous business decision every time. He was a man of high morals and consequently well-respected in his community. His only son, wishing to imitate if not surpass the father and his success, chose to separate his dealings from his father's. Therefore, the son began his own independent business venture. When the son made an unwise decision or an illegal business deal, his father cautioned him. But the son rejected the father's input, regarding it as interference. The son insisted on the freedom to make his own decisions and rejected the father's help, which he thought was coercion. Although the son's decisions often pained the father as he watched the son making many unlawful transactions, the father respected the son's wishes and allowed for the son's liberty. Finally the day came when the son was driven to file for bankruptcy. His illegal activities forced upon him a prison sentence. He lost everything he had, including his wife and family. Instead of taking responsibility for the wrong business decisions he had made, the son cursed the father and said he was cruel and evil for not intervening to save his business. On one hand, he insisted that the father not intervene. On the other hand, he became upset because the father did not intervene. Now, I ask you, does this young man have the right to blame the father, or should he blame himself?

Professor: Himself, of course.

Socrates: Then, this is the story that we must share with these modern process theologians, for they become like the son and cry foul against God instead of taking responsibility for their own actions and their own mistakes. They need to realize that humanity is located between the good, just, and free on the right which opposes the evil and distorted good which causes pain on the left. By intervening, the divine agent will always cause good and just deeds which will draw a person toward the right. The one who is in the middle however perceives this as coercion, as being forced to do only good. Instead, the one who is in the middle elects to embrace a misconception of freedom, which identifies humanity as free to make the wrong choices and cause evil, injustice, and pain.

Being free to do evil implies that one is free to strive toward and attain a distorted and unjust good on the left, while causing others misery and unwarranted pain. But once the evil deed has been committed as a consequence of this freedom of choice, such as the Holocaust, then the human cries foul against God for not intervening. But was this not the same human that cried out foul and coercion if the good and just side of God had intervened in the first place? What gives this human the right, then, after the evil deed is committed, to cry foul against God for not intervening? In other words, lad, from our distorted perspective concerning freedom, God is damned if he intervenes against our free choice to commit evil acts while God is damned if he has not intervened after we make the wrong and evil choice.

Professor: Fine, Socrates, let's acknowledge the guilt of humankind concerning the primary evils of morality, and of choice due to our abuse of freedom. Humans, however, are not responsible for the secondary evils which nature produces, such as natural catastrophes, cancer, heart disease, etc. Therefore, if there exists the Natural Artist which you identify as God, then God must be held responsible for the evils of nature, or shall we say, the evils of the Natural Artist.

Socrates: Now you are stating that humans desire no coercion or force from the side of good, but their desire to be free is a desire to allow them to make evil choices. How is it possible for humanity to simultaneously desire to force God's goodness upon their everyday life? Is it reasonable, I ask you, for humans to choose evil, and behave unjustly toward each other, and against God, while demanding God to behave just and good toward them? Can it not be that the evils of nature are forced upon humanity as a byproduct of their rebellious choices which go contrary to that which is good and naturally just?

Professor: The secondary evils of nature in the form of catastrophes and disease are consequences of the will of God, the Natural Artist. How do you reason that these evils are by the choice of humans?

Socrates: When rain causes a river to flood and damage many homes along its path, this is indeed the result of the evils of nature. But who, I ask, decided to build a house along the path of a flooding river, people or God? Or is God guilty for not warning those individuals of their unwise decisions? Of whom do humans inquire when they decide in their greedy nature to construct tall buildings upon a small parcel of land in order to maximize space? But when an earthquake rumbles and levels the building, do we blame greedy humans for the collapse, the wounded and the slaughter of many people living in the high-rises or do we blame God for not warning us concerning the consequences of building tall structures?

Professor: One can indeed argue that human greed and ignorance are partly to blame and should be held accountable for escalating the effects of the secondary evils of nature. One could even state that cancer is the byproduct of smoking cigarettes, air pollution, processed foods, etc., which are choices of humankind. But we cannot place blame for the origins of catastrophes upon humanity, since nature is responsible and should be held accountable for creating these evils, for it is within nature that these catastrophes originate.

Consider the story of the son who rebelled against his righteous father and was imprisoned for committing unjust and unlawful acts. If the father owned and governed everything, including the prison which incarcerated the son, should the father allow the son to continue to be punished? Should he disassociate himself from the son completely? Or would a compassionate father help liberate the son from his mistakes that forced him into bondage?

If then, Father God does exist, he should have compassion on his creation and freely reveal his goodness and justice to his rebellious people. Most religions argue the premise that humanity has rebelled against God and has abused its divinely given freedom. They claim that all people find themselves imprisoned in this world of evil, pain, injustice, and illusion. You, as a philosopher, Socrates, have a way of describing this illusion in a more comprehensive manner.

Socrates: Humans desire to be free to do evil but expect God to impose his goodness and perfect nature upon them, while they choose to live in their unjust ways at the same time. If God is good and free, then out of his goodness he allowed freedom of choice, which is our natural desire. Freedom entails choosing, and that must include choosing against God, which is sin. God, therefore, did not will moral disorder and rebellion upon his creation, he simply permitted it. He permitted it for the sake of the greater good, the good which is freedom; for he is one with good and freedom. Since freedom is that which is our natural desire and God is the one that is naturally free, then it is God who becomes our natural desire.

If humanity has rebelled and misused their freedom of choice against God, who is eternally constant and always good, then we realize that it is good and justified that rebellion be punished, hence everyone should take responsibility and no one should complain. Consider this: if God is omnipotent and has compassion for us, he would provide natural resources to cure every ailment. It is evident that natural resources such as plants and minerals are the source of ancient medicines as well as modern medicines. Even cancer should have a cure, although, as I am told, scientists have yet to discover the proper antidote. This of course might reveal that God has not forgotten his people in an ocean of evil and pain, but his healing qualities for ailments are indeed near to us all. The choice to find the good of his cures is left to us, since it is our desire to have freedom of choice.

Human rebellion and sin are not only evil in themselves but are the byproducts of the primary evils of immorality and choice. It is the ultimate source of human suffering which has produced the secondary evils of nature as well. If the dwelling of God consists of freedom and perfection on the right, how can humanity expect perfection on the left, which consists as we have seen of injustice and of behavior contrary to God? But why steer off course and contemplate the freedom of God that would be absolute, constant, and undeviating which would be incomprehensible to man. Do you suppose humanity is able to identify with freedom while living in this environment of distorted reality, and relative justice? What is this thing called freedom, lad? Is it descriptive that I may inquire of the scientist to weigh it, measure it, and describe it, or is it prescriptive, that we may debate its nature as philosophers, to understand its essence?

Better yet, how does the philosopher of history describe the use of freedom by humankind, that is, if freedom can be identified at all? Has freedom been used as a means of arriving at the right side of good, justice, and pleasure where it belongs? Or has freedom been misused and abused to cause evil, pain, and injustice, forcing humanity on the side of bondage? If it has been misused and abused, then humanity cannot know the true essence and nature of freedom.

Professor: There is a well-known declaration in America that states "Give me liberty or give me death." In this statement, one can identify that when we do not have freedom, implying we are dominated and coerced by an external force, then even death is superior when compared to living our lives in bondage.

Socrates: Since we all desire freedom, then all of us should help in providing it for our fellow man, and assist each other in attaining it.

Professor: Indeed.

Socrates: And if we cannot give freedom to our fellow man, or help him attain it, then we should at least be certain never to take freedom away from another or force anyone into bondage.

Professor: By all means.

Socrates: Forcing someone into bondage would be an act opposing the Natural Lawgiver that gives us our freedom, which is our freedom of choice. I therefore wonder; if freedom and reason are both identified on the right along with pleasure and good, why must death be exchanged for freedom, as your declaration states? Is it necessary for brutality and death to take precedence for a people to be free? Is our free will exercised when we kill our brothers and sisters in order to gain our own liberation? And why would a human being abuse free will and stain the soul by keeping another in bondage, with such force that only by acts of war and the brutal murder of the oppressor might the one who is oppressed become free. Is death necessary for the pleasure of freedom to take place? Must liberty through death be the means of moving toward freedom which is located at the right?

Professor: Freedom has its price and it is usually called death, Socrates. Triumph over bondage from the left has historically been guaranteed by guns, ammunition, killing, maiming, and bloodshed. Since you inquire of history, only through death and bloodshed was liberty bestowed upon the United States from the British.

Socrates: If there is a God who gave humanity freedom of choice which opposes coercion, what can we say concerning the human that forces and coerces another? Is that individual behaving consistent with or contrary to God?

Professor: Contrary, of course.

Socrates: Then which individual is in worse bondage- the one that forces or the one that is forced?

Professor: The one that uses force, for that one is behaving contrary to the Natural Lawgiver who gives freedom of choice.

Socrates: Then would you not say that freedom should be a natural right which is given by the Natural Artist? For once freedom takes precedence and men allow others the freedom to choose, humanity can be described to be in the image of God as opposed to being in bondage—which portrays man to be very unlike and even opposite to God.

Professor: It should, Socrates, but the one that imposes force and coercion resides on the left with injustice, believing in a skewed concept of freedom that to force another to comply seems good. Coercing someone to work gives the oppressor freedom from labor, financial freedom, and the freedom to consume another's toil, labor, and resources.

Socrates: Since we agree that freedom should be a natural right to all of humanity, what about those humans who oppose this natural law? We all desire good and justice and oppose evil and injustice. We all prefer pleasure and freedom and oppose pain and bondage. Why is it, then, that this same world contains so much of the opposites which we despise? Why do we desire one but get the other? And why, in the name of heaven, does the one who becomes free and liberated desire to force another into bondage, which we all despise?

Professor: Why indeed, Socrates? When freedom was finally established in this country, the same liberated people placed themselves in worse bondage by forcing the African-American into the shackles of slavery.

Socrates: Then freedom continues to be abused for the sake of evil. It seems, once liberated, instead of humankind striving toward the right as free men, they instead immorally exercise their newfound power which freedom offers, to enslave their fellow man.

Professor: It was not only the African American who felt the power of freedom abused. Through bloodshed the American Indian was also forced and coerced to be confined to the reservation. It seems that pain produces freedom, and bloodshed produces liberty. This is the history of freedom on our planet, Socrates. It is a history that describes the illusion of a human law which states that one must die for another to be free. The pain of killing and murder historically seems the only way out when it comes to arriving at the pleasure and good of becoming free.

Socrates: Amuse me, lad, and tell me that this abuse of freedom was not isolated only in this country of yours, but this nightmare of injustice is a universal phenomenon.

Professor: Universal indeed. It was even worse in your country of Greece where the ideals of democracy and freedom began. After 400 years of Turkish rule that had enslaved your country, only through war and bloodshed did the Greeks finally establish independence and receive liberty some 150 years ago.

Socrates: Then one is to assume that once liberated the Greeks in turn abused their freedom, enslaved and overpowered their fellow man, enforcing their value systems upon them?

Professor: Not quite. Your philosophy states that the powerful impose their justice and concept of freedom on the weaker. However, Greece was too weak after Turkish domination to impose their value system and justice upon their fellow man. But following the Turks, the powerful country of Germany in their distorted concept of freedom, justice and power, subjugated and coerced the Greeks and other countries on two different occasions: 1917 and 1941. Once again, through world war and terrible bloodshed, Greece and the other countries were able to rid themselves of the barbaric bondage of the Nazis. Once freed from the Nazis with the help of guns and ammunition from the British, the latter then found it necessary to remain in Greece in order to maintain liberty for the Greeks. Meanwhile, they were consuming Greek resources, of course.

The philosopher Karl Marx wrote his idea of ways and means of attaining freedom and justice for all. He called his liberating mindset "Communism," which helped "liberate" the Russian people from the bondage and oppression of the Czars. This newfound concept of freedom delivered by the communists grew on the grave of millions to a point where it held almost half the globe in bondage. Through intimidation and death, the Russians attempted to force and coerce the Greeks into this liberating system of equality for all. History has proven your philosophy correct, Socrates. The powerful will impose their concept of justice and freedom upon the weaker, always. As the old saying goes "power corrupts, absolute power corrupts absolutely." Nowhere else has this been more evident in recent years than by the ruling class of communism.

Socrates: Then what message does humanity send by the fact that Americans, Greeks, Russians and other nations celebrate special days of liberty and independence? Is it not a historical witness to humanity's hypocrisy? Humans want freedom without force, even from the side of good and justice. But once humanity obtains this freedom by abuse of such freedom, human beings transform themselves into hypocrites. They will enslave their fellow man. They fall into the universal trap of overpowering and imposing their value system upon their fellow man. We have previously agreed that justice, good, pleasure, and freedom are related, constant, and united at the right.

Professor: We did.

Socrates: We also agree that on the left we find the opposites, of evil-injustice, pain, and bondage.

Professor: Indeed.

Socrates: If on the left, one man's good deviates into another man's evil, and one man's pleasure becomes another man's pain, how can we state that freedom is on the right and constant, while all of this time you have been saying that one man's liberty is another man's bondage, one mans freedom is another mans death? Hence, in our environment of distorted reality, freedom must be but an illusion. Human freedom does not arrive freely with pleasure from the right side, but it arrives by butchery and bloodshed full of pain from the left. The concepts of good, justice, freedom, and, might I add, power, reside only with God on the right. Freedom is essential to justice, and good justice necessitates freedom, therefore only the divine one, who is free from error and bondage, can judge freely with accuracy and truth. His freedom includes possession of power, the power that freedom affords, yet is also capable of not misusing it. God's freedom must be constant and undeviating. Therefore, God must not possess a physical body to be coerced by the physical laws, and does not need to kill someone to liberate himself, which seems to be a universal human law.

Professor: Here in this country most Americans believe they are free since they are free to choose, free to vote, free to come and go as they please. They believe that we have progressed beyond this human law which portrays death bound to freedom.

Socrates: It will be hundreds of years from now before people will be able to judge, by the human standard of justice, this historical time period and decide on the freedom or bondage of your civilization. But I wonder, if we inquire of the poor concerning freedom, today, in this country, would the poor not wish to become liberated from the external force called poverty that dominates them? Would not the chronically sick person, who is coerced by external means called disease, which such a person does not desire, wish to find liberty from the force that keeps such a person painfully languishing in bed? If we inquire of women, will not many describe a desire for freedom and liberation from the external and historical coercion that male-dominated societies have imposed upon them? As you stated, the African-American desires to be free from racism, and the historical bondage which some believe is still endured today. The American Indian wants liberation for the Indian peoples and for Indian lands. The homosexual wants liberty to pursue and maintain a lifestyle. The Arab people want to liberate Palestine. The nation of Israel wants to keep Israel free from Palestinian rule. Need I continue, or do you still believe that you are truly free?

Professor: As you are describing it, Socrates, bondage is relative, since every individual is coerced by diverse means and dominated by different forces. Hence freedom must also be relative, therefore attained by relative and different means for every individual.

Socrates: Then enough of this schoolboy's philosophy lad, and let's reveal absolute bondage and coercion which are universal for all of humanity. For, no one can be truly free.

Professor: And how can we arrive at this conclusion?

Socrates: If there is a soul within the body, then is not the body the external force that is coercing and subjecting the soul to comply? Is this not universal bondage for everyone?

Professor: That is a big "if," Socrates. But, yes, if there is a soul within the body, then that could be a possibility.

Socrates: In this case should the mind or soul be a slave to the body, and the body be the master?

Professor: The mind should be the master of course. As we discussed earlier, reason should be in control of the chariot which we identified as the right horse. For reason is better qualified to keep us upon a straight path of righteousness as opposed to the bodily desires which you described as the horse on the left.

Socrates: But for many, if not all, the body is indeed the master to the mind, would you not agree? Which means humans are, for the most part, ignorant and unaware of their bondage. Observe those two people smoking cigarettes outside the door. Do you suppose they were forced to go outside and smoke, or did they freely choose?

Professor: First of all they are outside due to the fact that the museum does not allow smoking inside. But I get your point; they are primarily outside not because their mind chose to be outside, but because the body forced them to go there. The mind of many smokers desires to be free from the addiction of cigarettes, but the body of the smoker that is accustomed to the nicotine which cigarettes produce overpowers the desire and will of the mind. The body forces and coerces the mind of the smoker to continuously light up yet another cigarette.

Socrates: Then we can agree that the body becomes liberated from its needs which are necessary, once it has relieved itself from the coercion of hunger, from thirst, from the intimidation of extreme cold or heat upon it, etc.

Professor: The body should be liberated when it fulfills and satisfies its basic needs such as food, water, clothing, shelter, etc. The problem arises after the needs are met. After the necessities are fulfilled, then, follow the glutinous cravings, unquenchable passions, and insatiable desires.

Socrates: Should not the cravings and passions of the body be identified by the mind as desires and not needs?

Professor: They should, but for many the body demands its desires to be identified by the mind as needs. Hence the mind falls into bondage to the body once the mind misinterprets the body's desires as needs. Today, as always, Socrates, humans desire passionately to control and master nature, including the animal world. History also proves that humans derive satisfaction from conquering and mastering another human. And almost always there is even greater satisfaction found when the subject being mastered identifies and acknowledges the master himself.

Humanity will continue to behave unjustly and remain in bondage until we realize that first we must begin to master ourselves and have our minds conquer our own bodies. Humankind moans for freedom and cries foul against anyone's coercion, yet we are guilty of imprisoning the self as well as our fellow man. Humans are responsible for pushing and keeping themselves to the left side of bondage, coercion, and injustice. If there is an omnipotent being on the right that is all-powerful and free and who has allowed us freedom of choice, then it is that free being that we must imitate. The human who dominates, and subjects another human being behaves contrary to this image of the divine being or Natural Lawgiver that gives freedom of choice. If there is a God who judges, I would prefer to be judged as a slave in this world that has never forced or coerced anybody than to be judged a master that forces, dominates, coerces, and subjugates another. An individual, or master, begins to behave contrary to the image of God, the Natural Lawgiver, as soon as such a person takes away from another the freedom and the choice to be or not to be as that other person wishes.

As the stoic philosophers taught, freedom is part of the natural law that governs the universe and should also govern peoples' lives as well. This was the liberating good news that was offered to the vassal, the slave, and the poor by the stoics in ancient Greece two hundred and fifty years B.C. This is the liberating good news offered to a Vietnam prisoner of war who became our vice presidential candidate. Regardless if there is a God that is self-aware at the right of the spectrum or not, the fact is that desire for and movement toward the right of good, justice, pleasure, and freedom, without the abuse of power that freedom produces, should be the teleology or refined state of being for all of humanity. This is the description and location of the Logos to the Greek philosophers.

Socrates: And how does a modern philosopher describe the Logos of the ancient Greeks in today's world? It seems that you doubt its existence along with Dr. Lattison who is unwilling to accept such an intangible entity.

Professor: The Greek Logos, as I understand it, implies "the reason or purpose," the Natural Lawgiver, the ideal and justified good that is the paramount of freedom. Dr. Lattison does not disagree that such an ideal existence cannot be arrived at by humankind or that humanity lacks the potential of perfection; Dr. Lattison disagrees that such a one does exist in actuality, and that a self-aware Logos that is conscious of its own existence, of its freedom, of its goodness, and of its justice, is waiting to embrace a repenting humanity at the right side of your scale.

I say regardless whether the Logos is self-aware or not, the fact is, that is where our teleology and refined state of being should be. Will humanity ever liberate itself to freely make the good, wise, and justified choice toward the right of the true Logos; or, will we continue to abuse our freedom and cause evil and keep others in bondage?

Socrates: You stated earlier that humans want to be free to choose even if that entails choosing unjustly. Humans desire to be free to strive to the left of the distorted good which causes pain, and they also want to be free to strive to the right where the ideal and justified good and the ideal concept of freedom reside. If we compare the distorted good on the left, and the ideal and just good on the right, we realize that both can be bipolar opposites, yet both can be called good and free; yet only one can be the ideal good that is truly free. First, we begin with the understanding that the good on the left has a need. Therefore, it is not independently free. The authentic good on the right has no need, and is self-sufficient, and, in itself, free.

We concluded earlier that the distorted good on the left is in need of justice while the good on the right is in no need of such a thing, for its essence is naturally just. Therefore that which is free is free from compulsion, deficiency, imperfection, and does not lack anything including justice. It is just in its totality.

Acknowledgment of the lack of justice is only a part of the liberation process that the distorted good on the left is in need of becoming free. Along with justice, the good on the left has the need of desire to make it good, whereas the good on the right has no need for desire. In other words, when something becomes humanity's desire it also becomes a perceived good. It becomes a good simply due to the fact that one desires it, and is in pursuit of attaining it. Someone's desire to seduce another man's wife will become his good if he seduces her. But the fact that one might attain this perceived good is not grounds for making this good a justified good. A person's liberty to desire, and free will to attain a thing, is not grounds for making it good. Desires change from one individual to another and also change for the same individual over the course of time and under diverse circumstances, producing a relative desire which only describes a relative good.

The good on the right side however, which is identified as the Logos, has been, is, and will always be the complete, undeviating, and just good. It is in itself the ultimate and free good, which means it has no need of anything added to make this ultimate good a better good. And in particular this ideal good is not only not in need of justice, but is also not in need of desires to make it good. The Logos, therefore, which is good and just, should be desirable because its essence is of goodness and its nature is of justice. The fact that it lacks nothing in its totality constitutes it as free, whereas its polar opposite on the left becomes good only due to the fact that the desire and passion of attaining it makes it seem good. The human mind therefore can begin its path to freedom from its ignorance by realizing that desiring something does not make that something good.

The philosopher, however, who is free from such ignorance, is able to teach the rest to liberate their minds and strive toward the Logos which is righteous, ideal, and true good, and indeed is able to free humanity from the passions and bondage of ignorance. But as long as humans are bound to bodily desires which the left side offers, they will be unable to identify with or recognize the Logos, the ideal good, which only the mind and reason can produce. Hence, people will continue to live in bondage with their ignorant belief that is, "If I desire a thing, it must be good. If I am free to attain it, I must be truly free."

Professor: You will be glad to know that your pupils continued proclaiming your philosophy as Plato's pupil Aristotle states...

> *What appears to be good is the object of one's appetite, and what is good is the primary object of our will; and we desire things because we believe them to be good, rather than believing them to be good because we desire them....* [3]

Modern existentialists, such as the French philosopher Sartre, agree we are free to choose. But freedom, to Sartre, means condemnation, as each one of us is responsible for our evil choices, as I also believe. Although I am not a religious person and am therefore not held captive by any religious doctrine, your philosophy does seem to correspond with the ancient religion of Israel. For thousands of years the Israelites have told an interesting allegory concerning the abuse of freedom, and the "great fall." They believed that the almighty God who identified himself as Yahweh had offered the perfect environment for his creation. That perfect environment, of course, in his ideal state of being, included freedom, both for Yahweh and his subjects. No one was forced or coerced in Yahweh's creation at any time. Yahweh is described as allowing for freedom, yet is also a God of order and discipline, as is revealed in his law which states "you shall not eat of the tree of knowledge."

According to the Old Testament, this is precisely what humanity did indeed do. Consequently, due to the rebellion of his subjects, the tree of knowledge has become awareness of the side of injustice, evil, and pain which you describe as being on the left where humanity dwells. The promise that was made by Yahweh was "when you eat of the tree of knowledge you shall surely die." The spirit of Yahweh on the right is composed of life. Without that life-giving spirit, his fallen subjects, which is all of rebellious humanity, finds itself spiritually dead on the left. Therefore, God Yahweh offered freedom, and humanity accepted it, which means that humanity has been allowed knowledge with freedom to move to the left, which of course consists of pain, evil, injustice, and death. Consequently, the point of the story is, freedom was abused and humanity is now paying for it.

This captivating allegory of the great fall of humanity was described by the prophets of the Israelites in the Old Testament. The idea of allowing humanity freedom of choice and its subsequent abuse has been borrowed by the Christian and Muslim religions, which I might add are number one and two in total number of followers on this planet.

Suppose, for a moment, that I accept that the Logos, your ideal good, with justice that is self-aware, does indeed exist, and is identified as Yahweh of Israel. You have indicated that the Logos on the right is undeviating, constant, and the source of all truth. It does not possess matter. Therefore, it is immutable, since it is immune to the change governed by the laws of physics. The Logos is the Greek philosopher's terminology describing the active, unifying force of goodness and justice; the source of all reason for all things, that resides with and dispenses the natural law by which we must live. The Logos would be the transcending reason and purpose of all existence and unity of all things. The closest we can come to describe the Greek Logos in English is "the Word," but Logos has a higher meaning and there is no equivalent word in English. The sharing of a word from one human to another carries no dimensions in itself, but is able to communicate to the soul of the receiving party. The word is something lacking a body but is literally able to make one cry and another laugh, as it expresses meaning and reveals reason. The philosopher's Logos, therefore, is pure mind and spirit in its totality possessing the potential to speak from its innate goodness to our inner soul.

But this is where I, as a philosopher, part ways from all of the religious beliefs. All the religions that claim an absolute and undeviating just God on the right side should be in unison with one another concerning this immutable unchanging good. How is it possible then, for religions to deviate and change, one from another, while describing this undeviating and unchanging good which they call God?

Christianity, which originated 2,000 years ago with the life of Christ, claims that Father God from his throne on the right has sent his son Jesus Christ to save the world from their unjust and sinful behavior. As their holy scriptures indicate, Christians believe that Jesus was crucified, died, and resurrected three days later. His Father Yahweh is the immutable one who abides in his ultimate justice, goodness, and wisdom on the right of the spectrum.

Six hundred years after Christ, Mohammed made his mark upon world history in the Arabic world with his revelations from his idea of the Logos that contradicted the writings of the Christians. Mohammed and the Muslims call this same God, which the Jews call Yahweh, Allah. Allah is the immutable and ultimate good, the omnipotent and benevolent God identified on the right side of your scale, who is one with justice and also self-aware of his goodness. In contrast to the crucified Christ of the Christians, the Koran states in Surah 4 A 157-159 that Jesus was not crucified. [4]

How is it possible, I ask, for the mighty, absolute, undeviating, immutable, and constant one to reveal such a deviating, contradicting, and schizophrenic message to both Christian and Muslim? Either the Christian understanding of the immutable God is incorrect, or the Muslim belief concerning an undeviating God is incorrect. The only other alternative of course is that they are both incorrect, since it is obvious that both cannot be correct. Either Christ was crucified, resurrected, and was the son of God as the Christians scriptures indicate, or he was not crucified as the muslim scriptures proclaim.

The Hindu concept of the Logos completely contradicts the Greeks. For Brahman is the ultimate spirit of the universe. Millions of Hindu gods deviate and change matter, being worshipped as a snake or a cow, etc. This belief, which is found primarily in India, teaches that we all are separated from the divine as we live in our world of injustice. But with continuous reincarnations upon planet earth one can become better or worse, depending on one's previous lifestyle, until finally coming home to Brahman who is the ultimate good and just being on the right.

Ramakrishna who is "perhaps the best Hindu saint of modern times" reveals that there are "many paths to the same summit." He claims that "Indeed, one can reach God if one follows any of the paths with wholehearted devotion. One may eat a cake with icing either straight or sidewise. It will taste sweet either way." [5]

As the facts and evidence from all religions are analyzed, Socrates, one notices many deviating contradictions between all religions. One will come to the conclusion that either all religions are wrong, or only one can be right. And if this is the case then, that only one can be right, the only religion that can truly be wrong is the religion of Hinduism and Ramakrishna for stating that all religions can be right.

Socrates: Then your conclusion is that these deviating religions cannot describe that which is constant and absolute?

Professor: As I stated, either all are wrong or only one is right. Any clear-thinking individual that looks at the evidence will quickly realize that no two can unite and be correct, since they are contradictory.

Religions usually claim that humanity cannot impose its desire to force God to do anything, but I take issue with that. We were born on this planet without our consent or opinion; no one asked me or anybody else whether we wanted to be here or not. If freedom for God is also freedom for man, then force for man should be force for God.

In other words, if God forced me here on planet earth into inescapable evil, then God should be forced to allow me and the others that were forced here to experience the identity of his freedom, good, and justice. Freedom should not only be identified by the lack of coercion, and absence of force, but freedom should offer, and must be united to an enabling means. It seems that a free society usually offers an enabling means for the sick man that cannot afford a doctor. A free society should enable the poor to be fed and liberate their minds by educating them. If the Logos is aware of itself and of its freedom, then the

Logos should offer an enabling means for all of us to arrive at the right and rejoice in his ultimate freedom, justice and goodness. This enabling means to freedom, however, is where all of the religions disagree and deviate one from another.

It could be stated that the only liberated mind might belong to the agnostic or atheist that has rejected all of these contradicting gods. At least the agnostic or atheist attempts to cross over to the right side of justice and freedom on personal merit. This is contrary to the religions that go around forcing, coercing, intimidating, and killing people in the name of God, as all of these religions have historically done.

All of us are chained to Fortune. Some are bound by a loose and golden chain, others by a tight chain of baser metal; but what difference does it make? The same captivity holds all men in its toils, those who have bound others have also been bound.... Some are chained by public office, others by wealth; some carry the burden of high birth, some of low birth; some bow beneath another's empire, some beneath their own; some are kept in one place by exile, others by priesthoods. All life is servitude.

—*Seneca* [6]

So long as we do not feel that we are dependent on anything we regard ourselves as independent: a false conclusion that demonstrates how proud and lusting for power man is. For he here assumes that as soon as he experiences dependence he must under all circumstances notice and recognize it, under the presupposition that he is accustomed to living in independence and if, exceptionally, he lost it, he would at once perceive a sensation antithetical to the one he is accustomed to.–But what if the opposite were true: that he is always living in manifold dependence but regards himself as free when, out of long habituation, he no longer perceives the weight of the chains? It is only from new chains that he now suffers:–'freedom of will' really means nothing more than feeling no new chains.

—Nietzsche [7]

6

Illusion

I, Chuan Chou, once dreamed that I was a butterfly flitting about. I did whatever I wished! I knew nothing about any Chuan Chou. Then I suddenly awakened a Chuan Chou with all his normal trappings. Now I don't know whether Chuan Chou dreamed he was a butterfly, or a butterfly is dreaming that he is Chuan Chou.

—*Chuan Chou* [1]

Dr. Lattison: Socrates, in my crash course on Socratic and Platonic philosophy last night, professor Thomas used your allegory of the Cave to outline your philosophy. He told me that your student Plato records your allegory in the following manner...

Behold, human beings living in a deep cave. They have been there since birth. They are chained by the legs and neck and they cannot turn their heads. They can only see straight ahead. In front of them there is a very high wall which reaches the ceiling. Behind them there is another wall which is much lower. Further back, behind the short wall, there is a fire, which makes all of these people see their own shadows upon the wall in front of them.

All of the people, unaware that the illumination from the fire behind them is casting their own shadows on the wall, believe that their shadows are true reality when in fact their reality is but a shadow of actual reality. When puppets in the cave walk along the short wall behind the chained people, they also mingle their shadows upon the wall in front of the people. The chained people regard the illusion that the shadows of the puppets in front of them are true reality, unaware that the actual puppets behind them describe a more accurate reality. If someone drops a vase, while walking on the short wall, the chained people are convinced that the noise emanates from the shadows in front of them. Knowing no other world, all of the chained people believe in the illusions which the shadows produce.

If one of these people were to be unchained, that person would first notice that it is the fire behind the people which is producing the shadows. Once this same individual is taken out of the cave, and is able to see true reality of planet earth with the real light of the sun, the brightness initially would be blinding to the one who spent a whole life in darkness. But once the individual becomes used to it, and such a person experiences and compares both realities, then and only then is the individual able to judge that all along it was a life being lived in a cave of illusion. When this individual returns to the cave and attempts to describe to the chained people, that they are all watching only shadows and living in a distorted and false reality, what do you suppose the chained people would do to this individual? They would probably mock, laugh, and think that such a person is crazy. Certainly they would not believe him, and would probably kill him. [2]

This is how your pupil Plato, describes your lectures, Socrates. It seems you are convinced, and would like to convince others as well, that we all live in bondage and are chained to illusion. I assume that you are referring to your philosophical concepts of illusions, not the reality that the scientist studies.

Socrates: What is real in your universe, modern scientist, and how does one attain knowledge?

Dr. Lattison: Observations, measurements, and calculations that penetrate the senses are the only reliable sources that lead to true knowledge. Nature, for the most part, reveals itself to be predictable, in balance, possessing harmonious order. By simple calculations using mathematics, the scientist uncovers balance, order, and the beauty of knowledge, which we know as natural laws, or laws of physics. The word science comes from the Latin and literally means "knowledge." Only the scientist, using the five senses, has true knowledge of that which is knowable. That, of course, is the physical universe.

Socrates: Is it only the lifeless atoms of the physical universe that follow these natural laws yet produce life? Are humans not part of nature in this physical universe? Should not the mind of humans also be governed by the beauty and order of natural laws? Would you not think it as important if not more important, for the human being to function in a natural state of balance, harmony, and excellence, which would mean behaving in a righteous, just, and free manner toward other human beings and the Natural Lawgiver?

Dr. Lattison: Empiricism describes what is, and does not speculate what ought to be. As professor Thomas stated, a scientist offers descriptive truths, while a philosopher offers prescriptive truths. What is this state of human balance and excellence? And who is able to identify and describe it? You, yourself, challenged the philosophers of Athens to produce this ideal beauty of excellence, but no one gave you any verifiable results.

Show us this absolute, identifiable good that we also may believe not in theory, but in certainty.

Socrates: You seem to believe that the scientist is the only one that studies areas and objects of true knowledge, while the philosopher studies mere matters of opinion. Would you not agree that the one who has knowledge concerning something, such as two plus two equals four, cannot in any way be proven false, while the one who has only opinions concerning a thing must change beliefs once true knowledge that cannot be falsified is demonstrated?

Dr. Lattison: Historically, many times people had information which was generally accepted as knowledge, which was later proven false by new information.

Socrates: Therefore, these people never possessed knowledge but possessed only opinion to begin with; an opinion that was later proven wrong. Can you remember in particular when a scientist possessed knowledge concerning something that was later proven wrong?

Dr. Lattison: Yes, I can. As new information became introduced, tested, and verified, the scientist was forced to abandon previously outdated beliefs. This has indeed occurred many times.

Socrates: Then am I right in stating that the scientist who was forced to abandon an inaccurate belief possessed only an opinion, in the first place, and not knowledge?

Dr. Lattison: That can be stated, yes.

Socrates: Then would you not agree that it is the philosopher who studies objects of true knowledge, which are unchanging, such as the ideals of justice, good, freedom, etc., while the scientist studies objects of continuous change? An apple ceases to exist as an apple once it is consumed; a piece of wood is transformed once it is burned; even the sun and the earth will be transformed one day. A scientist, therefore, does not study objects of true knowledge, for the universe is in continuous flux and change. Within this universe of flux and change is also located the ever-changing physical body and the mental states of opinions, beliefs, and knowledge of all people, including the scientist. All of us are passengers upon a ship of scientific knowledge that is without destination, since it continuously changes course, as new information becomes available. A philosopher holds the anchor of the ship that studies the unchanging course within the universe of good, justice and freedom which are equal for all, and which remain the same yesterday, today, and forever.

Dr. Lattison: But if there is a God, which I am given no reason to believe, then why do you suppose he gave us this world of changing matter and our five senses to discover it? For it is within this corporeal world that we come to terms with justice, good, freedom, and especially pleasure.

Socrates: Highest knowledge does not derive from the senses, for the senses only teach concerning the transformation of matter. Even the animals can remember what is beneficial and what is harmful through their senses.

Dr. Lattison: What exactly are you implying by this statement? As philosophy is concerned, it has been stated many times that philosophers have never produced any bread for the people to eat but only ideas.

Socrates: It has been stated indeed, Dr. Lattison. Now, let us order a loaf of bread delivered to the museum and lets examine your physical universe, shall we. The bread will be divided in half, dissected into pieces, be transformed and cease to exist in a matter of minutes. Even the bacteria and the rats will eat some of the decaying crumbs in the waste basket. Then we shall order justice and freedom for the people and also their opposites, which are injustice and bondage; and, we will indeed detect a unanimous rush towards the philosophers understanding of truth.

The truth of the matter is that whereas the loaf of bread stimulates the taste buds and satisfies the stomach, justice stimulates the mind and freedom satisfies the soul. Only reason, which abides in the mind of human beings, is capable of arriving at the universal, eternal, and undeviating truths such as justice, freedom, etc. It is in these everlasting concepts that the anchor of true, constant, and undeviating knowledge is located.

Dr. Lattison: But you have not yet offered proof of the existence of this absolute truth with all of its attributes. By what reason do you arrive at this conclusion?

Socrates: If there is no absolute truth, scientist, as you seem to believe, then it would be the absolute truth that there is no absolute truth!

Dr. Lattison: I do not plan on entering a philosophical wrestling match with you, Socrates, since this is not my training and background. But you seem to be avoiding the question of offering empirical evidence through our senses that we all, universally, have in common, to believe this absolute truth of yours. I only attended one philosophy course in college and that was enough for me to realize that there are not many absolutes in philosophy, but rather there are many relative terms. My philosophy professor began the class by asking the students to describe and define this thing called "good." The professor drew a ladder on the board with ten steps on it and asked everyone to place themselves along this ladder. Number one step on top signified doing good and not causing evil and pain, while number ten at the bottom was to be identified with people doing evil, murder, pain, rape, etc.

After some confusing discussions between classmates, the professor offered guidelines by asking us to identify one human that produces or has produced good, who belongs on top, and then identify another human who produces or has produced the opposite, which is pain, and who belongs at the bottom. After some debate the class agreed that evil and pain on the bottom of the scale belong to people such as Adolf Hitler. On top of the scale my classmates placed people such as Mother Theresa, a Christian nun that gives of her time and energy bringing food and medicine to the needy and poor. Since we now had two identifiable characters in Hitler and Mother Theresa on opposite sides of the scale of good, we were again asked to place ourselves upon the same scale. None of us could claim to be near the status of the good of a Mother Theresa, yet no one dared even to consider taking a position near the evils and pain that Adolf Hitler produced. Thus, most of the classmates played it safe and opted for the middle of the scale at about five. After much persuasion, the professor convinced most to distance themselves from the evils of Hitler, and the students themselves, preferring to distance themselves from such a horrendous war-monger, placed themselves at a four and a half or four. Then the professor said, "Now let's inquire of Hitler himself, as to where he will place himself upon this scale." We agreed that he would have placed himself toward the top of either one or two on the side of good if not in the middle at four or five. "Thus you are all closer to Hitler than you think," the professor said with a smile.

Then the professor inquired about Mother Theresa and of our understanding as to her goodness and why we placed her on top of the scale, when suddenly an atheist student responded with a statement that shocked the whole class. The student stated that Mother Theresa and her Christian religion belong down toward the bottom of the scale along with Adolf himself.

Socrates: This is hardly the position of someone who helps the dying and poor for nothing in return, would you not agree, scientist?

Dr. Lattison: You stated earlier, Socrates, that every action we do has as its end some form of good that is identified with pleasure. Mother Theresa is after all in pursuit of the ideal good and eternal pleasure which, to her, is God. Mother Theresa's God promises her eternal good and everlasting pleasure following this life of giving and sacrificing of herself.

Socrates: We did agree that any human's action has as its end some form of pleasure. A small child desires to have pleasures fulfilled immediately, otherwise the child protests and cries. But an adult is mature enough to postpone pleasurable desires for the future. Could it not be that this woman is the most mature of all, simply by the fact that she is indeed postponing until the time is ripe? Her pursuit of God should not be a reason for the atheist classmate to place the poor woman with the man called Hitler. What pain and evil has she committed?

Dr. Lattison: The golden age of Greece began about 500 BC. For five hundred years, until the time of Christ, the great thinkers of ancient Greece sought rational explanations concerning the physical universe, and reality in general. These philosophers made tremendous discoveries in medicine, astronomy, mathematics, politics, art, philosophy, etc. Following this enlightened period, the Greeks embraced a new religion called Christianity, as did the Romans, probably more than any other civilizations.

Socrates: It interests me to know if it was the lay person or the philosophers of Greece that surrendered to this new religion. Was it simply a layman's religion or the thinking man's discovery of truth?

Dr. Lattison: I am not aware of any particular philosophers that bowed to Christianity. But it was with the introduction of Christianity that the Greeks ceased their scientific inquiry of the physical universe. They have been identified with the Christian Greek Orthodox church ever since. Romans also accepted Christianity and have continued to be identified with the Roman Catholic church. The intellectual pursuit of truth through science and philosophy was terminated by these great civilizations when they both bowed to Jesus Christ, a Jewish carpenter, as the Ultimate Truth. The atheist in class claimed that Christianity gained control of the sciences, art, and the intellect in general, ushering in the period known as the Dark Ages. Thus the human mind was brought into confinement and bondage.

Then around 1500 A.D., the renaissance from renascita or rebirth began. The exaltation of the human intellect was again of primary importance. The first birth was in ancient Greece, the rebirth in renaissance Italy. One of the motivating factors for the renaissance was the fall of Constantinople in 1453. Constantinople was the capital of the Greek Byzantine Christian empire. Many scholars along with their ancient Greek manuscripts fled Constantinople from the invading Turks and settled in Italy. By help of the printing press in Italy, scholars once again began to study and reproduce the classics. Reason, truth, science, and natural rights reigned once again, liberating humanity from the dark clutches of the church, which held a monopoly on science, literacy, art, and the intellect. These liberating concepts, which were suppressed in the Christian era, freed the individual of ancient Greece, and were re-established during the renaissance. These renaissance or born-again people began to question the authority and power of the church. Finally, they freed themselves from the "bondage" of Christianity.

It was during these times that the astronomer Galileo picked up his telescope and began searching the heavens, picking up where the ancient Greeks had left off seventeen hundred years before. Copernicus and Galileo agreed with the ancient Greek philosopher\astronomer Aristarchous, who maintained the belief in a heliocentric or sun centered solar system, and the idea that Socrates and Plato held that the earth spins on its axis. Consequently, Galileo was thrown in prison by the Roman Christian church. In 1600, Bruno was burned at the stake in Rome. In 1620 Vanini met a similar fate in Toulouse, France. These are only two among many atrocities which the church committed toward people who disagreed with them concerning matters such as the motion of the earth.

Copernicus and Galileo were ultimately proven right and the Church proven wrong. A few years ago, three hundred years after Galileo died in house arrest, the Roman Catholic Church pardoned and forgave him. But the scientific community has yet to forgive the Christian church for retarding progress and the bondage which it placed upon humanity, and especially toward the thinkers and scientists, such as their hero Galileo. Hence, Mother Theresa's religion, the atheist claimed, retarded progress for 1,700 years. Her religion has caused enough evil, pain, and retardation that both she, and her religion, should be identified toward the bottom along with Hitler.

You state all of humanity is in a cave of illusion, but the atheist believes it is Christianity that promotes the bondage of ignorance that has historically retarded the growth of intellect and knowledge. Through your philosophy, you reveal the evils of humanity that humans prefer to hide under the rug, such as the teleology of 100 million murdered in the last century alone. Since we must look at the truth of the matter, the sad statistic is that indeed such evil, death, and pain are primarily due to the abuse of scientific knowledge and apparatus. But it seems to me that the illusion is held by the philosopher or "idealist" who believes that humanity is capable of arriving at such an ideal existence of justice, good, and freedom.

Imperfect nature has produced imperfect human nature. It's that simple. There need not be any meaning to life other than what one chooses to make out of it. Now if your description of bondage and a cave of illusion is humanity calling injustice-justice, bad-good, and abusing freedom and power to produce bondage, then maybe we are living in your world of illusion. But the physical universe is here and now, and this, friend, is true reality and the only reality that is knowable. It is primarily the religions that have embarked in your idle ships of opinion. Ships of opinion and blind faith that lack sails of knowledge and a propeller to move them forward. Their quest for truth does not advance with the times and the evidence, but sits as a broken ship that goes around in circles. Many religions continue to believe in superstitious doctrine even in this age of scientific enlightenment. Regardless what the evidence describes, many times religions will deny scientific facts to accommodate their archaic belief system.

The evidence, for example, describes a four billion-year-old earth and a fifteen billion-year-old universe, yet some Christian fundamentalists, even today, choose to believe the earth is six thousand years old. Some believe the whole universe is only six thousand years old. The scientist is the one who is willing to modify an existing belief as statistics demand and the evidence requires. Therefore, only science is gradually guiding this ship of knowledge, attempting to find the straight-forward course toward truth as we obtain more facts and information concerning that which is knowable. Philosophers must ride this ship of scientific truths. Philosophers asks questions, many being universal and timeless indeed, but rarely does philosophy offer answers, since it seems many timeless questions will remain beyond the knowledge of humans.

Socrates: Why should blame be placed upon the philosopher? A philosopher describes the reality of a biased, unjust and lost humanity. Even though the philosopher provides a more excellent way of life, it is worthless unless the people first acknowledge the fact that they are lost, unjust, and deceived concerning the truth.

Dr. Lattison: Now that I think about it, Karl Marx, the last well-known philosopher, believed his philosophy had the answer. He attempted to move whole civilizations toward your ideal state of being on the right side. The philosophy he offered in his *Communist Manifesto* was meant to produce freedom, justice, harmony, and equality for all people. But, the fact is, his communistic philosophy produced quite the opposite. The reality was coercion, force, bondage, and suspicion between people and government, until one day his whole philosophy, like a ship full of holes, sank to the bottom of the ocean, hopefully never to be resurrected again. The only difference between your philosophy and Marx's philosophy seems to be that you believe an eternal being is waiting to embrace humanity on the right, or above, as most religions claim. Marx rejected the idea of an eternal omni-being, but he believed that humanity must strive alone to embrace each other on the right side of his ideal state of freedom, justice, and equality.

Socrates: I do lack information, and appeal to ignorance, concerning the ideas of this man Marx. But was it this philosopher's ideas that produced the opposite of equality, justice, and good, as you claim, or was it the abuse of power which humanity and in particular the ruling class falls prey to consistently? Is this not similar to the scientist who studies and reveals the balance and harmony of nature? Are not the same scientific advancements which the scientist discovers the very things that disrupt this balance by polluting the water we drink and the air we breathe? The scientist is not to be blamed because scientific discoveries have been abused. Likewise, it should not be the philosopher that is to be blamed for the abuse of ideas. The abuse of scientific technology produces pollution and imbalance.

This strangles the environment and causes ecological suicide, literally destroying the canvas of the Natural Artist, which is planet earth. What makes you then think that science will uncover the mind, which is of goodness, balance, truth, and harmony of the same Natural Artist and eternal being? It seems that science might very well be the last to identify the mind of God.

Dr. Lattison: How can one know that mind of God, which, if it really exists, would be transcendent and unknowable to humans? Let's first discover and understand that which is knowable and real before we speculate on that which is unknowable and unreal.

Socrates: And what in the name of heaven is more real than justice and freedom? How, I ask, do you know when something is real, scientist? Is it truly when you see something, hear something, or experience something by the use of the rest of the five senses? Is a thing really more certain the more intense the sense of perception available, and the more seemingly accurate the reality? In fact, yesterday I had a real experience, modern man. I was trapped in a neighbor's back yard and the gate behind me was locked. I heard something growling and suddenly I saw a rather large dog coming at me and barking furiously. The fear within took hold of me, as I saw and heard this barking dog ready to attack. The palms of my hands began to sweat, and my heart began to beat rapidly! Oh, in the name of God, how I did wish to be free from this confinement! At the same time that the dog was barking, I also heard a couple of loud knocks on the door. The knocks were so loud that it woke me. Then, and only then, did I realize that my true reality was only a dream.

My reality and sense perception of seeing a menacing dog, of hearing the dog growl, the feeling of sweat on my hands and my heart beating fast was an illusion. Only when I was awakened did I realize that it was not real. I was experiencing a distorted reality which had misled what I perceived from my senses to be correct. Although I was fully clothed and in the neighbor's yard in one reality, I was naked and in bed in the other reality. Yet in both realities, real and illusion, it was evident that freedom had remained the same and was discernible from bondage. Therefore that which remains the same is the true reality.

Dr. Lattison: Illogical, Socrates. This is hardly an argument for distorted reality and the senses being fooled. For it was only a dream, and in this dream it was only you who dreamed it, you, Socrates, and nobody else. You only thought you saw a dog and only thought you heard a dog and felt sweat on your hands. No one else agreed with you that this happened. And even you, now, must agree with the rest of us that that was not reality.

This external universe right now, Socrates, is reality. This world of matter is what we know and this, right now, is all we can know. For example, take this table in front of us. Philo, Professor Thomas, you, and I, do we not all unanimously agree that this table exists and is real, it is real by experiencing it through our senses? It is real because we see it; it is further identified as real since we can feel it, and we can hit it with our hand and hear it. The fact is, Socrates, that all of the people in the museum will unanimously agree that this table exists and that it is real. Its existence is verified through everyone's senses. This is reality and not an illusion. This reality is unanimously agreed upon by everyone in the museum; philosopher, scientist, cleric, lay person, and child alike.

Socrates: Let me follow you, friend. Suppose we went to this great statue here in New York which you call the Statue of Liberty. It is real because we all see it. It is real because we can feel it. We can even throw something against it and hear the sound that it is real. Therefore, all New Yorkers, some eight million people if I am correct, unanimously agree that the Statue of Liberty is real, since its reality penetrates at least three of our sensual organs.

Dr. Lattison: Indeed, all New Yorkers will agree with this reality as the senses describe it.

Socrates: Now suppose you ask an Athenian concerning the Statue of Liberty. Is it also real for the Athenian who has never seen it?

Dr. Lattison: To an Athenian, Socrates, the Parthenon at the Acropolis is as real as the Statue of Liberty is to New Yorkers. If an Athenian were to come to New York, that Athenian would agree that the Statue of Liberty is real, as is accepted by all New Yorkers, having experienced it through the five senses. Therefore the Athenian would be in agreement with all of the people here that this monument which resides in the external universe is of reality. Likewise, if a New Yorker went to Athens the New Yorker would also unanimously agree with all Athenians that the Parthenon is real in their world of reality. Therefore, there is unanimous disagreement with you, Socrates, and your world of illusion, dreams, and distorted reality. For this is reality in front of us, and around us, ready to be discovered, the reality of the physical universe.

Maybe we are unenlightened and do not fully possess the ideals of justice, freedom, good, and whatever else you choose to attach to this ideal state of excellence. But the fact is, we can only know the world of matter, energy, and motion. This is what is concrete and knowable. This is what scientists study. Now which do you suppose is relative and produces illusion-the physical universe or your idealist philosophical concepts?

Socrates: The truth, then, must be identified in the fact that, I, Socrates was slumped in a dreaming state in my isolated and lonely cave of illusion for more than two thousand years. Lonely in the fact that I, the fool, seem to have been there alone, with a few of my Greek pupils, all along. But now, with the help of modern science, I do recognize my fallacy and see myself breaking my chains of ignorance as I am resurrected from this cave of distorted reality. As I begin to ascend out into the world of descriptive reality verified by the senses, I become free of my childish beliefs and I can finally look up and see the sun and say "alas, reality!" After two thousand four hundred years of illusion and darkness, I now see the sun, and I am in full agreement with five billion people worldwide that that is, indeed, the sun. And both of my eyes are in accordance with ten billion eyes worldwide in unison, unanimously agreeing on this descriptive fact of reality.

Not only do I see the sun as the rest of the people on planet earth, but when I close my eyes I can feel the sun; more proof of reality since we now follow with a second sensual organ the feeling of the warmth of the sun as well. And if I continue to keep my eyes closed for a long period of time while facing east, I can feel the sun come up in front of me and set behind me, just as five billion people worldwide can also feel the sun daily. And if I open my eyes to this descriptive reality, I can see the sun rise up in the morning and set in the afternoon which is also in total agreement with five billion people worldwide. Hence the cave of illusion has been but a grave for Socrates, for modern science has resurrected me from my silly beliefs and has given me freedom from ignorance. Hence my tomb of obliviousness is emptied since the last fool has finally exited.

Dr. Lattison: Physical truth is all we possess, Socrates.

Socrates: It seems so, modern man, but I do ponder one question in your descriptive universe which seems to baffle me. The sun seems to possess a large amount of mass, and it seems to be quite a distance from planet earth. Tell me, if we were to begin at 12:00 noon when the sun is directly overhead, can you instruct me how fast the sun races around the earth to make one full revolution? So when one full day passes and 24 hours later the sun finds itself at high noon again?

Dr. Lattison: It seems that the sun is in motion and that it travels from east to west daily, but the truth is that the sun is stationary and the earth is in motion from west to east.

Socrates: Dear friend, what can you possibly mean, "the truth is?" Is this a different truth and reality than my sensual organs dictate to me? You tell me that I am in motion upon this planet, yet my sense of taste and smell and hearing are completely ignorant of this fact. My descriptive truth, as my sense of sight, describes to me is that I am standing still and that the sun is in motion east to west, while you are prescribing that my descriptive truth is a fallacy. Or are you describing that my descriptive truth is a fallacy, which means you are describing that my descriptive truth is really my prescriptive truth, or is it? You are not telling me this is an optical illusion and distorted truth, are you?

Dr. Lattison: The fact is, Socrates, that in this case, the senses are deceived. But take notice that it is the scientist who corrects this illusion that apparently seems to be real. Science produces true knowledge and reality that the sun is stationary and that the earth is in motion.

Socrates: Then you seem to be in agreement, scientist, that reason belongs to the mind and soul, producing knowledge and reality, while the senses produce opinions and illusions. Now describe this truth to me, I plead, modern man, since you have just convinced me not to rely on my senses to teach me truth, for they can be a false witness of what is real and true and of what is not, at least you might enlighten me which one of my senses I should rely on more and which ones less. Now tell me, at twelve o'clock noon a person six feet tall has a head that is six feet closer to the sun than are that person's feet, correct?

Dr. Lattison: Correct.

Socrates: And the Statue of Liberty, which is 300 feet tall, finds its head that much closer to the sun, which is directly above at midday, than is the bottom of its base.

Dr. Lattison: Definitely.

Socrates: Now if we can call the location of the sun directly above us at twelve noon "up," where are the people on the other side of the globe, along with their rivers, oceans, and mountains? Are they not found upside down and facing away from the sun compared to us?

Dr. Lattison: The Chinese people and other nations are indeed in such a position.

Socrates: This means that twelve hours later, we here in New York will have traveled so fast that we will find ourselves upside down, will we not? Our shoes will be six feet closer to the sun that has remained stationary in relation to us, and our heads will be six feet farther from the sun. Also, the Statue of Liberty, whose head was found some 300 feet closer to the sun than the bottom of its base was at twelve noon, will find itself upside down with its head that much farther from the sun and its base that much closer to the sun. Is this absolutely true?

Dr. Lattison: Indeed it is; the French astronomer Foucault with his Foucault pendulum has proven this fact.

Socrates: My sensory perceptions, of sight and feel, agree that I am standing still and that the sun is moving, modern scientist. It bothers me that the rest of my senses are completely ignorant of this motion of planet earth. My sense of hearing can only hear the unpleasant facts that my senses of sight and of feel are proven wrong. While my sense of taste has no option but to swallow this bitter truth, that the external universe is indeed an illusion as it penetrates my senses.

Dr. Lattison: Why are you surprised? You, Plato and other philosophers believed the earth was in motion 400 years before Christ. Why are you shocked?

Socrates: The shock, dear friend, comes from the fact that since the days of certain ancient Greeks, humankind, for the last two thousand years, believed that the earth was stationary and that the sun moved, and this fact was unanimously agreed on by all. Therefore, if we allow what is unanimously agreed by all to dictate truth by means of sense perception, then the whole world for thousands of years was unanimously wrong. But recently modern science revealed the earth to be in motion, which proves that humanity had universally fallen for an illusion of a great magnitude. Even today, unless a scientist explains to someone how the universe operates, and corrects the fallacy produced by the senses, will not everyone be held captive in the cave, believing in the illusion that the earth is standing still?

While everyone is chained in this bondage of universal illusion as the senses dictate, what would happen if one individual were to be let loose from this distorted reality and be found floating in outer space? Would not such a person see that the earth is indeed spinning and that the sun is standing still?

Dr. Lattison: Such a person would.

Socrates: And if this individual reentered this cave of illusion, or planet Earth, in possession of truth, and attempted to explain to the people the reality of the universe, which is the sun stationary and the earth spinning, what would they do to this individual? As you stated, friend, Galileo described the accuracy of reality and truth; that the earth spun on its axis and was orbiting the sun, and he was imprisoned was he not?

Dr. Lattison: That is a historical fact.

Socrates: Was not Galileo in this case telling the people the truth: that they live in a dream state of optical and sensual illusion? Surely all New Yorkers believe that the Statue of Liberty is real, but how would they respond if we were to ask every individual in New York that, based on sense perception, "is it the sun that is moving?" Do you believe everyone would unanimously agree that the sun is standing still and that all of them along with the Statue of Liberty will be hanging upside down in twelve hours? I hardly think so friend.

Imagine the disappointing fact that the body and mind of each individual possesses the five senses that are utilized, not only to teach us, but also to please us. Such a dualistic task forces the senses to simultaneously become friend and foe, enemy and ally, for everyone. For it is the same five senses that channel and offer humanity the good of pleasures from the external world, which also channel and offer humanity the pain of illusion when it comes to the greatest pleasure of all: truth. Therefore the same senses that are friends of the body seeking pleasure are enemies of the mind and soul that seek truth.

The scientist passes judgment by compiling information from the external universe, as well as using reason and wisdom which belong to the internal universe. The external universe fools the sense perceptions of five billion people on planet Earth daily.

Our senses can be deceived, and need modification to awaken from this dark cave of illusion to lead us into the light of truth and reality. Who is able to correct humanity so we do not live in a cave of illusion as we relate to the non-material world of our actions and behavior? Who has the authority to judge and tell us if our perception of reality is not real? Who should judge whether our desire of good is not good, or whether our understanding of a just act satisfying the self is injustice to another? One man's freedom is another man's bondage. Our actions producing pleasure can, and do, cause pain toward our fellow man. But when the philosopher describes the truth of this reality, how many are willing to listen and how many are willing to modify their behavior?

The scientist has assembled the information of the external world, and has passed judgment that we are all deceived and are in need of correction in our cave of illusion. Likewise, let us fervently hope that there is a transcendent God with justice, good, pleasure, truth, and wisdom. This transcendent God would have the natural right to assemble knowledge and pass judgment on all of our seemingly justified actions. Many of these actions are only a deception and a false reality, and are in desperate need of correction. However, even if God's truth, with all of its divine attributes from the right, were standing directly in front of us who are on the left, we would almost certainly think that God's truth were false, senseless, and unjust in our cave of distorted reality. This is precisely what we did with Galileo.

Since the job of the scientist with his or her instruments is to study the physical, external universe for physical truths, then let's allow the scientist to explain only the truths of that external physical universe. We cannot, however, allow the scientist, who does not know and cannot satisfy the truth-seeking desires of the soul–such as justice, good, freedom, pleasure, and truth–to tell us that there is no soul within. Has not the scientist learned humility by proving the external universe to be a false witness to the senses, and to stand in awe of this thing which we call consciousness? The scientist does not study it and does not know its substance or origins. And since the scientist cannot study the consciousness of humans, by what right does the scientist pass judgment that the consciousness of God does not exist? By scientific measurements and calculations of the physical universe, the scientist guarantees us that everyone is unanimously deceived concerning physical truths. How can the scientist, then, be so sure of the opinions of science concerning the divine truths which belong in the internal universe that science cannot study, measure or calculate? Let's hope in the name of goodness and justice there is a God who possesses truth, and by his judgment he has found Hitler unjust, though Hitler found himself just. Let's pray to God that all of the injustice that has taken place and gone undetected upon planet Earth does, indeed, bear consequences in the afterlife when the soul of the unjust on the left attempts to unify with the soul of the just who is found at the right end of the spectrum. Also, let's pray to God that those who found unjust pleasure at the expense and pain of others do not go unpunished when they attempt to unify with the Being which is ultimate pleasure, ultimate justice and ultimate good.

When a scientist states that there is no God, is the scientist speaking from knowledge derived from the senses, which have proven themselves as a potential false witness and an enemy of the soul that seeks for truth; or, is the scientist only speaking from opinion? If the scientist is speaking from opinion then this opinion can be corrected and modified. But if the scientist is speaking from knowledge then the scientist must have perfect knowledge of everything there is to know concerning the essence of God. The scientist must have a perfect knowledge of justice, freedom, and all of the other divine attributes. When the scientist states that the Natural Artist does not exist, is the scientist not passing absolute judgment that the absolute good and just does not exist? This means the scientist becomes the final authority on justice superseding God and his existence.

Whoever undertakes to set himself up as judge in the field of Truth and Knowledge is shipwrecked by the laughter of the gods.
—Albert Einstein [3]

He who finally sees how long and how greatly he has been made a fool of embraces in defiance even the ugliest reality: so that, viewing the way of the world as a whole, the latter has at all times had the best of wooers—for it is the best who have always been most thoroughly deceived.
—Nietzsche [4]

7

Love

Something exists in the understanding, at least, than which nothing greater can be conceived... And assuredly that, than which nothing greater can be conceived, cannot exist in the understanding alone. For, suppose it exists in the understanding alone: then it can be conceived to exist in reality; which is greater. Therefore, if that, than which nothing greater can be conceived, exists in the understanding alone, the very being, than which nothing greater can be conceived, is one that which a greater can be conceived. But obviously this is impossible. Hence, there is no doubt that there exists a being, [God], than which nothing greater can be conceived, and it exists both in the understanding and in reality.
—St. Anselm [1]

Socrates: Tell me professor Thomas, does not humanity universally measure the value and beauty of everything in the physical external universe in monetary numbers? In particular, the more beautiful something is, the more desirable it becomes and the more desirable it becomes, the more expensive it is. A beautiful and well-designed home in an attractive part of town will be more expensive than a not so beautiful home in a less desirable area, will it not?

Professor: It will.

Socrates: This painting on the wall by the painter Monet is very desirable, since this is the only original one painted by the master. As I am informed, its monetary value is in the millions of dollars. Is it not also this same monetary value which we place on all things found elsewhere in the physical universe? For example, the value of a desirable, unique-cut diamond is symbolized by the fact that it is much more expensive than the flawed diamond, is it not?

Professor: That is usually the case.

Socrates: Therefore, the more beautiful and desirable something is, the more expensive it becomes. The more precious something is, the higher its monetary value. This is how we measure beauty in the physical universe, is it not?

Professor: This, Socrates, is a law of economics, of supply and demand. There are only so many precious diamonds, and by their sheer beauty the demand for them is much greater than the supply; therefore their monetary value is higher.

Socrates: In this case, modern man, since we measure objects of surpassing beauty by the higher price, the highest beauty possessing the highest price, then as a rule only the wealthy can afford the most desirable and artistic things of beauty. By these laws of economics, what would be the price if there existed something which we all, old and young, universally desire? And how high is the monetary value of something, which we all, rich as well as poor, want to obtain?

Professor: If there is a commodity that is not in surplus which we all desire to obtain, then its monetary value, one might say, must be so high that most of us will not be able to afford it. What is this precious item to which you are referring, that possesses such beauty that we all desire and long for?

Socrates: Love, modern man; the desire to love, and the desire to be loved. The universal love that an infant desires from the mother and awaits from the father; the joyous love that parents share with their newborn child; the loving home to which the family member returns, the love which two childhood friends have shared throughout their lives. What is the price of precious love modern man?

Professor: Love has no price, Socrates.

Socrates: So you say that love must be free and cannot be bought and sold?

Professor: Indeed.

Socrates: Now I don't suppose modern scientific textbooks in chemistry or physics deal with the concept of love, do they?

Professor: No, they do not.

Socrates: Then love is not located in the external, physical universe possessing matter, since scientists cannot measure, divide or weigh it. But philosophers can measure it to a certain extent, can they not?

Professor: You ancient Greeks had a better understanding of measuring love than we modern people have, for the Greeks utilized eight different words to describe what we, today, call love. The Greeks described different kinds of love so thoroughly that they seemed to be opposites. This is true of "eros love" and "agape love." Correct me if I am wrong, but eros love is when someone desires to attain something of beauty from the physical universe based on a sensual and emotional relationship. This includes possession of another person. We have distorted its meaning, calling it only erotic love. Agape love does not desire to possess, but describes a desire to give. That is, to give to the beloved, without expecting anything in return, desiring only the happiness and well-being of the beloved. This is the love, as you stated to the ancients Greeks, Socrates, that includes sacrifice; the giving of the self.

Socrates: Let's consider the essence of love, professor, shall we? Now, suppose we find two neighboring children who each have $50.00 to buy lunch at school for the next two months. One child decides to give half of the lunch money to a poor child across the street who does not have any money and cannot afford lunch at school, while the other child was forced by a parent, the father, to give half of the lunch money to the same poor child. Which one of these was an act of love?

Professor: The act of the first child, of course; the one who gave freely. An act of love cannot be forced. The giving or receiving of love cannot be coerced, either.

Socrates: Since force and coercion are opposites of love, and since force and coercion are also opposites of freedom, then love and freedom are united on the right, the side of the Natural Artist, in opposition to force and coercion on the left.

Now, we find two sons-in-law who decide to visit their father-in-law in the retirement home. The first son-in-law decides to give of his time to visit with the old man, regardless that it is his only day off from work this month. The second son-in-law decides to visit his father-in-law with the hope of gaining some inheritance. Which one of these actions was an act of love?

Professor: The first one, of course, Socrates; the one who sacrificed and gave freely of his time. Unlike the second son-in-law who placed a price tag on his giving, hoping for something in return. Giving of his time, and sharing of his love with the father-in-law was artificial, selfish, and certainly not agape or unconditional love. Agape love cannot be self centered.

Socrates: Now tell me, modern man, since everything tangible which we desire in the physical universe, such as a nice car, a beautiful house, an expensive dinner, a painting, or a precious diamond, increases in monetary value by supply and demand, how is it that love, which we all desire, is so inexpensive, and has no monetary value? Does not this contradict the laws of economics, of supply and demand? This now means that not everything desirable and beautiful has to increase in price, for the beauty of love is free.

Professor: Most definitely.

Socrates: We all prefer to be loved and accepted rather than hated, despised, and rejected, but since love is free and we all desire it, then all the people upon planet Earth should be immersed and enveloped in total love, simply because it is free and we all desire to obtain it.

Professor: Unfortunately, the world is not immersed in love, Socrates, but only traces might be found here and there.

Socrates: But why the difficulty and elusiveness of attaining it? There must be a problem with humanity, lad, for the law of love remains constant and free as it always has been. How is it that humanity desires it and cannot obtain it, since it is free?

Professor: While the law of agape love is to give, rather than take, our human nature goes contrary to love. Our nature is to take rather than give. When we do something for another person, we almost always expect something in return. When we spend a dollar, we will give it to the merchant who will provide us the most return for our money. When we give of our time, we will give it to the employer who will return to us the highest wages. Even a wealthy person who gives money to charity usually does not give beyond a safe limit, beyond which a feeling of loss and of personal jeopardy occurs. Does not the wealthy person usually give of the leftovers, or of the excess?

Nothing has changed since ancient times, Socrates, when you proclaimed to the Athenian philosophers regarding who has seen ultimate beauty and inquired where such beauty can be found. Where can it be found? The most likely place where agape love might be located would be in the heart of a mother who will give of herself for her child and expect nothing in return.

Socrates: In this case, modern man, you must agree that love is found in the deepest part of the human heart, in the internal universe where even science is forbidden to venture. Within this universe of consciousness and mind lies the concept of love, and this concept of love possesses such value that it defies all the laws of the external universe where everything increases in price by demand. It seems that the laws of the external universe do not govern the internal, where the desire for love is high, but is without monetary value. You must agree then, that the private universe of each individual, where love can be found, is more precious than the external universe of matter where the most desirable material gadgets are predominately for the wealthy. So, if love is free, then it also belongs with freedom, good, justice, and pleasure on the right. Similar to the other divine attributes, love has remained constant and unchanging due to the fact that it has maintained its luster of equality for all, since it continues to be free.

Contrary to the external universe, in which the wealthy bathe in excess, and possess most of it, the freedom of love being located in the internal universe is equally available to the poor as well as the rich. It is attainable for the educated as well as the uneducated, equally distributed to the minority as well as the majority. The internal universe, therefore, is more precious, and should be considered the higher education as is studied by the philosopher and lived by the refined mind of the wise; while the external universe, which is studied by the scientist, is lived by the naive and the brute.

Professor: Unfortunately, Socrates, very few people today study philosophy, since there is no demand for philosophers. As I stated, we study computers, marketing, business, and accounting in order to produce, market, and sell products which are primarily gadgets of the external universe. Like bees in a hive, humanity swarms to take possession of the goods that the external universe offers, believing if they attain riches they will be able to buy pleasure, good, freedom, love, and sometimes even justice that was unattainable when they were poor and unknown. In fact, the external universe cannot offer these attributes, since they are not for sale. The external universe will only offer them the pain of illusion once they discover that their newfound wealth cannot afford these virtuous qualities. Many times we see very wealthy music and movie stars, or famous athletes, that neglect their own wife, children and families. Instead they turn to drugs, alcohol, million dollar cocaine habits, and other instruments of illusion, purchased in the external universe, while masking their pain.

But how can one be certain that these ideals of justice, good, freedom, and love, that are desires of the soul within humankind, do indeed exist in reality? For if they exist, then this would be the character and composition of God. Can we know for certain without taking a big leap of faith?

Socrates: You do not need a leap of faith to believe that human beings exist, and that they possess essence produced by their existence.

Professor: No, not much faith. But what are you implying here?

Socrates: The existence of a rose, for example, is that it is, and has a being, while the essence of that rose is not that it is, but what it is. For example, the essence of a red rose is it's deep red color, which it transmits to the eye of the beholder; also its essence is the beautiful fragrance which it emits to the nose. First, we have existence, that something is, then we have essence, which describes what it is, or what it sends forth beyond its existence, such as red color or a specific fragrance. The essence of man, then, must be what man produces. We can see that man produces a rational mind of creativity and will. This creative essence of man is witnessed in the chairs, tables, buildings, and all art. Man's essence is also the ability to produce love. Therefore, the existence of man is that humanity is, and the essence of man is also to produce artwork, as human creation verifies. Man's essence also produces love, as may be seen in the love of a mother for her child.

In this case the existence of God is that he exists, and that he is, while the essence of God is his creativity and will, witnessed in the trees, plants, animals and humans. The essence of God must also be love, and God must have passed down this essence of love to man. Therefore man's essence is creativity but is also love.

Professor: I completely disagree, Socrates. First, God's existence, his being, whether or not he is, cannot be proven scientifically. And second, I'm not sure that his essence of love can be proven philosophically either. Scientists, with all of their technology, today do not know if there is a divine agent behind the living things of nature. But if God does exist, I don't believe that what I call nature and what you call God possesses the essence of love.

Socrates: We just agreed, lad, that humans have the capacity to produce love, and are part of nature. How can you, then, claim God or nature possesses no love?

Professor: The reason God's essence of love cannot be proven is simply this: if God possesses love, within his private universe of thoughts and ideas, then it could be stated that God's love is inferior to the love of humans, especially to the love that a human mother possesses for her child. A mother who loves her child in her private universe of thoughts and consciousness does not keep her love for the child to herself. She expresses her essence of love in the external universe, perceived and verified by the five senses. Only when the mother's actions display love does her essence of love become identifiable as such, in the eyes of her child. Likewise, the essence of the mother's love by her words once spoken and produced into the physical universe, will be received by the ear of the child when the mother tells the child of her love. Only in the external universe, by her actions, when the mother embraces the child, will she exhibit love and give the child the ability to feel her love.

Similar to the essence of the rose that transmits color and fragrance through the physical universe to the eyes and nose, likewise the mother's actions, producing her essence of love, are channeled through the external physical universe revealing love to the sight, hearing, and touch of the child. Therefore it is necessary that essence uses the physical universe as a means of communication, proving the existence of something in the internal universe. If God possesses the essence of love, why can we not see it, feel it, or hear it, in our common public universe, Socrates? If the mind and essence of God is love, and God has a will, then God's will should be to reveal his love in our public universe of sense perception.

If I agree with you, Socrates, that God gave humans his essence of love, then why is the mother willing and able to reveal her love for her child in the external and public universe, whereas God does not? Consequently, a child is able to verify a mother's love with its senses, while God has left us ignorant of his essence of love. How can one verify God's love? If God possesses love, he is not willing to reveal it. To possess love in the internal universe of God's mind alone seems a lesser reality, than if God's love was also expressed in the physical, objective universe. Since the law of love is to be free, as you state, then God must demonstrate his love and make it equally free, knowable, and available for all, rich and poor, educated and uneducated, minority and majority, not only for the trained philosopher who spends a lifetime pondering such issues.

Socrates: You claim that the essence of love, which exists in the mind alone, must be inferior by virtue of the fact that it belongs to only one reality which remains within the mind; but once love is acted out it becomes authenticated and more real by existing in two realities. Hence, two realities are more authentic and better than one.

Professor: Indeed.

Socrates: Then, how appropriate for you to ask me to reveal the existence of God, only to have you convince me, and the others here, that you agree with the fact of God's existence.

Professor: By what process did you come to this conclusion?

Socrates: You claim that the thought of love inside someone's mind is not enough to produce the reality of love, but the thought of love which first existed in the mind must be acted out in the external universe; hence that which exists in two realities is the greater reality.

Professor: I believe that is what I stated.

Socrates: Notice this statue. First, it existed only as a concept or an idea in the artist's mind, but now, once sculpted and finished, it exists in the greater reality, which is both in the mind of the sculptor and the external universe. Therefore, what remains in the mind alone is a lesser reality, as opposed to what exists in the mind and becomes real outside the mind. To belong to two realities, the internal and external realities together would be the greater reality. Now, in my mind, I conceive of the idea of ultimate justice, good, and ideal agape love, that belong only to the ideal divine being. The mind, therefore, is capable of conceiving the idea of God, which is the greatest conception. Since what belongs only in the mind is inferior, but the greatest conception the mind is able to produce is the ideal being of justice, good, and love, which is God himself, thus, superior. Then God must exist outside the mind, for, as you stated, to belong to two realities is the greater reality. If God did not exist outside the mind, then the greater conception of good and love is only within the mind, which would make the mind the greater reality by itself. And you have already stated that the thought that exists only in the mind is the lesser reality; hence you must agree that God does exist, not only in the mind, but both in the mind and outside the mind, which would be the more authentic and greater reality.

Professor: Congratulations! You set me up for the ontological argument and I fell for it. But are you not falling into the fallacy of deducing existence from essence? You seem to be implying that God's existence can be transcendent and above us, in his greater reality, but his essence could be eminent and within us in our reality. When my students ask me if there is a God, am I not contradicting myself if I state God is in the world, and God is not in the world? God is on the right side of justice but he is also on the left side of injustice?

Socrates: Does it have to be either or, black or white? Suppose you have worked up a thirst while climbing a tall mountain. Halfway up the mountain you find a stream of water flowing down from the top of the mountain into a puddle. You decide to drink some of the puddle water and also fill your canteen. When you climb to the top of the mountain you find the original spring of water that is the source of the puddle halfway down the mountain from which you drank. Now, which do you suppose is more desirable to drink, the unblemished spring water on top, or the muddy puddle water?

Professor: The spring water on top, of course. Everyone would prefer to drink the pure, and spotless water.

Socrates: And if you were forced to drink from the puddle water, will you not desire and request to have some water from the spring added into the puddle water?

Professor: Indeed, adding water from the spring will make the puddle water more clean and pure.

Socrates: But since you prefer to drink the water from the spring, it would be unacceptable, and irrational, to add even one drop from the puddle water to the good water, would it not?

Professor: Certainly the dirty puddle water will enhance its existence if we increase the percent of the spring water. On the other hand, the spring water, which is pure and clean, cannot enhance its existence by adding even one drop from the water in the puddle. The pure water therefore has no dealings or affections and cannot be enhanced by the impure water.

Socrates: Now, lad, you have seen that the spring itself, atop the mountain exists and has it's being. You do agree that the spring itself, does not exist within the puddle half way down the mountain?

Professor: Undoubtedly, the spring itself is found only above and separate from the puddle.

Socrates: Although the spring is not found in the puddle, the essence of the spring being the water which the spring emits, is indeed found in the puddle, is it not?

Professor: It is.

Socrates: As the pure essence of the spring flowed out, down toward the puddle, it gradually became diluted with some dirt, leaves, and contaminated by germs and bacteria. Although the puddle water is obscured by contaminants, the essence of the spring water can indeed be found within the dirty water.

Professor: It can.

Socrates: By purifying the debris from the dirty water we will find the essence of the pure water, will we not?

Professor: We will.

Socrates: Therefore, modern man, God's existence, and being, can be above, and not within us, just as the spring itself, is above and away from the puddle. But God's essence of love can be within us, just as the essence of the spring is to be found within the puddle of water. Just as we need to purify the puddle water to find the essence of the pure water, we also need to purify ourselves from our unjust and sinning nature, to realize that the essence of God's love does, indeed, lie within. The fact that one cannot discern pure water in the puddle does not signify that the puddle does not contain the essence of the spring. Likewise, if you believe you cannot see the essence of God's love around us, it does not signify that it cannot be found within us. First, we must purify the water to find its true essence. Likewise, we must purify ourselves of our unjust behavior to find the true essence of our existence, our teleology, our refined state of being, our purpose in life. And when we do, only then might we find the nature of God's love.

Just as we would desire pure spring water be added to the puddle to enhance its existence, we should desire and request God's essence of love to enhance our existence. Just as not even one drop of the impure water can enhance the existence of the pure spring water, likewise not even one of us, unpurified and unrepentant, on the left side of injustice, is able to enhance the existence of God on the right. He is the spring and essence of good, holy, pure, love, justice, and freedom!

As the dirty water needs to draw from the spring water above, we likewise need to draw from God's pure nature and essence from above. Therefore, God's being can be transcendent, and above us, just as the spring is located above and away from the puddle, while at the same time God's essence can be within us, just as the essence of the pure spring is found within the puddle.

Professor: Well said, Socrates. But you must be informed that your philosophy goes contrary to modern philosophers such as Nietzsche, Hume, and Hegel who have been some of the most prominent philosophers of the last two hundred years. Your philosophy also contradicts the existentialist philosophies of Sartre, Camus, and others of this century. Your description of good and evil goes against the grain and attacks the heart and soul of the religions of the far east, especially the Taoist.

Nietzsche and Hume, for example denied the existence of God, with the "God is dead" announcement. Nietzsche, who coined that phrase, was in pursuit of a superhuman condition for humanity, now that we need not rely on God any longer. While you claim God is not dead, but is alive and vibrant, and that man must humble himself to identify the supernatural, or shall we say God; that would be more natural. And what would be more natural, or supernatural, than that which is composed of the divine natural attributes you have been describing, such as freedom, love, etc.? Hegel believed that the mind, or soul, which has recently developed within human beings, will gradually continue to develop to a refined state of being consisting of pure excellence, and divine status. This could take millions or billions of years, but this is what the philosopher proposed. However, the way you describe it, the chances of this occurring are as ridiculous as the puddle climbing to the top of the mountain and becoming the spring itself!

The philosophy of the French existentialist Sartre states that existence precedes essence. In other words, one is thrown upon planet earth, into this polluted puddle, if you will, and this is all there is. His philosophy proclaims that there is no spring which produces essence of ultimate justice from above. He did not believe there was a source or fountain of love producing the essence of good. Sartre postulated that there exists no previous essence, and that the essence of one's being and reality will consist of what that individual being decides to make of it. You are what you decide to become. The only thing to look forward to is death, and when it's over, like an athletic event, all of the points, penalties, and fouls, that were produced and accumulated in this game of life will be wiped from the scoreboard. In this scenario there are no winners, but all losers, with no meaning to life whatsoever. He even wrote a book titled *Nausea* using such morose words as anguish, forlornness, isolation, etc. Your analogy of the spring and puddle opposes this idea of existence preceding essence. On the contrary, it describes essence to precede existence. Your premise is that all of us exist with the conclusion that the essence of man must become one with the essence of freedom, good, and love that are eternal, which preceded our existence.

Another Existentialist philosopher, Camus, stated that "existence is absurd." That the world is not absurd and humanity is not absurd independent from each other, according to this philosopher, but when the two encounter each other, only absurdity is the outcome.

Socrates: Why such pessimism, lad?

Professor: His reasoning is based on the belief that there is no hope. Humanity desires the good things: love, justice, and pleasure, but the world offers the opposite: pain, prejudice, and injustice, so that when humanity and the world embrace, which is mandatory, only absurdity results. These existentialists continued with the claim of modern philosophers that "God is dead."

Socrates: If this philosopher identifies himself with all of humanity as living in absurdity, which is to live in complete irrationality, by what means does he logically state his conviction that God is dead?

Professor: That I could not tell you. The Taoist believe that there are two equal and opposing universal forces, such as masculine-feminine, darkness-light, good-evil. This is clearly evident and well-described in their symbol of yin and yang. But your philosophy maintains the opposite of their belief, for it seems that you proclaim good and evil to be opposites indeed, but not at all equal to each other.

Socrates: Is it indeed a wise man that claims the notion that there is no good without evil. Or do you suppose it is possible for good to come out of evil?

Professor: Many philosophers and theologians believe, and have attempted to describe, the potential for good to come out of evil. Didn't you claim that purification could indeed take place from this evil existence?

Socrates: But others also proclaim that good is opposite and equal to evil.

Professor: If there were no short people and everyone was of equal height, there would not be any identifiable tall people. If there were no poor people there could not be wealthy people. Does not good, to be identified as such, necessitate the existence of evil?

Socrates: The fallacy here, of course, lad is that you and these philosophers believe that the good has a need; in this case a need for evil, to verify the existence of good.

Professor: What's wrong with believing that there is no good without evil? It seems one would need the other for both to have identifiable existence. And what is wrong with stating that good can come out of evil?

Socrates: Is this not similar to stating that there is no identifiable pure spring unless there is a polluted puddle? What should be stated is "There is no identifiable puddle water without the existence of the spring." The existence of the spring does not depend on the puddle water, but the existence of the puddle water depends on the spring. Likewise one cannot state the false doctrine that there is no good without evil but what should be stated is "there is no evil without good." For evil needs good to exist, whereas the good has no need, and in particular, good need not be dependent on evil to exist. Did we not state earlier, lad, that good is one with, and must offer, freedom, but along with the good of freedom is offered the potential to abuse it? Once freedom is abused, it becomes evil. Hence evil is a distorted good and a distorted freedom that is without justice and without love.

Evil is a spoiled good, as the puddle is spoiled water. Good needs nothing, as the spring needs nothing. The puddle needs to draw from the spring while it distorts the essence of the spring, as evil needs to draw from the good as it distorts the essence of the good. Never can these two be equal opposites. But only those that live in the puddle in this cave of illusion fall for the false belief that evil is equal to good or that good will somehow come out of their evil behavior. The only possible chance for good to come out of evil is if the original source of good, such as the essence of the spring, penetrates the murky puddle water in its form of pure essence. This means the water of the spring, in its pure and undefiled essence, must penetrate the puddle through an extraordinary, and more natural entrance, and not through the contaminating means of trickling down the mountain. Otherwise, how can we on our own identify, and fully understand what is truly good while living in this bad environment? For any action to be authentic of any human that is on the left, it must be justified and deemed as such by the side of good on the right, and not by others who belong on the same side of the left, who lack knowledge of the good. How then can we state that good can come out of evil?

> *Until the person is able to abstract and define rationally the idea of good, and unless he can run the gauntlet of all objections, and is ready to disprove them, not by appeals to opinion, but to absolute truth, never faltering at any step of the argument–unless he can do all this, you would say that he knows neither the idea of good nor any other good; he apprehends only a shadow, if anything at all, which is given by opinion and not by science; dreaming and slumbering in this life.*[2]

And in these shadows, professor Thomas, would include the good that is love.

Professor: Then you seem to be stating, Socrates, that good cannot come out of evil, as the spring cannot come out of the puddle, but good can come into evil, as the spring comes into the puddle. For example, if someone had seen the side of good, let's say, was taken out of the puddle to the top of the spring, drank of it, and brought down a bucket of the pristine spring water and offered it to us. Being unfamiliar with the possibility of pure, undefiled water, we would ridicule and ignore the bringer of the perfect water. As the allegory of the chained people in the cave describes, most in the puddle, except some philosophers, cannot even identify that we all live, swim, and drink in polluted waters. Even if the Natural Artist were to appear upon planet Earth, and proclaim his masterpiece of nature, we humans, bathing ourselves in our own artificial art, imitation justice, artificial good, false freedom, and distorted love, would reject his truth and laugh at him, as we would laugh at the one offering us the pure spring water.

As a seeker of truth which way do I turn? Ancient Greek philosophy is in contrast and opposition to modern psychology and philosophy. The ancient Greeks, such as yourself, were in pursuit of identifying the Logos in its ideal essence. Today, psychology and philosophy state that there are no absolutes, especially justice. Your philosophy states that we need to live in harmony and balance with the universal moral law. Modern philosophers such as Nietzsche state that there cannot be a moral law, for to have a moral law is to pass sentence on existence.[3] Aristotle, in ancient Greece, a student of your pupil Plato, stated that although good is not a common term it is something of that kind we are seeking.[4] Modern-day existentialist Sartre states "Nowhere is it written that the good exists."[5] There is no spring pouring out truth; that is what his modern philosophy teaches. Existence is absurd.[6] "God is dead."[7] Ancient Greek philosophy tells humanity to be humble while in pursuit of truth. Modern philosophy has exalted humanity to relative truth as if each ones idea of truth is a valid one.

Which way do I turn, Socrates? If only God had described his existence, I would be a man free from nihilism, which is the belief that the universe and life have no purpose or meaning. If I cannot liberate my mind concerning the existence of God, my life is absurd and God remains but a fiction, as modern philosophy describes. For without this knowledge, I am enslaved to bondage, to the pain of ignorance when it comes to the ideals of truth, justice, good, freedom, love, and pleasure, which would identify God. If God is truly free, he should liberate us from our ignorance concerning his existence.

But if God does exist, with all of his divine attributes, one essence of God cannot be separated from another essence; they all must be united into one.

Mothers may offer agape love but humankind in general divorces itself from the ability to produce love, choosing willingly or ignorantly to produce pain and misery for each other. Man does not emit truth but many times the essence of man emits the opposite, which are lies. Hence, once God produces his essence of love, then that essence cannot be separated from the rest of his attributes. For God's act of love must include and reveal an act of justice, good, freedom, truth, and pleasure all combined in one; otherwise God will be identified as being plural or divided. One cannot divide God's essence of good, justice, freedom, or love, as one cannot even divide one of these attributes from the others. This means an identifiable essence of God that becomes descriptive is an absolute revelation of the existence of God in its totality. But humanity lacks such an absolute, descriptive revelation. It seems philosophers will continue to have many timeless questions, but very few answers!

As professor of philosophy Dr. Soccio states,

> [T]oday I have more questions and fewer answers than I did twenty-plus years ago when I was bitten by a philosophical gadfly named Socrates. And yet my questions of today are more satisfying than my answers of yesterday.[8]

Philo: So what are we to do as philosophers? Are we to terminate this discussion once again and leave the unanswered timeless question pending?

Socrates: Who are you, lad? You have not uttered a word all of this time?

Philo: My name is Philo. I am a modern disciple of Socrates. I wonder if we have analyzed all there is to analyze, and have we exhausted all means and avenues searching for truth? I am curious, as to which flag we raise behind our ivory towers contemporary philosopher; the flag of ignorance, or of defeat. Can we not possess an answer to these timeless questions and become followers of truth and the right doctrine? These were the questions and answers raised by Socrates and revealed by timeless truth itself.

Socrates: You seem to have an insight to truth, Philo. By what means did you arrive at this conclusion of right doctrine?

Philo: By what means indeed, Socrates? What is the means by which the ancient Greeks sought of transforming humanity from the left side of injustice to the right side of justice? Do we have a way to transport humanity toward the right side of righteousness? Professor Thomas stated earlier that freedom requires an enabling means, but who can offer us such an enabling means, except freedom itself? Dr. Martin Luther King, a hero who attempted to provide freedom and justice for a people in bondage, was imprisoned for the love of freedom and for justice for his people. In his own words he sought for the "means" which should be "as pure as the end." [9] Only by pure means can we arrive at the end that is pure in itself. We must all purify ourselves. Otherwise, the end will continue to remain obscure. Dr. King requested from his prison cell that we model ourselves after "Socrates" and become seekers of truth. Consequently humanity, which removed Socrates by poison, gave King its means of freedom and love by planting a bullet in his head. Mahatma Ghandi, for the love of his Indian people, sought to find freedom and justice against bondage and imperialism through peaceful means. He also believed that "If we take care of the means, we are bound to reach the end;"[10] consequently, he also received a bullet to the head from a loving humanity. If such are the consequences of the human struggle to find the means of attaining justice and freedom in our human existence, what is the pure and enabling means of arriving beyond human toward the ideals of these concepts that are united with the divine? The enabling means that keep us to the left of injustice and bondage are very familiar, overflowing, and in superabundance in humanity. For humanity knows all too well its own nature of war, stealing, cheating, lying, raping, murdering.

But freedom-bearing doves, and champions of justice, such as Socrates, King, and Ghandi, have revealed and described the evils of human nature through their deaths. Human beings look for love. Yet, agape love is where truth and justice reside. But a man's lips will tell a woman "I love you" to seduce her, while his thoughts say "I do not!" How can one find harmony and balance in one's self, and in things as grand as the universe and the moral law, when there is yet an imbalance in the short distance between the mind which says "no" and the mouth which says "yes?"

Socrates: Then it all begins within, Philo. What one's mind thinks needs to be in harmony with what one's word says. We agree that eros love which is of the physical universe cannot be the enabling means of transforming the self toward the refined state of agape love, which is together with truth, justice, and pleasure on the right.

Philo: Human beings lack the resources to arrive at the spectrum of truth on the right, for it entails genuine love, which physical passion and lies cannot offer. It requires legitimate justice, which money cannot buy, and authentic freedom, where human bullets do not apply. Due to the inability of humanity to arrive at truth, truth utilized genuine love from the right to triumphantly arrive into our polluted and distorted reality in pursuit of a lost humanity on the left. For he is not far from us; for in him we live and move and have our being as some of the poets of ancient Greece and the pupils of Plato write, "For we are all his offspring."

Professor: What is this babbler talking about, Socrates? He seems to proclaim a strange God. If truth has indeed revealed its love, truth must have revealed all of its other attributes as well. Need we listen to this talk, or are we to assume all modern professors of philosophy, who are the seekers of truth today, were bypassed by this truth of his?

Socrates: Let's allow him the freedom to speak, professor. Is not philosophy the art of listening to new information and ideas of others? What is this truth which you proclaim, Philo? I recommend we stroll to the park across the street, where it is quieter, so that we can hear more concerning this matter. Do we all agree?

It is true, that a little philosophy inclineth man's mind to atheism; but depth in philosophy bringeth men's minds about to religion.
　　　　　　　　　　　　　　　　—Francis Bacon [11]

One may go wrong in many different ways, but right only in one, which is why it is easy to fail and difficult to succeed—easy to miss the target and difficult to hit it.
　　　　　　　　　　　　　　　　　　　—Aristotle [12]

The Veil

If you admit that we can't peer behind the [veil], how can you be sure there's nothing there?
—Time Magazine[1]

Professor: Well Philo, we are curious to hear what you have to say about this absolute and universal truth of yours.

Philo: Professor Thomas, let us differentiate between existence and essence. You discussed earlier with Socrates that existence states that something *is* whereas essence describes *what it is*. Now, before we analyze the existence and essence of the greatest existence and most refined essence of being, let's begin with the lowest possible form of essence and existence of, say, a rock. We do agree in fact that the existence of a rock is that it basically takes up space upon our three-dimensional universe; that it is lacking a living essence.

Professor: Simple enough.

Philo: A flower depends upon its own physical substance for its existence as the rock, but is of a greater essence since it breathes nitrogen, emits oxygen, emits a scent, which places it above the essence of a rock. Agreed?

Professor: Granted.

Philo: Now, an animal, such as a dog, has its own physical substance taking up space upon our three-dimensional universe as do the rock and the plant, but its existence is not dependent on being rooted into the ground. It is mobile, having power to move about. It consumes food in different locations and leaves its essence of digested food behind as a trail of its existence. Even a blind man may identify the dog's existence by the sound which it produces. The unique attributes and characteristics of the five senses are not found in the rock or the plant, but belong to the higher species of animals and humans. Now the human has its physical existence, as the rock, plant and animal. But human essence is not only of motion and sound, which also belong to the animals. The essence of humanity includes creativity, the will to produce, the ability to communicate in language and the expressions of art. Humans have the ability to reason, inquire, and contemplate philosophical questions. They have the capacity to connect different branches of study to arrive at truth. Such characteristics are nonexistent in the other species. Communication distinguishes and separates the human species from all others. Now, as we move upward along the scale of existence which produces essence, would you not agree with Socrates, that to move beyond the essence of humankind we must come to the reality and essence of God, the Natural Artist, whose divine essence includes justice, good, love, freedom, and other higher qualities?

Professor: There is nothing I would like more than to agree with Socrates that the essence of God is composed of these divine attributes. But I would agree under one condition. You have shown that the higher species possess essence of the lower species, but the lower species lack the refined essence of the higher species. You, therefore, seem to have bypassed the essence of humankind to arrive at the refined essence of God. Did you not claim that the essence of humankind is shown in its ability to reason and communicate?

Philo: That is an observable, descriptive fact.

Professor: Then I would be delighted to discover a refined justifiable purpose and reason for the existence of humanity. My belief that the universe has no special purpose or meaning but is simply the end product of an unintelligible accident still stands. Before we arrive at the refined essence of God's attributes, we must face the fact that without communication God lacks the essence of lower species such as the human species. As we move up on the scale of existence, it seems that lower species lack a more refined essence that higher species possess.

It is unnatural for a plant to move, but it is natural for the animal to move. Likewise, it is unnatural for the animal to communicate through language, literature, and paintings but communication is developed in the higher essence of man. Since it is natural for humans to communicate, it would have to be natural for God, in the higher existence, to have the ability to communicate. Now check your descriptions of essence revealing existence and tell me what is missing. The nature of the rock is to be lifeless which is simply to take up space.

Philo: That's about it.

Professor: As we move up, the nature of the plant is to be and live.

Philo: Indeed.

Professor: Moving up, the nature of an animal is to be, live and move.

Philo: An observable fact.

Professor: Still moving up, the nature of man is to be, live, move, reason and communicate.

Philo: Equally an observable fact.

Professor: We then move to the higher existence of God, whose nature must include to be, live, move, reason, communicate, and express higher qualities such as justice, love, goodness, and freedom. Since man's essence is communication, why, then, has God not communicated his essence of these higher qualities? If God lacks communication which humans possess as a lower species, how can God's nature possess the ideal essence of justice, freedom, love, etc.? God must possess the lesser essence of communication before God can possess essence of greater qualities.

Philo: If God described his existence through his essence of the higher qualities such as love and justice, would you agree that such communication must leave a universal, life-changing impact upon humanity, greater than any other communication the world has ever seen or heard?

Professor: Indeed, Philo. But as I stated to Socrates earlier, the uncommunicated good is an unknown good. The unknown and uncommunicated good is a lesser good than the ideal good, that would have communicated itself. Hence the ideal good of justice and love, if it existed but was uncommunicated, would not exist in its ideal form. The ideal form would need communication.

Philo: Then you are saying that it is mandatory that God possesses the ability to communicate in order to proclaim his essence of ideal attributes revealing his existence? I wonder what means of communication would be satisfactory to you, or humanity in general, to comprehend God's communicated goodness and justice?

Professor: I assumed this is what you had intended to divulge to us and why we now find ourselves here in the park.

We have agreed that humans do not possess the highest ideals of justice, freedom, and love but do possess the lower essence of communication. How can God, who does not possess the lower essence of communication, possess a higher essence in its ideal form?

Ask any religious man this question: "If God would appear in front of us, how could we know it is God?" By what substance and composition would God communicate himself? Physical substance is for rocks, plants, animals, and humans. Would God communicate by a miracle? The skeptic will ask, "How do I know that it is not a magician doing magic tricks in front of us?" Would God communicate his existence by healing someone's infirmities? In this case, a modern doctor would be God in a primitive society. Will God reveal himself by presenting his ideals of justice, love, and good? It seems that more injustice is found upon this planet.

Our knowledge of justice is subjective. We see only relative good. And it is with great difficulty we try to arrive at truth. The burden of proof, neighbor, is upon you to relate God's communicated and descriptive attributes. Unless God first expresses communication, I cannot determine whether or not he possesses the greater qualities that belong to a more refined existence, higher than our own. What sort of communication would the divine utilize in order for everyone to verify that it is God's communicated good?

Philo: I believe your question, Professor, is this: "If God communicated his essence of divine attributes, how can we humans, on a universal standard, identify such a valuable essence leading up to the true and absolute existence?" But how do you suppose humanity values anything? Are there not human values or a moral law implanted within all of us that describe right from wrong, one that we value, although we don't follow it all of the time?

Professor: I am not so certain many are willing to accept the moral law within humanity as a descriptive, communicated good from God. When the Sophist philosophers debated with Socrates 2,400 years ago, they valued the moral law as relative and changing from one tribe, civilization, political system, and religion to another. But Socrates, whom I believe lost that argument, has maintained, as he still does today, that there is a universal, divinely inspired, absolute law.

A relative law could be illustrated by two drivers, a young man and an old one driving along on the freeway. If we allow these two people to drive as their conscience describes, then a young man in a well built sports car possessing quicker responses justifies himself for speeding along at eighty-five miles per hour. The old man with much slower reaction time in an old car also justifies himself for driving forty miles per hour. Both drivers might appear unjust and a hazard to yet another driver that is traveling sixty miles per hour. Consequently, the state has eliminated any misinterpretation of a relative speed law, and has established a descriptive, absolute, and indisputable speed limit. A relative humanity on the left side needs absolute and indisputable laws and directions from the right side of God's justice. Take the issue of abortion, for example. As you probably know, in many countries of Europe, such as Germany, abortion is illegal, while in the United States it is legal. If we allow everyone to describe their own idea of right from wrong, justice from injustice, and good from bad; humanity, for the most part, will justify itself. We justify our actions according to our age, education, traditions, religious and political system, laws, and ethics. You see, Philo, we need an absolute law so that we may value the descriptive nature of divine origins, and not relative prescriptive laws of someone else's morality.

Philo: Then you are claiming that the right side of the divine should have provided an absolute communicated law that everyone should value and be subject to, similar to the absolute and descriptive physical laws?

Professor: Indeed, Philo, the nature of communication which the lower species of humanity possesses is a requirement in the higher nature of God. Communication would be mandatory before I may accept and value any law as absolute and therefore divine.

Philo: The physical substance and composition of matter within a rock, plant, animal, or human is universally subject to the laws of physics. Whether rock or human, if it is thrown off a bridge it has no choice but to fall straight down as the descriptive laws of physics demand. Likewise, humans have no other choice but to age and die as all other animals do because the descriptive biological laws demand it. But in the laws of morality, in doing good or bad deeds, man is not forced to do good ones. The laws of goodness do not impose forced goodness but the laws of goodness demand freedom and choice.

A person in the conscience may say "no, this is wrong" while that one's actions proclaim "yes, I knew that it was wrong but did it anyway." Now if there is a God on the right side who is defined by justice and good, Socrates stated that in God also is the essence of freedom. This means, then, that God must have allowed us the freedom to abide, or not abide by his laws, to accept or reject them. For if we were forced to behave morally as the physical and biological laws command us to behave physically, we would be commanded by the laws originating from the side of the good to behave with virtue toward all. If there were no choice in the matter we would and could not choose to be good, but would have to follow the mechanical laws of goodness.

This means that forced goodness cannot be authentic goodness, for true goodness is one with and must contain freedom. But if we were forced to be without choice then Hitler had no freedom of choice in his actions as he equally had no freedom of choice in the outcome of his height or in the color of his hair. Now I ask, could it be that the divine side of justice has revealed and communicated his absolute laws, but you have chosen in your freedom to reject and not abide by God's standard of justice and goodness which his laws describe? Your rejection is only possible, of course, because of the freedom of choice which the right side of God has allotted and bestowed upon you.

Professor: Tell us about these absolute and universal descriptive laws of God, so that we may also know them, Philo. For if there is such a communicated right and wrong by a divine standard, then everyone must be subject to these laws as everyone is subject to the physical and biological laws. If God's laws exist, then even those that freely choose to disobey God's absolute and undeviating laws must bear the consequences of rejecting his laws. Hence everyone must be subject to these laws regardless if one chooses to accept them or reject them. Now where are these descriptive laws you seem to be referring to?

Philo: These are the descriptive laws which the Jews, Christians, and Muslims accept as a divine revelation and illumination of God's justice upon humanity.

Professor: Then you are referring to the Old Testament law declared by Moses which we also know as the Ten Commandments. Does this also include the six hundred plus, additional laws, revealed in the Old Testament? If so, then by what reasonable conclusion am I to believe that these are God's absolute and universal laws? Is it simply because Jews, Christians, and, Muslims accept them as such?

Philo: Well, what is the alternative? Either God, from his side of justice, imparted these laws to Moses, or Moses created them himself.

Professor: Practically every civilization has produced a moral lawgiver similar to Moses. Hammurabi in ancient Babylon, Solon in ancient Greece, Confucius in China, etc.

Philo: If God gave his laws to Moses, then these are authentic, absolute and constant divine laws, and not a mere human, moral law. Although Socrates in his time was unaware concerning the absolute divine laws described to Moses, Socrates was wise enough to understand that there must exist an absolute divine law. Therefore, the Sophist philosophers who disagreed with Socrates were right concerning the relative moral law as it concerns humanity, but ultimately Socrates was correct in the overall picture, for an absolute law existed. In those days Socrates was uninformed that the lawgiver was identified as Yahweh of the Old Testament.

Professor: But what makes Moses so special and different from other great lawgivers of other civilizations? Hammurabi, the lawgiver of Babylon, existed at least 300 years before Moses.

Philo: He did. But Hammurabi lived in a civilization that worshipped an array of polytheistic mythological gods that have not endured the test of time, and have disappeared from the face of the earth. Moses revealed the one, true, and constant Yahweh, whose word and laws are still found alive and vibrant even today, enduring the laws of change for these thousands of years. If all others were of divine origin where are these other lawgivers, their laws, their gods today? For to be of divine origin which remains constant, we must conclude that the law would not change to satisfy the mutating passions and desires of a relativistic humanity. Whether you accept the laws or not, you do not question the fact that the Old

Testament itself claims that these are the laws of God? These laws were the heart and soul of the nation of Israel for more than a thousand years before Christ, were they not?

Professor: Undoubtedly.

Philo: Neither can you deny the fact that not only the Jews, but the Christians and Muslims have all accepted these to be indeed God's laws?

Professor: I believe they do, yes.

Philo: Then, you see, if Moses did not receive these laws, as his writings indicate, then he created these laws himself. This means that he deceived the people of Israel, the Christians and the Muslims who for thousands of years have accepted his forgery with the mistake that these laws have divine origins and the stamp of divine authenticity. If these laws were a creation of Moses, he was a clever forger and liar.

Professor: The man could have simply been a great moralist and attempted to induce an ethical and moral standard upon his people.

Philo: But Moses gave directions in one commandment not to lie, did he not?

Professor: That might be one of the better known commandments.

Philo: Then Moses, the great moralist, who directed his people not to lie behaved immorally, breaking his own law by lying to the people that these divine commandments are from God, when in reality he knew that they were not. In this case, the world's best selling book is not describing the just nature of God and his laws but the lies and forgery of Moses. The only alternative, of course, is that Moses was deluded into believing that they were actually from God when they were not.

Professor: Then let it be, Philo. I will momentarily accept that the Ten Commandments and the rest of the biblical laws are a revelation from God; and thus, Moses does not contradict himself when he claims not to lie. But does not one of the commandments say not to murder?

Philo: Indeed.

Professor: Then if these are the divine revelations from God, as you state, why did God murder people in the Old Testament for no rhyme or reason? Did not God, in this case, break his own commandment not to murder? In the book called *Atheism: the Case Against God,* George H. Smith states...

> *The first problem with omnibenevolence is reconciling it with the biblical portrayal of God who, in the words of Thomas Jefferson, is 'a being of terrific character-cruel, vindictive, capricious and unjust.*[20]

Words such as unjust, cruel, and vindictive contradict the ideal reality given by Socrates of an eternal and just God whose truth must be undeviating and constant. I would need to see consistency in the God of Moses to accept what you are saying as truth, Philo. If we must value God's goodness, love, and justice as absolute and constant, as Socrates proclaims, then we must identify the descriptions of God's nature with consistency, which is a required essence of the absolute.

Philo: But what is value, professor, and how does one measure it? Can the scientist weigh it, or divide it? Does not value require a free choice in order to value that choice over other less valuable choices? A woman who freely chooses a diamond ring over all other rings which she considered purchasing does not hide it but displays her valued choice in the public arena. Likewise, the young person who chooses a valued sports car over other cars publicly displays a value choice to friends and neighbors and even to strangers. The Greeks did not conceal their valued Parthenon, but built it upon the center rock in the heart of Athens. So did the French with their Eiffel tower, as we did with their present of the Statue of Liberty. Likewise, God displays his choice of revelation of his laws in the physical arena, written in the world's best-selling book, that has been translated into more languages than any other book. The value of choice is the precious and prized value which God offers to humanity giving us the freedom to choose to value God's justice and laws, or to reject them if we choose.

Professor: First we must consider the fact that Socrates reveals human ignorance, injustice, and falsity as perceptions of truth. Could it not be that these Biblical Laws, although morally good, have developed into the world's best selling book due to the distorted reality and illusion of humanity perceiving something to be of God, but in reality being the creation of man? This would mean that humanity has elevated such public value of the laws of the Bible, in which case they do not have their origins from divine revelation.

Philo: Ironic that we should agree that humanity is indeed in a cave of illusion as Socrates reveals. If these are the direct divine laws in the Old Testament, as I trust them to be, then I live in the reality of truth and you live in the illusion of distorted truth simply by rejecting that which is true. But if these are not God's direct, divine laws then I live in the illusion of Moses' lies and in that case you live in reality. But I am curious to know, since the only certain fact is that one of us is indeed wrong and the other right, who would you say is capable of weighing this issue on the scales of justice? For if there is no God my mistake is irrelevant, but if you are wrong then your mistake is of great consequence. You stated that as we have no choice in the physical and biological laws, we equally have no choice in the moral laws. If one chooses to freely reject the moral or biblical law then that individual will have no choice but face the consequences due to his rejection of the law.

Professor: You have failed to address the issue of how a just God could condemn murder in one law but breaks his own law and murders people? By what means can God justify his actions?

Philo: Going back to the example of the state and its laws, we know that the state has absolute laws for speeding on the freeway. Imagine if it did not. Someone traveling at one hundred and twenty miles per hour could not be guilty of speeding if there was no established descriptive law.

Professor: This is surely the case.

Philo: But once laws are established then the speedster is pronounced guilty only due to the fact that there is an existing law. Therefore, such lawbreaking individuals cannot proclaim ignorance of the law in front of the judge. For the laws of the state are enforced from border to border, imminent although invisible. The essence and force of the law even flies invisibly within an airplane thousands of feet above ground, and the essence of the law of the state was even present upon the moon along with the astronauts. If one astronaut injured or murdered another then it would activate and arouse the law to take action once the astronauts returned.

Professor: What you are telling me Philo is that when I die and leave all physical substance behind, but take my imperfect soul and being to the presence of your God of justice, he will judge me by his laws. But I say before he judges me, I believe that he first must justify himself of breaking his own laws of murder! Then I will justify myself of any crimes I may have committed. These contradictions do not communicate a God who is constant, undeviating, and eternal as the philosophy of Socrates demands.

Philo: Is it not the philosopher's law of contradiction that no statement can be both true and false, or that something can be and not be at the same time and under the same condition?

Professor: Yes, ever since the times of the ancient Greeks. This is my problem with the God of the Old Testament. As the atheistic book stated, the nature of God is revealed as "cruel, vindictive, and unjust," while God should be forgiving, righteous, and just.

Philo: Socrates utilized this law of contradiction earlier when he challenged the essence of freedom. You stated to Socrates that people generally prefer to be free to do evil than to be forced to do good. Someone might challenge the goodness of God by asking, "Why does God allow a man to rape a woman instead of intervening to stop the rapist?" Such individuals are breaking the law of contradiction, are they not?

Professor: Indeed, Philo. Once someone states a preference for being free to do evil and to not be forced to do good, one cannot then complain to God that God did not intervene to stop a rapist. For if God intervened to prevent an evil act then the freedom to do evil is violated. Therefore, you can have one or the other but not both. To have both breaks the law of contradiction.

Philo: Likewise one could state that either Moses received these laws from God or he did not. Moses could not have both received the laws from God and not received the laws from God at the same time and same conditions. But if Moses did, indeed, receive the laws from God as about half of the people upon this planet believe, then you seem to be implying that God is contradicting himself by implementing a law against murder yet behaving contrary to his implemented law by murdering people.

Professor: An absolute and eternal God must be absolutely and eternally consistent, which troubles many in the Old Testament's portrayal of God.

Philo: You must realize that it is your argument against God in this case which is illogical and inconsistent.

Professor: By what logical standard? How am I inconsistent?

Philo: By a consistent and justifiable standard that is the byproduct of the laws of all nations. What happens to a prisoner that attempts to escape from prison before he has served his complete sentence? Does the state reward such prisoners or punish them more severely?

Professor: It would punish them more severely, of course.

Philo: Could you imagine any civilization that would reward its prisoners for attempting a premature escape from prison?

Professor: If there ever existed a civilization that offered prisoners the reward of reducing their sentence by attempting to escape, then you would have every single prisoner attempting to escape in order to be rewarded.

Philo: Sheer chaos?

Professor: More like anarchy.

Philo: Illogical?

Professor: Absolutely.

Philo: Then we identify this universal and consistent standard: the laws of the state decide when the time is right for the lawbreaker to go beyond the prison wall. It is not the decision of the unjust to cross this barrier to the side of the just when such a one so desires.

Professor: Unquestionably. I could not imagine a society without such a law.

Philo: No indeed. But this is precisely what you are imagining when you imply that God states not to murder but that God murders.

Professor: I'm afraid you just lost me, Philo. What does the consistent law of a more severe penalty toward a prison escapee have to do with God's inconsistency when he states not to murder but murders? How do you reconcile the two?

Philo: Once the state produces laws, it follows with a consistent and absolute right to raise a prison wall. This prison wall separates those that the state sees as just from the ones that the state sees as unjust. The unjust, of course, are those who have violated its laws.

Professor: True. There must be a law revealed before a separation between the just and unjust can exist.

Philo: Does not the human behave similarly to the state when someone has reasons to assume that another man is a murderer or rapist? A law-abiding individual would not usually invite a perceived murderer to his house for breakfast.

Professor: Not very likely.

Philo: Neither do we allow a perceived child molester nor a rapist to stay with our children and wife while we are away for the weekend.

Professor: Agreed.

Philo: The fact is, first there must be laws to identify the innocent from the guilty, and then follows the prison wall of separation between the innocent who are just from the guilty who are unjust. And in case of a known lawbreaker who is not found separated by a prison wall where he belongs, we separate ourselves from such unjust individuals and place an invisible wall or barrier between ourselves and such lawbreakers.

Professor: This is usually true.

Philo: Was this not the case with O.J. Simpson, one of the most famous football stars, who was accused of murdering his wife? The jury of twelve found him not guilty and thus he avoided being separated by a physical prison wall. But most Americans who believe he is guilty, raised an invisible wall of separation between themselves and Simpson.

Professor: This has indeed occurred.

Philo: Is it easier then for the just man to exit his invisible wall of separation which he has erected and visit the unjust man's house, or is it easier for the unjust rapist to pass beyond this invisible wall of separation and visit the just man's house?

Professor: The unjust man seems to have no problems having the just man visit his house since the unjust man has not raised an invisible wall of separation between himself and the just man. But the just man who has indeed raised an invisible wall of separation would not desire to have the unjust rapist cross this barrier and enter his house.

Philo: Likewise then, you agree, if the state decided to examine the prison which it has constructed, it can freely enter within its walls and bars when it justifiably chooses.

But the unjust imprisoned man is not free to exit this wall of separation as he wishes. If a guilty individual attempts to break across his prison wall of separation prematurely, it is a universal, consistent law that the prisoner will pay a greater penalty, requiring a greater sentence than his original term. Hence only the state that possesses the laws has the freedom to be on both sides as it desires. And only the state which makes and enforces the laws is able to pardon the lawbreaker, as the laws of the state mandate.

Professor: Certainly true.

Philo: Do these descriptions of the good and just along with their freedom to be on both sides as they wish, not correspond to the allegory of the spring water on top of the mountain? Which states that the good spring water can be found within the bad puddle water but the bad puddle water cannot be with the good spring water?

Professor: Remind me.

Philo: The spring water on top of the mountain is pure, good and refreshing. Accordingly, humanity universally erects an invisible division and separation between the good and clean water on top and the dirty water below in the puddle. This parallels the just and good man that has erected an invisible wall of separation between himself and the unjust man. The just man is free to exit his invisible wall of separation and come to the bad man's house as the good water is free to come into the dirty puddle water. But the unjust murderer and child molester is not welcome to pass our invisible wall which we have erected, just as the puddle water is not welcomed into the good spring water we are about to drink.

Professor: This is typical of humanity.

Philo: We would not consider adding dirty puddle water to the spring water we are about to drink unless the dirty water first be purified. Otherwise, it would be unacceptable by our standards to unite the two. Likewise, the desire of the state toward the prisoner is that he will be repentant and a changed man prior to his being released and permitted to rejoin society. Both prisoner and water need cleansing of their polluted nature prior to uniting with the side of the righteous and just. God, therefore, is analogous to the pure and spotless spring water, for he is righteous, pure, and just. His nature would demand the purification of humans just as humans demand purification of the dirty water. God's laws therefore decide when the time is right for anyone to unite with his side of justice, just as the laws of the state decide when the time is right for the unjust lawbreaker to unite with the just. Now, since God has produced laws and has thus described a separation between his just nature and our injustice, what must God do if anyone were to attempt to cross to his side of justice prematurely, unpurified and unpardoned as the right time of his law requires? You stated that the state is consistent and justified when it executes a more severe penalty toward those who attempt to cross their wall of separation prematurely.

Professor: I did.

Philo: Is God not consistent and justified then, for serving a more severe penalty, as his law mandates, upon such individuals?

Professor: If this is what God's laws mandate, then he would be justified, and it would be consistent.

Philo: And if God's law states that death is the more severe penalty against such individuals, then God's laws and reasoning are consistent and justified, do you not agree?

Professor: I see what you mean.

Philo: It is not the nature of God, then, that is inconsistent, but it is your perception of the nature of God which you indicate is inconsistent. Earlier you stated God was inconsistent and illogical in stating not to murder, but murdered; now you state that God is consistent and logical. First, God reveals laws proclaiming him judge. Then he reveals a stiffer penalty toward those that disrespect his laws by attempting to cross his divine side of justice. And the Old Testament declares that the more severe penalty is death.

Professor: Your argument seems to be flawless, Philo, except for one problem. The state has indeed descriptive and absolute laws and has therefore the right to separate and divide the just from the unjust by a physical, observable prison wall. But one human who perceives another human as unjust does not raise a physical observable wall of separation but an invisible, subjective wall of separation toward the other human. The reason why the state raises a physical observable wall of separation and the human an invisible one, is because state laws are authoritative, descriptive, and enforced.

The human who only perceives injustice toward another human possesses no absolute descriptive laws, and no authority to enforce his relative perceptions as justifiable. Now since you believe that the laws of the God Yahweh in the Old Testament are descriptive, authoritative, and enforced, how can human beings possibly know when they are crossing into the presence of God? Can one know this as clearly as when dirty water is added to the spring water? Or, can human beings know this as clearly as prisoners can know they are acting contrary to the laws of the state, when they break across visible walls of separation.

Since this separation of God and humanity seems to be an abstract concept extracted from the laws, how does the layman understand such a theoretical division? How does the layman even begin to understand that he is in need of purification and that God's nature demands it? God, whom you believe has produced descriptive laws declaring an unjust humanity, should have produced an observable, descriptive, physical separation. He should not be in need of human philosophical rhetoric to justify his laws and separation between our injustice on the left and his justice on the right. Therefore, there should be a physical division understood by any lay person between a just God and an unjust humanity. The way it is now, only a philosopher can understand such an abstract, invisible division between justice and injustice, God and humanity.

Philo: Once again you are speaking from opinion and not knowledge, professor. You seem to be ignorant of the fact that a physical veil of separation did, indeed, exist in Israel in the temple of Jerusalem as the Old Testament describes. Once the descriptive laws of God were introduced; immediately, a physical separation between his justice, along with his laws, was located on one side of the veil, and unjust humanity, described as unjust by the laws, were found on the other side of the veil.

Professor: If there exists such a descriptive separation, I admit, I am not aware of it.

Philo: Then you must agree that it is by faith and without examining the facts that you believe that the God of the Old Testament is inconsistent and unjust. God used the physical universe to communicate his laws and his justice to humanity. He used the same physical universe of sense perception to show his separated nature of justice from injustice. He demonstrated this by a physical veil of separation. By this veil of separation, his justice and separation is revealed equally to the layperson and the philosopher.

Professor: Are you saying there was a physical veil of separation? If so, where was this veil located? If it did exist, was it simply a symbolic portrayal of justice and injustice or do you believe the actual presence of almighty God was behind the veil? And, if this were a literal division which no one was able to cross, how can any human arrive at the knowledge of the nature and essence of God who remained transcended and beyond human contact behind this veil?

Philo: The veil was located in the temple of Jerusalem, as commanded in the law of the Old Testament. Only the high priest who first became purified himself through a special ritual was able to cross this veil once a year carrying the blood of the sacrificed animal to spill upon the laws. This was the sacrifice which God prescribed as the means of forgiveness for the people from the guilt proclaimed by the law. This was not a permanent solution as it must be repeated each year.

Professor: Then the high priest should describe for us the form, composition, and nature of the divine, the ideal essence of justice, love, good, and freedom whom he met behind this veil.

Philo: The Bible states that the essence of God appeared behind the veil in the form of a cloud without dimensions, shape or form. Just as freedom, love, justice, and good possess no form or shape.

Professor: Then let's agree with you Philo that this veil in the temple of Jerusalem was literally a division between the injustice of man and the holiness of God. You stated that the laws of the Bible are universal, verifying guilt upon all of humanity. I assume this would also include the Romans?

Philo: Everyone, including the Romans.

Professor: The Romans must have certainly been unpurified, unrepentant and found guilty by the laws. So why do you suppose in the year 70 A.D. God allowed the Romans to sack and totally destroy the country of Israel?

I assume the Romans must have sacked the temple and even trampled upon the veil altogether, entering into the side of the righteousness and purity of holy God. Did they not?

Philo: They did.

Professor: Then we must accept the fact that this physical separation existed in symbolic form and not literal. Do not most civilizations produce a holy site which people revere and respect as holy ground?

Philo: This is a custom of most, if not all, civilizations.

Professor: Once we do a historical analysis and compare many holy sites along with their sacred relics in different parts of the world, we notice the only consistency history offers is that at some point the power of God diminishes and disappears. The glory of God, along with the sacred relics, runs away with its people and God's chosen clerics when an invading army crushes that country and tramples upon their holy sites. It happened to the holy sites of ancient Israel as well as to the holy sites of American Indians. It has happened to holy sites of Tibet by the Chinese, as it has happened to holy sites elsewhere. It seems Yahweh protected the country of Israel, and his temple, along with his veil of separation from the Romans about as much as the Great Spirit that offered the American Indians rain, protected them, their land, and all of their holy sites, from the invading U.S. cavalry.

Philo: The location of the actual separation is still regarded as a holy sight by Jewish clerics. Not only can we read about the existence of the physical veil of separation in the Old Testament, but visit the actual location in the ancient temple of Jerusalem.

Professor: And you see no inconsistency here, Philo? The laws continue to exist describing divine justice in the world's best selling book, but this physical separation that was a byproduct of the laws was thrashed and trodden down by the Romans?

Philo: Again I ask if you are speaking from knowledge or from opinion, professor. You demanded for God to possess the essence of the lower species, which is the ability to communicate. I tell you his laws do communicate right from wrong, justice from injustice. God utilized laws to communicate to the ancient people, and continues to communicate through his laws to modern people. God has used a wall of division and a veil of separation to communicate to all of humanity, ancient and modern people alike, and he continues to communicate through this veil of separation even today.

Professor: You seem to be implying that similar to the state which produces laws and thus divides the just from the unjust by a prison wall, likewise God has produced laws and a veil separating himself from an unjust humanity. This veil seems to be the point beyond which no human being could possibly pass and cross over into the presence of justice, good freedom, love and the rest of the divine attributes. If anyone attempted to cross this division they were supposedly stricken dead as a greater penalty, similar to the state that imposes a stiffer penalty when the unjust prisoner attempts to cross the prison wall.

Now lets look at the evidence prior to drawing a conclusion. The fact is indeed that it is claimed that the Old Testament laws have been ordained of God and are of divine origin. It is also a fact that this veil of separation ceased to exist after it was trampled down by the Romans. Based on these facts, it seems to me that this was a theoretical division, a means of teaching humanity that we are imperfect and that a separation between our reality and the ideal attributes of divine reality eludes us. We therefore must accept this veil, as a figurative means of communication not a literal one.

Philo: Since we are to examine the facts prior to our drawing conclusions from them, you should be informed that you have drawn conclusions without considering all of the facts.

Professor: Then enlighten me as to which fact did I not take into consideration.

Philo: You must not be aware of the historical impact and symbolic legacy that this veil of division has left upon humanity. Many thousands, in fact hundreds of thousands of veils of separation continue to exist, even today. These veils continue to remind modern people concerning the division of the just from the unjust, the separation of God from humanity. These veils are even found throughout the United States, from Alaska to California, from Florida to Maine. Here in New York, hundreds of reproductions of this veil of Jerusalem exist. Some of them are twenty feet high and forty feet across. Their purpose is to declare this division of the righteous from the unrighteous; the separation of the absolute reality of God from the relative reality of man. Now I do not suppose you can tell Socrates where these veils are located in case that he might desire to examine one himself.

Professor: No I am afraid I am unaware of this fact.

Philo: It was the descendants of Socrates in Greece that chose to reproduce this veil declaring the division of the sacred from the worldly. The Greeks were present in 70 A.D. when the Romans sacked Israel, destroyed the temple, and desecrated the veil. But for the last 2000 years all Greek Orthodox Churches display a veil of separation reminding its people of the great divide. Anyone who enters this historic church will see that towards the front of the church, there is an altar. Separating the altar from the people in the church is a partition stretching from the left wall of the church to the right wall. It separates the people on one side in the church from the holy altar in front of them. Only a door in the middle of this duplicated veil allows the people to see the altar.

But the question remains; what was the motivating factor that propelled the Greeks to duplicate this physical veil of separation? Why did the Greeks face all of their veils east toward Jerusalem, pointing to the place of the original veil?

> *[And] the vail shall divide unto you between the holy place and the most holy.*
> —*Exodus 26:33* [3]

> *Which hope we have as an anchor of the soul, both sure and stedfast, and which entereth into that within the vail....*
> —*Hebrews 6:19* [4]

9

The Modern Philosopher

To lose what I owe to Plato and Aristotle would be like the amputation of a limb.
—C.S. Lewis [1]

Professor: The philosophy of Socrates, Philo, erects a philosophical wall of separation between human nature and God's nature. On the left, is man's relative justice, goodness, freedom, and love. On the right, is the nature of God with his absolute justice, goodness, freedom, and love. Now the relative nature of man is descriptively verified by our existence, while the absolute nature of God is prescriptive and remains but a theory. I can't see how the Old Testament laws and a simple veil of separation incorporate attributes such as love, freedom, pleasure, and truth.

Philo: Socrates made this philosophical division in the fifth century B.C., but the Old Testament was translated into Greek at 250 B.C. There was then correspondence between the philosophy of Socrates and the Old Testament. Both a philosophical separation and a descriptive division existed. The Greeks could now read about a physical separation displayed in this veil in the temple at Jerusalem. The philosophy of Socrates was gradually proving itself correct; that two diverse realities were in existence. The relative human reality was separated from the absolute and divine. Humanity was below and God above.

Professor: It seems that there are many similarities between the physicists' unified field theory and the philosophers' or Socratic unified field theory of truth.

Philo: I am afraid I do not follow you.

Professor: Are you familiar with the unified field theory with which physicists such as Albert Einstein attempted to combine and unify different branches of physics?

Philo: If I remember correctly, Einstein attempted to unify gravitational force, electromagnetic force, and strong and weak force into a single unified theory.

Professor: Then you must know that Einstein failed in uniting them as all other physicists have also failed. Their failure is due to the fact that such unity remains an impossibility with present human knowledge. Is such unity not similar to the philosophy of Socrates that attempts to unify the ideal essence of justice, good, love, freedom, pleasure, truth, and an omnipotent nature to a single transcended divine being?

Philo: That would be a reasonable comparison between the unattainable desires of the physicist and the philosopher.

Professor: Both Socrates and the Old Testament claim that humanity on the left possesses relative love, justice, freedom, etc., but you state that the Old Testament describes that behind this veil of separation existed a unified singularity. This monotheistic being was composed of justice, good, truth, freedom, love, pleasure, and omnipotence all in one.

Philo: Then you realize that there is a definite relationship between the philosophy of Socrates and Old Testament descriptions concerning the essence of God.

Professor: But you see, Philo, if God, behind this veil of separation, is omnipotent, this means that God is all-powerful. This includes the power to communicate and reveal his unified nature that would be composed of justice, good, freedom, truth, pleasure, and especially love. Before you attempt to integrate all of these divine attributes to the one source behind this veil, do you agree that two of these attributes are that the divine must be all-powerful and all-loving simultaneously?

Philo: I have no doubt that both of these attributes of love and power are parts of the whole which composes and unifies the nature of the divine.

Professor: And I assume you believe that the divine is communicating his omnipotent and benevolent nature to humanity?

Philo: Indeed I do, professor.

Professor: Then let's first examine only these two unified aspects of God: benevolence and omnipotence. Let's see how humans in their relative reality identify and understand these absolute attributes. A human parent who loves a child would do everything possible to protect that child from a painful infirmity such as cancer or leukemia.

Philo: Yes, a human parent would indeed do everything possible to protect or to heal a child.

Professor: However, suppose a human parent possessed the power to completely heal their child free of cost and the healing is without side effects, but chose not to. Then we would say that such a parent does not truly possess love for the child. We would think of them as cruel. Now, if God is simultaneously omnipotent and benevolent, why do you suppose God does not use his mighty power to remove evil? We agreed that a human parent would, if possible, heal a child from the painful ailment of cancer. Does God lack power, or does God lack love? Look around us and you will verify that either God has not used his power to remove evil, since pain and evil continue to exist, or God has the power but has chosen not to use it, which as we have agreed would not be loving.

Philo: This is the argument of modern philosophers, such as David Hume. Socrates will consider it as I do, a schoolboy philosophy, for such discourse does not belong to true philosophers but to pseudo-philosophers.

Professor: That is quite a statement against Hume. Are you unaware that he is regarded as one of the best of modern philosophers? And considering the fact that the question of unifying omnipotence and benevolence in one God remains unanswered and thus continues to be debated in philosophy schools, I am curious to hear how you can make such a statement against the philosopher Hume.

Philo: Let's analyze Hume's question and see if it is worthy of a philosophical debate or not. God must exercise his omnipotence, according to Hume, in order to possess an all-powerful nature, which is essential. Would Hume have been satisfied if God utilized his power to remove cancer and leukemia? Would Hume be persuaded that God existed if God used his omnipotent power to remove natural catastrophes such as tornadoes? And would Hume have been convinced there is a God if God removed all evils that cause pain such as heart disease, kidney disease, or Alzheimer's disease? Is this not what Hume is stating?

Professor: The two qualities of omnipotence and benevolence united and descriptively verified is a requirement of God. This is what Hume stated. Yahweh, of the Old Testament, who is claimed to possess both of these attributes, must have descriptively communicated both of these qualities if he is God. If God has failed to reveal to humankind his two qualities of power and love, how then can you prescribe that the remaining qualities such as justice, freedom, good, and the rest are also united with God?

Philo: There arises the problem of limitation and restriction when attempting to identify God as expressing omnipotence and benevolence simultaneously.

Professor: Limitations! You are limiting God, the all powerful one? How can you make such a statement, Philo? What limits God in describing his benevolent and omnipotent nature to humanity?

Philo: The problem of limitation is not with the nature of God, for God is unlimited and unrestricted. Limitation is in the restricted nature of man. The problem of limitation and restriction is especially identified in the philosophy of Hume's misunderstanding of God. Hume limits God to removing evils of cancer, leukemia, natural catastrophes, heart disease, etc. God acting and removing all natural evil is what Hume desired in order to verify God's omnipotent nature. If God chose to act out his omnipotence and remove all evils of nature, then God, according to Hume, would also be simultaneously describing his benevolent nature.

Professor: The fact that both of these divine qualities united and combined have not been descriptively revealed and communicated is indeed what Hume states. But how do you see Hume limiting and restricting God since you state that God is unlimited and unrestricted?

Philo: If God were to utilize his omnipotence and remove all pain-causing agents which seem to have satisfied Hume in identifying God, must not God also remove the pain-causing murderers? Or shall God allow the murderers to continue living? Should God, who removes all pain-causing agents, also not remove the rapists, or should God allow them to continue living and raping? Why is Hume limiting and restricting God to removal of only the secondary evils of nature and not the primary evils of humanity? Should God be restricted not to remove the cheaters, swindlers, thieves, kidnapers, extortionists? What about the drug dealers? Does God's omnipotence also remove the drug dealers or do we restrict God into allowing them to continue dealing and ruining children and families? When Hume states that God lacks omnipotence, or simply has not described it to humanity, is not Hume limiting God? Supposing God chose to use his omnipotence and removed all pain-causing agents, could you identify one or two individuals that deserve to be spared due to their good, righteous and loving nature? Such perfect individuals must not have caused any pain to their fellow man. Are there such individuals worthy to be passed over by God's omnipotent, evil-cleansing nature? If God were to exercise his omnipotent nature, can you imagine the nature of any humans that would remain spared, standing, and alive? Why, their nature would be composed of the ideal essence of good, justice, and love. In such just, good, and loving individuals worthy to have God's cleansing pass over them, God must identify within them his own nature of good, justice, and love and indeed bypass them. For in their nature of ideal justice, good, and love, they are one in essence with the nature of the divine. But you and I both well know that not one human exists with ideal attributes. Hence both of God's natures of power and love acted out simultaneously are impossible, due to man's limitations, verified in the fact that humanity would be wiped out by God's omnipotence and thus not be able to identify God's benevolence. If God were to utilize his omnipotent nature first there is a good possibility Hume would have been the first one to be removed for rejecting God's benevolence and leading people astray.

Professor: Wait a minute. How did you ever arrive at the conclusion that Hume rejected God's benevolence? How could Hume reject something uncommunicated and nondescriptive?

Philo: But how could God simultaneously be omnipotent which requires mankind's extinction, yet at the same time be benevolent? As I stated, if God exercised his power to remove all wrongdoers, no human would be left alive to verify God's benevolent nature.

Professor: Then you are telling us, Philo, that God is both omnipotent and benevolent. But are you also saying God is limited in describing both attributes due to man's limitations and inability to endure God's omnipotent nature? Is this not a cop-out, Philo, justifying God for his inability to communicate both omnipotence and benevolence?

Philo: Not at all. Hume limits and restricts God to only the two natures of omnipotence and benevolence. Due to Hume's misunderstanding of divine attributes, he ignorantly omitted the third essence that is essential to both divine power and divine love. In order for benevolence and omnipotence to be descriptively communicated, there is the third essence of God that must be present that binds both love and power and also separates the two.

Professor: And what might this binding and dividing essence be, that communicates God's power and love yet divides them?

Philo: Not only does this particular essence separate and simultaneously unify omnipotence and benevolence, but it overrules the ideal essence of justice and is the pinnacle of all power. It is of the most refined essence belonging to the one that is composed of freedom, for this is the essence of mercy. Human justice strives for equality, demanding retribution, fines, and penalties from the unjust toward the just. Many times someone's unjust actions require severe punishment. In some countries, such as the United States, horrendous crimes of injustice are punished by the state with the death of the unjust. But God's justice of punishment against an unjust humanity must be overridden by God's refined essence which is to forgive, and have mercy, which is the pinnacle of love. For to forgive is more powerful than to destroy, and to pardon overrides justice which requires punishment and retribution. The essence of mercy describes love, while simultaneously describing power. Love, mercy and power; all three combined, describe God. The philosopher's timeless questions of benevolence and omnipotence along with mercy were verified thousands of years ago in ancient Greece. It puzzles me to see modern philosophy professors in America pondering these timeless questions that have been descriptively communicated and revealed.

Professor: Nothing has been described so far but your philosophical rhetoric and jargon, Philo. You rhetorically evaded God's omnipotent and benevolent nature by including mercy as uniting the two. Descriptive answers to these questions are demanded from you, Philo, since you claim that such answers do descriptively exist. But if these timeless questions united in one divine source did exist and were answered in ancient Greece, do you not find it odd that Socrates here remains ignorant of these answers unified into a monotheistic singularity? And what is this new and strange connection you are attempting to make between the Old Testament and Greek philosophy? What does Jerusalem have to do with Athens? Are you telling us that the Greek philosophers identified omnipotence, love, and mercy through the laws Of Yahweh in the Old Testament? If so, I must admit it would have been quite an accomplishment.

Philo: You are wrong, philosopher. The philosophers of Greece did not identify omnipotence, love, and mercy. But they did identify love, mercy, and omnipotence, in that order. The Old Testament was only part of the source which revealed these attributes.

Professor: Then are we to assume that God has communicated these three attributes of omnipotence, love, and mercy but we have failed to identify them by not placing them in their correct order as the Greeks and you just did? Do you mean to infer that the rest of God's divine attributes have been described, but modern philosophers such as Hume and myself are oblivious to such divine attributes?

Philo: Modern philosophers continue to carry the torch of wisdom and logical thinking on the human level. However, concerning God's wisdom, reason, and truth, I would say that, yes, modern philosophy is ignorant of God's communicated attributes.

Professor: Then let's momentarily abandon these modern ignorant philosophers which you seem to have difficulties with and inquire of the wise ancient philosophers of Greece. Allow me to quote from a modern philosophy college text book which I utilize in class:

Socrates asked the following question: Are actions right because God says they are right, or does God say actions are right because they are right? [2]

How do you answer Socrates, Philo?

Philo: The question seems to be if there is a divine existence above. Is there a reality separate from our human reality, or, shall we say, a division between humanity on the left and God on the right? If there are two separate realities, then a human action that is a just and good action such as giving to the poor, is just and good because God on the right side justifies such an act to be deemed right because it is right. But if the right side of God says to the Hindu "Do not eat cows" as the Hindus claim God told them, why do Jews, Christians and

Muslims eat cows? And if God tells the Muslim and Jew "Do not eat pork" as they claim God told them, why then do the Hindu and Christian eat pork? The question remains, is it truly God speaking or someone saying that God spoke these things?

Professor: We see then that humans can communicate through language and also communicate through action. One may say "I will kill you" by language and we might believe his words to be true. But if he does kill his friend then we know by his actions that his words are true. Likewise, Socrates taught that to die with justice is a greater good than to live with injustice. But it was his actions that confirmed and verified his words. Actions speak louder than words and have a tendency to leave a greater impact.

Philo: I could not agree with you more. A mother says she loves her child, but when she pushes her child to safety from the path of an oncoming car and is struck herself, then her actions verify and authenticate her love. All of the bystanders will indeed verify her love for her child.

Professor: This reminds me of the analogy which Socrates presented earlier concerning the two neighboring children. One who freely and willingly gave half of his lunch money to the poor and hungry child while the second child was forced by his father to give half of his money. We agreed that the one who gave freely performed an authentic act of love compared with the child who was forced to give.

Philo: We did agree.

Professor: We also agreed that the son-in-law who gave freely of his time to the father-in-law described an act of authentic love compared with the second son-in-law who secretly desired an inheritance from his father-in-law in return for the giving of his time.

Philo: I do remember.

Professor: But how would you respond to this scenario, Philo? The first child decided to give some of his money to the starving child, requesting nothing in return, while the second child was promised a brand new bicycle. If the second of these children were to give some of his money to the starving child would you not say that the child who gave more freely was performing a more genuine act of love than the child who was promised a new bike as compensation by the father?

Philo: I would agree that the first child's action is deemed as authentic love.

Professor: Then you see Philo, the first child gave freely and his action was right because it was right. While the second child's action was right because his father said it was right, or that the compensation of a new bike from the father made it right in the eyes of the child. Thus, you see neighbor, even a good, loving, and justified action by an agnostic such as myself, or the same action by an atheist such as Dr. Lattison, the scientist, is of equal if not superior merit than the same action of the religious man who believes in God. For if I decide to drive my terminally ill neighbor, who is unable to drive, to his chemotherapy clinic every week, I do it freely and expect nothing in return. But I do wonder, when a believer of God decides to drive such a terminally ill individual to the hospital he could certainly be influenced by the fact that he believes God will compensate him with a reward or an entrance into heaven. Hence, the atheists' action is right and good because it is right and good, while the same action of the believer is right and good because God says it is right and good. The God-fearing believer's righteousness is many times attached to fear of God or to the promise of a greater reward in heaven. When in fact it should be given freely, while expecting nothing in return.

Philo: If there is no God, Professor, which would negate any absolute authority of goodness and is the standard of justice, then I would agree with your statement.

Professor: Have you seen any Christian television shows? "Give," they say, "and God says that he will multiply ten times over." Not only is compensation offered in the afterlife but God seems to say that he will compensate a cheerful giver in this life as well. Ten times over, Philo. How does the Christian God judge the atheist who freely gives to the poor expecting nothing in return compared to judging the Christian who demands or expects ten times over? Because God says so?

Philo: But since there is an absolute good and an ideal standard of justice that belongs only to God, then your statement is in the same vein of ignorance and misunderstanding which Hume also labored under.

Professor: And what might this ignorance and misunderstanding be, Philo?

Philo: Your ignorance is in omitting the descriptive essence of God. Everything is not judged by the goodness and justice of man for the goodness and justice of man is but a relative illusion composed of ignorance on the left. Instead, everything is judged by the absolute goodness and standard of justice of God who possesses the ideals of good, justice, mercy, love and omniscience.

Professor: We have grown weary of hearing words from many religious books revealing a transcended God somewhere above and beyond us prescribed as just, loving and merciful. Please explain this descriptive standard, Philo, that will help us to realize that the action of the atheist who drives his neighbor to the hospital every week is a wrong action.

Philo: We stated that the good and just man is usually free to pass the invisible wall of separation and enter the bad man's house and not vice versa. The spring water is free to enter the dirty puddle water in direct contrast to the dirty water entering the spring. The state with its laws is definitely free to cross the prison wall and enter the prison as it desires. Since the good, just, and pure, have the right and freedom to be on both sides, then likewise, God utilized his freedom to penetrate beyond the veil of separation and enter the evil, ignorant and relative reality of humanity on the left.

Professor: Words, neighbor, nothing but words. A demonstrated act, however, is as a painting, worth a thousand words. If this is the case that God's nature is imminent within humanity on the left then God should communicate his essence of divine attributes by descriptive actions and not philosophical theodicy and human rhetoric. If such absolute actions exist, describing omnipotence, benevolence, mercy, justice, and good, then that would be the standard of all human actions and affairs. That act would be the yardstick of justice and the criteria of good. That would indeed describe the existence of the absolute and righteous on the right and reveal the relative and unrighteous on the left. But if such an absolute standard is described by deeds in contrast to the words of religious books, then am I to assume that the great philosophers such as David Hume, and others who spent their lives searching for truth, and who were in daily pursuit of the absolute, ultimate existence, have somehow missed it? These philosophers built solid foundations of reason and built bridges between ignorance and reality. Have they been oblivious to such authentic actions and communicated deeds, which reveal the divine, absolute, and authoritative good?

Philo: These are not philosophers but mere schoolboys who have built bridges of illusion in the quicksand of ignorance. We must return to the real and authentic philosophers of ancient Greece to identify truth, as truth revealed and communicated itself in word and deed, Professor.

Professor: What is this truth of yours, Philo? Are you not speaking from prejudice, subjectivism, and a biased perspective against these modern philosophers, due to the fact that you were born and raised in Greece?

Philo: I am not evaluating the ignorance and schoolboys' philosophies of Hume and the others from a prejudiced Greek perspective. The words judging these modern philosophers come from a prominent American philosopher, Mortimer Adler, author of at least twenty-three books on philosophy. Adler, is chairman of the editorial board of Encyclopedia Britannica, director of the Institute for Philosophical Research in Chicago, and senior associate of the Aspen institute for Humanistic Studies. I believe, the philosopher Adler, whose credentials speak for themselves, has the ability to objectively critique and evaluate these modern philosophers.

> *Modern philosophy has never recovered from its false starts. Like men floundering in quicksand who compound their difficulties by struggling to extricate themselves, Kant and his successors have multiplied the difficulties and perplexities of modern philosophy by the very strenuousness-and even ingenuity-of their efforts to extricate themselves from the muddle left in their path by Descartes, Locke, and Hume. To make a fresh start, it is only necessary to open the great philosophical books of the past (especially those written by Aristotle and in his tradition) and to read them with the effort of understanding that they deserve. The recovery of basic truths, long hidden from view, would eradicate errors that have had such disastrous consequences in modern times.*
>
> —Mortimer Adler [3]

> *The ancients knew something which we seem to have forgotten.*
>
> —Albert Einstein [4]

10

Divine Love

What, after all, is the reality of our motives, intentions, thoughts, attitudes, and the like? For example, we readily speak of love, dream of it, build lives around what we take love to be. But what is love, after all?

—*Kenneth Gergen* [1]
Professor of Psychology

Philo: What is your definition of the word Logos? Does it not mean reason as well as discourse? Is not Logos the reason behind the universe, the reason of its own existence and of all of existence, the reason and meaning of the physical, biological and moral laws, the unifying force of all reality and truth, and the very word of God.

Socrates: Logos is, indeed, reason and discourse.[2]

Philo: The ability to reason and communicate by language, literature, art, etc., which is found developed in human kind, the lower species, must be found in the nature of the Logos, or God, who is of the higher order. Since God must possess both essence of communication and reason, which he allotted to humankind and allotted creativity and will, then God must be the most reasonable being there can possibly be. Therefore this most reasonable being must have reasonably communicated his existence to humanity. If this is so, that God has indeed reasonably communicated his existence to humanity, do we not agree that such communication should be reasonably described to the poor as well as the rich? The communication of the Logos would be equally descriptive to the educated as well as the uneducated.

Socrates: That would be a fair and reasonable description of any communicated good.

Philo: The major difference between ancient Greek philosophers, such as yourself and Plato, and modern philosophers, is the limitation and restriction that modern philosophers have imposed upon the Logos. Reason of the absolute, they say, is non- existent. They maintain that there is no absolute, only relative reality, while Greek philosophers, in general, humbled themselves while in search of identifying with reason, which is naturally built into the human soul or mind, to be in accordance with the Logos or reason of the universe. Humans are reasonable creatures possessing the ability to communicate, thus the universe should be guided by reason or Logos–the communicated good. They were seekers of the ultimate good which is truth, absolute truth. As Aristotle states "It is the good that we are seeking." In contrast, modern philosophers such as the existentialists have designed their own version of the reality of good and truth, by stating that "there is no ideal good" to be found. Greek philosophy concedes reason to the Logos, the unifying principle of the whole universe, the absolute truth. Modern philosophy, however, elevates human reason beyond all other reason and has in general disregarded the existence of an ultimate reasonable being, citing that the Logos or God has not communicated his being, nature, and existence to humankind.

Socrates: Quite strange, would you not say, Philo, for the artificial artist to make the absolute statement that there is no absolute truth, and to pass absolute judgment that the absolute or Natural Artist does not exist?

Philo: This lack of reason within, or behind, the universe denies that there is any purpose or meaning for our existence. Modern philosophy accepts only a relative concept of truth. What was true yesterday might not be true today. What is true in one part of the world is not true in another part. What is right for one society is not right for another. They claim that there is no absolute, such as justice, as you stated, that is the same yesterday, today, and forever.

Socrates: But you somehow seem to combine or unite this local deity of Israel called Yahweh to the Logos, or universal reason, of the philosophers of Greece. The Logos is not a local deity, Philo. The Logos, is the everlasting universal force, the one, true, and only life giving agent, righteous in nature; the unifying principle of justice, good and love. The Logos is the principle of all laws including those laws by which move the stars, sun, moon, and planets. How do you rationally equate a local deity called Yahweh in Israel to the universal reason of the Logos?

Philo: Greek philosophy is based upon reason, as both yourself and Plato prescribed. The Logos "is" and the Logos is "reason and truth." The prophets of Israel were compelled by Yahweh to speak his commands to the people that they would know that he is, and that he has a being, for his name Yahweh means "to be." Therefore the Logos that is reason, in Greek philosophy, is the being that has revealed himself as Yahweh in Jewish theology.

Socrates: But the Logos is not a tribal god whose nature is to be subjective to a particular small band of people, bound and contained by the physical borders of the tiny country of Israel. The Logos possesses a universal essence whose existence and being even the borders of planet earth are incapable of containing.

Philo: Then your Greek philosophy states that the Logos has an eternal existence and that it was, will continue to be, and exists in the eternal "now." This would mean that the Logos is God, will be God, and has from the beginning been God.

Socrates: The Logos is the only substance that possesses absolute and undeviating essence. Contrary to the nature of humanity where everything is relative including justice, good, and from what I am told, even time, has been proven to be relative and not absolute.

Philo: The Greeks believed that the Logos, in its ideal state of being, transcends our human reality. The Jews in Israel were likewise instructed that the state of Yahweh transcends human reality. With the difference being that of a direct revelation of laws and a veil of separation describing God's transcendent, absolute, and perfect nature separated from humankind and its lesser reality of relativity.

Socrates: The Logos would indeed be the author of the laws and maybe the laws of the Old Testament do indeed reveal this deity proclaiming him a lawgiver. But let's not forget that the Logos is much more than laws, for only the revelation of laws do not reveal Yahweh as the universal essence of love, freedom, mercy, and omnipotence that belong to the Logos. I sincerely question the connection you are attempting to make between this Yahweh of the Old Testament and the Logos of the Greek philosophers.

Philo: We stated that the nature of humankind is the ability to reason and communicate; another aspect of the uniqueness of humankind is personality. The higher order and superior nature of the Logos must then contain the essence of reason, communication, and personality. Pantheism states that God is everywhere, in every physical manifestation, which would mean that everything that possesses matter, or even energy, possesses

God. Wisdom tells us that we must look for reason, communication, and personality from the divine, for communication and personality are essential to the divine being, as opposed to the divine being limited to the manifestation of lifeless matter and energy. Consequently, the personality of the Logos or Yahweh is much more than a set of laws and a veil of separation. He is composed of all divine attributes which elevate him to the transcended nature of divine status, possessing justice, love, and in particular, personhood. Justice combined with love and personality cannot be located and identified in dead, lifeless matter. This is where pantheists are looking for God, such essence is only found in the unity of the living God who is the Logos of Greece and Yahweh of Israel.

Socrates: By possessing personality, will and communication, each human being is capable of describing their own personality, as we identify in their speech and their deeds. Am I to assume that you believe that the Logos or Yahweh possessing will, communicated his personality and became descriptive and thus known to humankind in word and deed?

Philo: By reason alone the Greeks concluded the existence of the Logos hundreds of years before Christ. The Logos, or reason, communicated himself, his personality, and nature in person. Thus Yahweh of Israel and the Logos of Greece are one. God Yahweh himself, Hebrew scripture tell us, then communicated his being, born of flesh, becoming incarnate upon planet earth.

Socrates: If this is so, and the Logos came to planet earth and crossed this veil of separation it must have been the most astounding and bewildering entrance! One would not expect the Logos from the right side of the veil of separation, composed of justice, good, and love, who is constant and eternal, to enter planet earth as an issue of physical desire, human passion and sexual intercourse!

Philo: Absolutely not, Socrates. Just as the spring water will not enter the dirty puddle, since it would pollute itself by the ordinary means of trickling down the mountain. Likewise, the indication that the Logos or Yahweh God is not of our nature and is holy and pure, penetrated this veil of separation and made his entrance by being born of a virgin. Thus, God proclaimed that the divine does not need sexual intercourse, physical passions, nor human effort, to produce the Logos. Therefore, his spiritual substance is of divine nature from the right, identified as his Father, but his physical substance is of human nature from the left identified as his mother.

Socrates: The Logos incarnate? Quite an astounding reality in our cave of illusion that would be!

Philo: The bridge connecting Yahweh of Jerusalem with the Logos of Athens begins to appear when one realizes that the Hebrew prophets wrote the Old Testament in Hebrew, but the New Testament, describing the life of Christ, the Logos, was written in Greek. It was after the Logos became flesh that, for the first time, Jews began to describe Yahweh as the universal Logos of the Greek philosophers. As we read in the gospel of John where the English translates Logos as the Word...

In the beginning was the Word, and the Word was with God, and the Word was God.... In him was life; and the life was the light of men. And the light shineth in darkness; and the darkness comprehended it not.... And the Word was made flesh, and dwelt among us.[3]

Since the Logos is reason and discourse, is not the gospel writer in effect stating, "In the beginning was reason and discourse and reason and discourse was with God and reason and discourse was God and reason and discourse became flesh." If it is true that reason, or the Logos, became flesh, which history confirms in that many of the Greek philosophers identified this as so in Christ, then modern philosophers' inability to identify the universal reason with the Hebrew prophets and the Greek philosophers exposes modern philosophers as unworthy and unqualified philosophers.

Socrates: But if true, that the Logos became incarnate, then that event must be the heart and soul of human history! The Logos must have left an unrivaled legacy upon planet earth.

Philo: No human born of two parents has left a greater impact upon world history than God in Christ. There are more people who carry his name as Christians than anyone else. More literature concerning the incarnate Logos than any other literature, more paintings, more followers, more churches are dedicated to him. Since the Logos is constant and undeviating, he continued to be called Yahweh as he walked planet earth; however the word "Shua" is added after his name, Yahweh, which means "saved." Thus Yahweh became Yahweh Saves or Yahshua. Here in America the name Yahshua is shortened to Jesus. You stated earlier that a human judge, to be identified as such, needs an existing law prior to entering his court. Likewise the law was established which verifies and describes Jesus or the Logos as judge before he entered planet earth. The name Yahweh is not contained within the borders of Israel, but since the incarnation, for almost two thousand years, Yahweh has been sacredly recognized far beyond it's borders. A very common expression by Christians is "Hallelujah." This word is composed of two Hebrew words hallelu and Yahweh. Hallelu means worship and Yahweh means God. Thus this statement literally means "worship God." One may hear this expression even here in America which is on the opposite side of the globe from Israel. The Greek philosophers' prescriptive reasoning of the Logos, the true and eternal essence of existence, possessing the qualities of law and order, is the same Yahweh who descriptively reveals his law and order in the Old

Testament, and descriptively revealed his personhood, incarnate, in the person of Christ as the New Testament records.

Socrates: How would the Logos from the right side of righteousness communicate his personal nature and prepare humanity on the left for such a bewildering revelation? How could the One from the true reality enter this cave of illusion without being misinterpreted, misidentified and misunderstood?

Philo: How, indeed, Socrates? Would a human father planning to visit his rebellious children not inform them of his coming? Would the father not prepare his children for his arrival by sending some letters concerning the date and time of his arrival and since they have not seen him, maybe describe his physical stature that they might recognize and identify their father when he arrived?

Socrates: It would seem the appropriate thing to do.

Philo: This is precisely what Yahweh, the Logos, Father God did, for he divulged letters, through the prophets, of announcing his coming to his lost children upon planet earth.

Socrates: And where might these letters be located, Philo? I would like to examine them myself. For such a bewildering revelation must be universal and objectively available to all, not a subjective revelation obscure in an ancient museum available only to archaeologists and historians.

Philo: These letters of arrival, which were spoken through the prophets of Israel, are located in the books of the Old Testament, the worlds best-selling book of all time. More books have been reproduced which contain God's communicated letters of arrival than any other human literature.

Socrates: You have been describing this Old Testament as a book of laws. But now you state that in this Old Testament I may find the letters and promises of the coming of the Logos, who is identified as judge?

Philo: The Old Testament contains both, Socrates. It reveals God's laws along with the physical veil of separation, as well as revealing his divine, coming nature. It describes his genealogy leading to his birth, the location of his birth, etc. In over thirty-nine separate books, which complete the Old Testament, the arrival of the Logos is described and communicated by dozens of prophets in a time span stretching some twelve hundred years prior to his arrival.

Socrates: Is this not contradicting the laws of philosophy, Philo? The picnic table in front of us is indeed a table, therefore it cannot be a table and not a table at the same time. Something cannot be and not be at the same time. Was he God or was he human? How can you state that he was both?

Philo: It is one of the most confusing paradoxes. How was Jesus, God, as he claimed and how was he praying to God at the same time he was here? Since he was praying to God while he was here then how was he on this side of the veil of separation in concrete, finite form and still be one with the abstract and infinite, behind the veil at the same time? As we look at this wooden picnic table in front of us we notice that it is composed of its own particular substance. Suppose the people across the street in the museum had never been outside the museum and were unaware of anything that existed outside of their surroundings, including this table. If I were to cut out one third of this table and take it inside the museum where the people have no knowledge of such substance, then the substance of the remaining two thirds of the table out here in the park is found transcended and beyond their sense perception.

Socrates: That would be true. The remaining two thirds of the table out here would be beyond them.

Philo: Yet the one third of the table that is composed of a foreign substance would be, to the people inside the museum, imminent and within their sense perception. Therefore, two thirds of the table is beyond them, yet one third is within them. Likewise, God is transcendent, abstract, and beyond our sense perception, but in Christ became imminent, concrete and within our understanding by sense perception.

Socrates: The incarnate Logos. What an incredible reality that would be!

Philo: A couple of hundred years following the incarnation, Athanasius, a Greek philosopher and theologian, wrote a book titled, "On the Incarnation." A book that is still read today.

Socrates: And these Greek philosophers such as Athanasius found no inconsistency of the Logos existing beyond and transcended yet imminent and within?

Philo: No, and neither does the great modern scholar, C.S. Lewis, who wrote the forward to Athanasius's book for the modern reader. [4] There are only a handful of absolutes which modern science can verify, such as the speed of light. Likewise, there are only a handful of absolutes in philosophy, as you ancients taught, such as the part is never greater than the whole to which it belongs, as part of the table in front of us is never greater then the whole table. Regardless of how big the part is, it will never be greater than the whole.

Socrates: Definitely the part is never greater than the whole to which it belongs.

Philo: But you agree that the part of the table, which is not greater than the whole table, is one with the table?

Socrates: Certainly the part of the table is one with the table.

Philo: Then you also agree that the part of the table on which I am resting my hand is the table?

Socrates: Most assuredly. The part of the table your hand is on is the table.

Philo: Therefore, Socrates, just as the part of the table is not greater then the whole table, likewise Christ, being part of God, is not greater than God. But although the part of the table, which is not greater than the whole table is one with the table, likewise Christ, who is not greater than God, is one with God. And just as the part of the table where I am resting my hand is the table, likewise if anyone rests on Christ they are resting on God. Just as the part of the table and the whole table are one, Christ states of himself, "I and my Father are one." [5] Therefore, it is an equivalent testimony when Christ states "he that hath seen me hath seen the Father...." [6] Which is analogous to stating he who has seen the substance of the third of the table in the museum has seen the substance of the table that transcends them.

Socrates: What you are saying, Philo, is this Jesus is of one and the same substance as God, the Logos, which is the one unifying principle of the ideals of good, love, and truth. He embodies constant, eternal, and ultimate justice. If so, then the essence and composition of Jesus must be a foreign substance to a humanity that lacks absolute knowledge of such divine ideals such as undeviating love.

Philo: And what is love, Socrates? We all desire it, but has the scientist ever measured it or described what it is? Does he know its substance and composition? Humans relate to physical love, which is eros love, whereby we take or use another person's body to satisfy our appetite of physical passion. But the motivation of agape love is not to take but to give, even to sacrifice, one's body for the sake of the beloved. As the philosophy of Plato states, love is to die for another.[7]

The young man values his choice of sports car and the woman her diamond ring; both are displayed in the public universe for all to see. Likewise the value of God's choice to act out his love was made evident in the physical external universe. He crossed the veil of separation in order to proclaim love in action and thus, he became crucified high on a cross for all to see, that they might come to know the truth. Love is that which must be freely given, "No man taketh [my life] from me but I lay it down of myself"[8] he stated. Neither scientists nor philosophers have satisfactorily described love, but the incarnate Logos has made love descriptive indeed.

Socrates: Most fascinating, Philo. Then I assume that these crosses that I see on top of churches are a witness of this divine sacrificial love?

Philo: Many of the ancient philosophers spanning the globe, five hundred years before Christ, were in pursuit of identifying with the reality of absolute love. But had anybody seen such beauty prior to or after the sacrificial love of Jesus? Truth is relative, modern philosophers tell us, but take notice how absolute and universal the truth of sacrificial love is maintained. Five hundred years before Christ, Buddha used the following words to describe love:

> *As a mother, even at the risk of her own life, protects and loves her child, her only child, so let a man cultivate love without measure toward the whole world....* [9]

Such love, according to the Buddha, is the best state of mind. The sacrifice upon the cross thus became that ideal act of love that Father God without measure produced for his children throughout the whole world. The second most famous oriental sage was Lao Tsu, who also lived some five hundred years before Christ.

Lao Tsu describes love in the following manner...

Only he who is willing to give his body for the sake of the world is fit to be entrusted with the world. Only he who can do it with love is worthy of being the steward of the world [10]

Thus five hundred years after the lives of Socrates, Lao Tsu, and Buddha, Jesus described his worthiness to be steward of the world since he was willing to, and did give his body to fulfill that desired ideal, agape love, for the sake of his love for the world.

Although the act of Christ spoke louder than his words, both deeds and words of the Logos have continued to be communicated in the Bible which is the book that contains and describes the nature of God. The Bible, which as one might expect, has become the world's most published book and it describes love in the following manner:

This is my commandment, that ye love one another, as I have loved you. Greater love hath no man than this, that a man lay down his life for his friends. [11]

The commandment the Savior gave us is to cross our walls of separation and love, forgive, and give to our fellow human being.

Socrates: And what has humanity learned, Philo?

Philo: What has the married couple who have vowed to love each other only to raise a wall of separation between themselves learned, Socrates? Christ crossed this veil of separation as the paradigm for us to model. But over fifty percent of the married couples in this country will not cross their veil of separation to give and forgive, but will usually send their attorneys across to fight and take as much from each other as they legally can.

Jesus taught to cross the walls of differences separating humanity, and by his act of sacrifice validated his words. His example is to give of oneself as he did to the point of death. But governments and politicians have historically raised invisible walls of separation against neighboring nations. They command not forgiveness to cross, but armies with their bullets and ammunition. Such divisions and unwillingness to forgive have murdered more than one hundred million persons in this century primarily due to war. What have we learned, Socrates? A group of nations even erected an invisible wall against another group of nations called 'the Iron Curtain.' No one was instructed on crossing and forgiving, but hydrogen and atomic bombs and other nuclear weapons were fixed to penetrate this division.

Alas, finally in human history, due to the incarnation of the Logos, the evils and relative reality of humanity have been revealed and understood. For although God raised a veil of separation between his justice and our injustice, he crossed it and sacrificed himself. He has established the one archetypal love and righteous standard of forgiveness. As the Logos descriptively crossed his veil that was separating us, he invited all of us to cross our veils separating humanity by race, color, creed, gender, sex, and physical borders. "Love your enemies as you love yourself." "Do good to those who hate you," he stated. But is anybody listening, Socrates?

Socrates: If true, then it could be stated that this would be the unveiling of the divine essence of love, Philo.

Philo: We discussed that what remains in the mind alone, such as love, is a lesser reality than that which is in the mind and acted out, and thus exists and corresponds in the universe of both realities, first the subjective reality of the mind and second the objective reality of the external universe. But God described that what exists in three realities is the greater reality than the two to which humankind is limited. For love that is first in the mind and reality of God became expressed in the second reality of the objective external physical universe, and has thus penetrated the third reality which is the mind of humanity. Human wisdom, therefore, states that that which exists in two realities is greater than one reality, but God's wisdom states that that which exists in three realities is the ultimate reality, for it includes divine reality. The highest component of divine reality is ideal, sacrificial love, which has not remained eternally transcended and prescriptive, as many religions claim, but has been made imminent and descriptive, as God proclaimed.

The prophecies of the Hebrew prophets materialized when the essence of divine love was finally proclaimed upon planet earth as they had foretold. The desire of identifying the essence of love by the genuine yet humble masters such as Socrates, Plato, Buddha, and Lao Tsu, had finally been manifest in descriptive, sacrificial form. The fact that divine love was expressed in the physical universe of matter should satisfy even the modern scientist! For the God that gave us our five senses to understand the universe around us came into our universe of senses and perceptions to describe and define his essence of love from his side of the universe. This is the act of sacrifice which displays absolute, constant, and undeviating love.

Socrates: Professor Thomas made an interesting statement, that both philosophers and physicists are in a peculiar dilemma. He described that the physicist has been frustrated by his inability to unite the four separate laws in the one single "unified field theory." Likewise, he described that the philosopher is frustrated by his inability to unify a divine theory, which is to unite the many divine attributes to one singularity.

Suppose we agree that this was indeed the incarnation of the Logos God, who revealed his nature of love. Is this the singularity, the unifying principle of all divine attributes?

If so, how does his omnipotence unify with love in this incarnation of Christ? And how is it that modern philosophers have been oblivious to such divine, revealed essence?

Philo: The Logos of the cosmos, the reason who sustains the universe, the existence of all reality, made his nature of love descriptive and empirically revealed. He, therefore, reasonably and logically communicated his benevolent nature to humanity. This reveals that communication is indeed within the nature of God, for he is the Logos, and that all the divine attributes we have discussed and identified belong to one source indeed.

Socrates: It is hard to imagine then, why modern philosophers, such as David Hume, could possibly misidentify this descriptive, communicated nature of love.

Philo: David Hume is in pursuit of identifying all-love and all-power simultaneously. If he is a loving God, states Hume, then God must utilize his all-powerful nature to remove all evil. Only in such a scenario is Hume willing to verify God's omnipotent nature. Hume's argument has compelled, yet misled, many intellectuals such as Dr. Paul Davies, a theoretical physicist, into agreeing with him.

States Davies:

Omnipotence raises some awkward theological questions. Is God free to prevent evil? If he is omnipotent, yes. Why then does he fail to do so? This devastating argument was deployed by David Hume: if the evil in the world is from the intention of the Deity, then he is not benevolent. If the evil is contrary to his intention, he is not omnipotent. He cannot be both omnipotent and benevolent (as most religions claim). [12]

Socrates: You do notice the three divine attributes of freedom, omnipotence, and benevolence identified with God in this argument and that...

Philo: Yes! Which is where the fallacy of the argument is exposed. First by the abuse of the word "freedom" as it concerns benevolence, and second by omitting the word "mercy" which separates yet unites benevolence and omnipotence.

Socrates: Please, explain, Philo. You must agree with Hume that both omnipotence and benevolence are to be united and in one essence with God.

Philo: I do agree. But we already stated if God behaved as Hume demanded and used his omnipotent power to remove evil, then not only the evils of nature in the form of disease and ailments have to be removed, but God would also have to remove all of humanity, since humans are also filled with evil, pain-causing activities, and moral ailments. In this case, if God utilized omnipotence to remove all evil, no human would be left to witness God's benevolent nature.

Socrates: Then let it be, Philo. Suppose this Christ was the Logos describing omni-love. Where is the solution, then, identified in this dilemma? Hume's argument seems to be valid only in the fact that evil, and pain causing agents continue to exist. Pain-causing agents derived from both natural and moral qualities. Do you not agree that evil continues to abide in humankind, even after the revealed nature of the Logos?

Philo: The nature of divine love was made evident in the first incarnation of Christ. We read about divine, purifying love in the four gospels of the New Testament. But omnipotence, or God's eradicating nature against evil, both natural and moral, is revealed in the last book, the book of Revelation. This is when God returns and thus fulfills his omnipotent evil-cleansing nature.

Socrates: How do you split the "one," Philo? You made a nice analogy earlier as you described the part of the table which is never greater than the whole table, yet is one with the table and is also the table. Likewise, you stated that Jesus being part of God, is not greater than God but is one with God; thus, he is God. But since tables are finite and divisible, how does the "one," the "infinite," the "undivided" become split and divided into two parts? One part love, another part power? In particular one part "before" and another part "after?"

Philo: If the right side of God forced us to be good, compelled us to make the right choice, and coerced every action to be a good action, then that could not be an authentic good on our part; for it is a forced good that is without freedom. And since freedom is one with the good, then we must be free to be good, and in particular, free to identify the ideal good. Since freedom is one with the good, and both freedom and good are united with love, then we must also be free to love and free to identify the goodness of divine love.

God, from his right side of divine attributes, penetrated our left side, in the first incarnation, which revealed ideal, sacrificial love. Humanity on the left is therefore free to choose evil and free to choose good; free to call God "unjust, cruel, and vindictive" as the atheist's book describes God; and free to use his name maliciously. We are even free to harm other persons, verified in the killing of 100 million in this century alone. Free to accuse God of causing evil, of not being benevolent, and of lacking omnipotence.

Humanity is also free to repent, ask for forgiveness, and purify itself. For those that desire not to identify their evil nature, choose not to repent, choose not to change their ways, reject the one that loves them, desire no mercy from the merciful one, or attain forgiveness from the one that forgives, the omnipotent one reserves the right to take his ultimate vengeance by force.

You stated earlier, Socrates, that humankind thinks in pictures and images. If we hear the phrase Statue of Liberty, we do not spell it out in our minds, but imagine it in picture form. Likewise, God communicated in picture form, which is the most common and universal language. In the first incarnation of God, Jesus is identified as "The Lamb." However, in the book of Revelation, revealing the apocalypse, God's vengeful nature against evil, both natural and moral, Jesus, "of the tribe of Judah" is returning as a lion.

By communicating through symbols such as a lamb and a lion, God universally communicates to all; the uneducated as well as the smallest of children. Even a child understands the universal truth that humanity would unanimously prefer to be in the presence of, and facing a lamb, as opposed to being confronted by, and face to face with a lion! If Hume had distinguished between lamb and lion, and that God's attributes of love and power symmetrically, logically, and chronologically are separated within human history and human time, then Hume would not have made the gross error of misidentifying the benevolent nature of God.

Socrates: So this is where your answer lies, Philo! This is why you have been insisting all of this time that omni-love, mercy, and omni-power are not only made descriptive but are revealed in this particular order.

Philo: Indeed, Socrates. Benevolence, combating evil, was made descriptive; first, that evil may be conquered by humankind, based on freedom, choice and love. Omnipotence, combating evil through forceful means and coercion, will occur later in the future. We now live between the nature of love, symbolic of the charitable lamb, and the nature of power, symbolized by the vengeful lion. One divine attribute removes evil by freedom, the other by force. Therefore, God's nature of mercy and forgiveness is presently offered to humanity. It is mercy, the pinnacle of freedom, that is erroneously omitted from Hume's argument. An essential detail to which Dr. Davies also falls victim.

Socrates: It seems that Dr. Davies has not only fallen for the fallacy of drawing conclusions by neglecting certain premises, such as mercy, but has also fallen for Hume's distortion of truth, due to Hume's ambiguities and abuse of language, which I must admit runs wild and rampant, suffocating the nature of reality and truth in this modern society of yours.

Philo: Jules Henry confirms the abuse of language by modern persons, as he is cited by Dr. Soccio, professor of philosophy...

Ancients of our culture sought clarity: Plato portrays Socrates tirelessly splitting hairs to extract essential truth from the ambiguities of language and thought. Two thousand years later we are reversing that, for now we pay intellectual talent a high price to amplify ambiguities, distort thought, and bury reality... One of the discoveries of the twentieth century is the enormous variety of ways of compelling language to lie. [13]

As it concerns God's removal of evil by force, God does "not fail to do so" as Davies quotes Hume, in Hume's abuse of language, but both Hume the philosopher, and Davies the physicist fail to identify the fact that God accomplishes the task of removing evil through love. Also, "evil is not the intention of the deity," as Davies quotes Hume again, but as a good and loving mother whose arms never close, but remain open towards the abusive child. Freedom's noble nature is that it also remains open, thus offering the potential for abuse. This is the intention of the deity.

It is mercy, which is one with freedom, that sets apart the lamb as it liberates from the lion, and it is mercy that guides us to the lamb and saves us from the lion. This is the meaning of the term, commonly used in the churches, "to be saved" or "salvation." One is to be saved by benevolence from omnipotence, or simply stated, to be saved by God the lamb is to be saved from God the lion. Not only the philosopher but a child can identify with sacrificial love.

> *But there is something else which we can truly say about the good man. Many of his actions are performed to serves his friends or his country, even if this should involve dying for them.... And surely this may be said of those who lay down their lives for others; they choose for themselves a crown of glory.*
> *—Aristotle* [14]

> *But God commendeth his love toward us, in that, while we were yet sinners, Christ died for us.*
> *—The Apostle Paul* [15]

11

Divine Justice

In the idea of the Good, Plato has given expression to a vision of an absolute source of truth and goodness.... The Idea of the Good is Plato's conception of the absolute, the perfect principle of all reality, truth, and value. For two thousand years, when Christians thought of God they envisioned the divided line and the ascent out of the cave through the power of reason and the power of love to Plato's Idea of the Good.
—*T.Z. Lavine*
Professor of Philosophy [1]

Socrates: If it is the case that Jesus reveals the divine essence and nature of love, then the complete unity of divine essence of love and mercy, united with the good, freedom, and in particular justice, must also have been simultaneously revealed.

Philo: Who is the universal judge, Socrates, and what is justice? In an unjust environment we find fragmentation, distrustfulness, division, suspicion, and separation; whereas in a just environment, we should find freedom, wholeness, harmony, compatibility, peace, and agreement. Humankind aspires to obtain and desperately craves justice. Our own Declaration of Independence states that "the pursuit of happiness" is to be attained through "liberty and justice for all."

Socrates: Then how does humanity find justification in its self-righteous, filthy acts, so that we may find harmony, wholeness, peace, and compatibility with God, Philo?

Philo: How does one define, thus, identify "liberty and justice" and in particular "justice for all?" If the ideal nature of absolute freedom and justice are found on the right side of the spectrum with humanity on the far left, where is our hope? And who has the ability to recognize, identify, and thus describe the absolute nature of justice? As we stated earlier, we can easily and effortlessly recall other people's acts which results we perceived as unjust toward us, but we would have to search very hard to remember when someone's act delivered justice and good to us.

Reason tells us that justice is a relative term within our reality. The fact is that the wealthy, and in particular the ones in power, have consistently abused justice throughout human history. And when we, today, begin to believe that we have made some progress, and are behaving justly, Socrates appears, reminding us that we have unjustly killed over 100 million people in our century alone. All of our injustice is revealed however by God, who has made our injustice descriptive by placing a physical veil of separation between humanity and himself.

If justice is on the right and humanity on the left, then by what means is humanity capable of arriving at such a state of perfection? How can humanity penetrate this veil of separation and arrive at its desired state of being?

Socrates: What other means is there, but by the hope of love, Philo?

Philo: Therefore, "justice for all" as our constitution desires, would be best achieved by the law of love. As Jesus himself stated "Love your neighbor as you love yourself."

All of humanity on the left side of injustice desires to attain attributes found on the right side, such as ideal justice. But it is our nature of sin and rebellion against God that has forced a veil of separation between humanity on the left and the divine essence on the right.

As you stated, Socrates, justice begins to reveal its essence through love. One behaves justly, by simply not interfering with another person in their pursuit of happiness. One who not only does not interfere, but goes out of his or her way to help others attain happiness, does so out of love. As Mortimer J. Adler echoes the thoughts of Aristotle:

> *Justice only requires you not to impede or frustrate others in their pursuit of happiness. If you go beyond that to help them in their pursuit, you do so because you love them as you love yourself.* [2]

Socrates: If I am following you correctly, Philo, you seem to be attempting to unite the two divine attributes of love and justice in this incarnation of Jesus.

Philo: I will allow you to make this decision, Socrates; but before we identify divine justice we must identify the ideal judge. Human nature demands that a law be established and be in effect prior to a judge being identified as such. Likewise, the Old Testament law was established before the incarnation of Jesus, which identifies him as judge.

Socrates: Granted, Philo, that if this Jesus is the Logos-the universal nature of justice, the judge of all humanity-then such a revelation brings us to a curious dilemma.

Philo: And what might this dilemma be?

Socrates: Once the laws of any state are established, so is an established and identifiable judge. But laws are designed first to teach, and second to pass judgment; that is, to pass judgment upon those who are not taught and do not follow the commands of the laws. I ask, then, if this Jesus is the judge of the universe identified as judge by Old Testament law, and these same laws are first to teach us, and second to pass judgment, then I must know, what is the judgment he passes upon humanity by God's standard of justice? What is it that the laws demand from the law-breaker?

Philo: It is clearly stated: All sinners are guilty by the law; all are condemned to die by the law. The Old Testament laws assure us of this. Graveyards validate it.

Socrates: Then do you not see a possible conflict and maybe even a contradiction within this Jesus as God of both love and justice? We agreed that once a state produces a law, then, that state also produces a judge.

Philo: We did.

Socrates: Then you stated that the revelation of the law, prior to the empirical revelation and incarnation of the lawgiver, identifies this Jesus as judge.

Philo: The scriptures assure us of this.

Socrates: We also agree that once any state produces a law, not only must that state produce a recognized judge, revealed by the law, but the state, in order to impose its laws, raises a physical wall, a prison wall, between the just and the unjust. The unjust are identified as such first by the existence of the law, and second, by a prison wall which has separated the law-breakers.

Philo: This is universal.

Socrates: Then you made the claim that analogous to the state and its prison walls, which follow the laws, an actual physical veil of separation was erected by God following his laws, separating the just from the unjust.

Philo: As the scriptures state, Socrates. Between the nature of God on the right, and a fallen humanity on the left, God indeed erected a physical veil of separation, descriptively verifying this division.

Socrates: Then you state that with the incarnation of the Logos, God made descriptive his nature of love, by crossing this veil of separation and sacrificing himself.

Philo: Yes, absolute love!

Socrates: But now you state that God is judge whose nature is justice, and that God's law demands the penalty of death upon all of humanity.

Philo: Yes, it is stated as such.

Socrates: Then do you not see a conflict or contradiction between God's nature of justice demanding death and God's nature of love which requires mercy, which is freedom and is the opposite of death? How can you reconcile both of these attributes?

Do you not see the dilemma, Philo, that God's nature of love demands mercy and forgiveness for all, but God's nature of justice demands death upon everyone. If this Jesus is love, his nature is to forgive. If he is the judge that passes judgment, his nature is to destroy. How can he express love to humanity, which he is to destroy, by his required penalty of death? If death upon everyone did not occur when he arrived, as his law demands, he is not judge. If he did not forgive and spare humanity from the law of death, he is not merciful and loving.

Philo: The nature of love was made manifest indeed in the crucifixion, Socrates. Simultaneously, the nature of judgment, which by the law is death, was also manifest.

The penalty of the law was death upon everyone, and was to be paid when the judge arrived. But the law of love is compassion, mercy, and forgiveness, which was to spare people from the law of death. In order for God to exhibit his judgment of death upon all as well as his love of grace, mercy, compassion and forgiveness, simultaneously, he lashed out his justice of death and justified not only humanity but himself! By receiving the penalty and judgment of death upon himself, sacrificing himself in our place, he produced ideal justice and revealed his infinite love for all.

With this divine act, God described that mercy is the pinnacle of justice and that love conquers all, including justice. Thus the God of love is a merciful God, whose nature is composed of justice and is universal judge.

Our human injustice called sin divides, and has pinned us on the left, divorced by a veil of separation that obstructs us from coming close to the divine on the right. But Christ, who is justice and love, has united us with God.

Socrates: So we are to believe that the ideal nature of justice, that eternal yearning and longing of humanity, the desire of all nations, which the universe prefers, desires, but is frustrated by its elusiveness, became known, thus, found upon planet earth. An astounding revelation, Philo.

Philo: To the ancients, Plato stated that "Justice is the interest of the stronger." [3] And today, nothing has changed, as Dr. Gergen, professor of psychology states in interpreting certain practitioners of the critical legal studies movement: "The justice system serves to protect certain classes and interest groups at the expense of others."[4] But within world history the righteous essence of justice, identified in the eternal Logos, described that, his divine justice is to protect the weaker group or class, which is humanity at his own expense. This is in direct opposition and contrary to human nature, which is to protect the self or their own interest group at the expense of others, in the name of justice. Human justice is a relative term that serves the ones with power and wealth as they see fit. Divine justice revealed that it serves the weak and powerless as the judge of the universe sees fit.

"Cross your walls of division and love each other, as I have loved you," is his message. Give as I have given to you, cross your borders of hate and forgive your neighbor as God crossed his physical border and is willing to forgive us. But the commandment is not only to cross our walls of separation as he did, but that we should tear down and remove our veils of injustice, walls of racism, sexism, and class. In particular our barriers of injustice, not only towards each other but against God, against his nature, his incarnation, and his revelation.

Socrates: Then you assert that in Jesus, God's divine essence crossed this physical veil of separation, thus empirically revealing love, mercy, and justice in the incarnate Logos?

Philo: It was more than crossing the veil of separation; it was tearing down this physical division between the just and the unjust, reconciling the left side of relative truth and fragmented reality with the right side of absolute truth and undivided reality. The Old Testament reveals laws, and a physical veil of separation between God on one side and humanity on the other. In the New Testament the book of Mark, chapter 15, describes that during the crucifixion, at the point of death, during that universal act of love, justice, and mercy, "the veil of the temple," dividing humanity from God, "was torn in two from top to bottom."

We also read in the 27th chapter of the book of Matthew...

Jesus, when he had cried again with a loud voice, yielded up the Ghost. And behold, the veil of the temple was torn in two from the top to the bottom.

In the 23rd chapter of Luke the gospel also records...

And the sun was darkened, and the veil of the temple was torn in the middle. And when Jesus had cried with a loud voice, he said, Father, into thy hands I commend my spirit.

Therefore absolute justice became absolutely revealed. Reconciliation and peace, between the two sides, was made manifest and empirically revealed. He completely replaced the division of the veil becoming the bridge between humanity and God.

Socrates: What is all of this information which you are revealing here Philo? For the past two months no one has described anything of this nature. Professors and scholars from your prestigious universities with whom I have dialogued seemed ignorant of these things, or at least have failed to divulge them to me.

Philo: Universities today are producing business executives, marketing strategists, computer programmers, engineers, and scientists, most of whom lack basic understanding of philosophy, history, art, much less theology and other humanistic studies. Our schools, in the name of human justice have even made it illegal to teach the Bible, the world's best selling book, to our students.

God's laws and commandments, the prophecies of his arrival, the diverse means of communicated symbols, the physical veil of separation, his physical incarnation, along with his nature of justice, mercy, and love is not communicated in our universities, but is communicated and taught in the Christian Church.

Socrates: If this was indeed the ideal good incarnate, as you claim, then, are you telling us that his being, becoming perceived, physically described, and his nature and existence communicated in written form is not the only means of communication? Are you now saying that God communicated himself through other means beyond the scriptures?

Philo: We did state that reason and communication are attributes of humanity; therefore, if there is a God, whose essence by definition would be superior to human nature, then we would expect him to possess reason and the ability to communicate. If he gave us the ability to create artificial art while he creates natural art, and is composed of natural and ideal justice, is it possible for humankind, the artificial artist, to possess and utilize reason and communication and for God not to have such attributes?

Socrates: Then enlighten us concerning his diverse means of communication, that we may also know.

Philo: If humans communicate by diverse and abstract means separating us from the animal kingdom, God must have the same ability. Does not humankind communicate by symbols? A ring worn on a certain finger is not worn for aesthetic beauty or as a status symbol, but it communicates that the individual wearing the ring is married to their spouse.

Humankind also communicates by rituals, tradition, and symbolic acts. As Mary Douglas, a Durkheimian anthropologist has been said to state...

Ritual is more to society than words are to thought. For it is very possible to know something and then find words for it. But it is impossible to have social relations without symbolic acts. [5]

The tradition or symbolic act of shaking hands, for example, communicates greetings between two people. In business circles this tradition communicates agreement between two parties. Likewise, God communicated via traditions, rituals, and symbolic acts. Not only did this veil in symbol form communicate separation, but the symbolic act of the tearing of this veil empirically revealed reconciliation and unity, forgiveness, and acceptance. Since that historic date, the nature of God was to be known beyond the borders of Israel, for the veil was removed as his nature has indeed become known ever since.

For over one thousand years prior to the coming of Jesus, God had communicated to the Jews through many symbols and symbolic acts. Such was the case with the traditional sacrifice of a lamb every year. This symbol was known as the "passover lamb," that was sacrificed in the annual ritual known as Passover. When Jesus arrived, he himself was sacrificed on that Passover Day, fulfilling the symbol of the lamb. Thus, he became communicated as the symbol of the lamb, sacrificed on the traditional Passover Day, in the symbolic act of sacrifice.

Professor Thomas made the statement earlier that the uncommunicated good is an unknown good, and that the unknown good is a lesser good than the communicated good. He therefore concluded that the ideal good does not exist. I do wonder. Before he made this statement did he consider the communication which the Bible offers? It is the world's most published book. It continues to be communicated in the churches on a regular basis, and is taught daily in the Christian schools. Did he consider the fact that what is written in the Old Testament was also communicated in symbols, traditions, and rituals?

Since our American culture lacks rituals, art, history, culture, and traditions reaching back thousands of years, it is easy to understand why our American, evangelical churches utilize scripture alone, as they communicate God's nature to their congregations. "For faith comes by hearing and hearing by the word of God."

Contrary to American culture, the history and culture of the Greek people reaches back a thousand years before Christ, and the Greek Orthodox Church dates from the days of Jesus himself. This Church continues, even today, with the legacy of communicating through diverse means besides the scriptures as it utilizes symbols, tradition, ritual, and art.

Practically the whole New Testament gospel, depicting the life of Jesus, is enacted, thus communicated, in dramatic form within this ancient Church, which in typical Greek and Jewish fashion is permeated with and enriched by poetry, philosophy, symbolism, rituals, and art.

Did Professor Thomas consider the fact that what is communicated to the ear by the New Testament in written form, in thousands of churches in New York, is also communicated to the eye, through ritual, tradition, and symbols, in hundreds of thousands of churches world wide?

Socrates: If all of this is true, then he seems to have drawn a conclusion without considering important evidence. Is it not human nature to draw conclusions based on emotions and opinions?

Philo: The veil existed in the temple of Israel describing laws, injustice, and separation. In the Orthodox Churches the reproduced veil continues to exist with one difference. Every Sunday the priest passes through the veil, breaks the bread and wine upon the altar, and comes out from behind this veil and offers communion to the congregation. The congregation, in the meantime, has inched forward, coming before the veil to partake of the mystical supper of his divine essence. As they partake of his divine nature, what do they witness but the Savior breaking through the veil by means of his broken body, spilled blood, and torn veil. Would they dare commune with the one who tore this justified veil of division while they have erected invisible, thus, unjustifiable walls of separation towards their fellow man? Thus, in this case the veil is utilized as a "symbol" enhancing and communicating the tradition of communion between both sides.

Our relatively new American nation and culture prevents us from preserving through culture the legacy of thousand-year-old traditions and rituals. Within most of our American Christian churches however, we do find the ritual of communion. This two-thousand-year-old tradition continues to be an integral part of communication to God's people.

Whether one hears the message concerning the nature of God in one church through the ear, or also sees it in symbol form in another through the eye, or even experiences God's sacrificial nature through the sense of taste, the message is the same. That is, that this veil revealed that God, the light of the world, whose light is composed of justice, illuminating humanity with love, radiating mercy, and truth, freely penetrated the veil to the side of darkness consisting of obscure justice, shadowy love, concealed mercy, hidden truth, and bondage. This is the simple message of the Bible.

The reproduced veil is not only utilized as a symbol in the Orthodox Church, it is also utilized in a symbolic act. The night before Easter Sunday on Good Saturday night, nearing twelve o'clock midnight, this church is in complete darkness. The congregation wait, all holding unlit candles, as the church is pitch dark and the symbolic veil of separation is closed. Then, precisely at midnight, the priest, holding a lit candle, exits from behind the veil of separation. As he opens this division, celebrating the resurrection, he lights everyone's candle. The church immediately radiates light. The light that originated behind the veil now illuminates and enlightens a darkened humanity. Therefore, a darkened humanity living under obscure justice, shadowy love, concealed mercy, and hidden truth may symbolically identify with the light of the world that tore the veil in half two thousand years ago; thus communicating his goodness, justice, and love.

There are hundreds of thousands of Orthodox churches worldwide, besides the Greek, such as the Anthiocan, Serbian, Russian, among others. This means that at 12 o'clock midnight, hundreds of thousands of veils, are simultaneously torn all over our planet in a glorious, liturgical ceremony, consisting of lights, symbols, art, and poetic worship, communicating the scriptures in a symbolic act revealing God's divine justice which reconciles a fallen humanity.

The ideal good, then, is the communicated good, which continues to be communicated by diverse means that satisfy humankind's abstract means of communication. Professor Thomas, however, concluded that "The uncommunicated good is a lesser good than the communicated good," while Jesus, the incarnate good himself, stated "Do not call me good unless you realize God is good."

But without knowledge of this communicated good, then what remains as the absolute and ideal good? As you stated, a modern scientist certainly does not study such attributes. Modern philosophy and popular humanistic thought state that there is no absolute good. Good is relative they say; what might be good to me might not be good to you.

Can we envision any human action which we all unanimously agree to be good by the sheer fact that such action would be, and must be, good for all of humanity? The good act of Christ taking the penalty of death upon himself and expressing ideal love and justice for all produced the reality that finally in human history one act became a universal good for all. This act became the absolute standard of all good, the perfect measurement of all actions.

Socrates: Then an action is not right because God says it is right, and neither does God say an action is right because it is right. But if all of this is true, then God's demonstrated act of right is right, and all else falls short of that manifested right. For without that act of righteousness, all other acts are subject to relativism and personal interpretation.

Philo: Professor Thomas proudly stated that an atheist or agnostic, driving his cancer-stricken neighbor to the hospital once a week, without expecting compensation in return, is a good act that must be deemed good by God. But in his classroom, the Professor convinces his students, God's children, to reject God and not to come to know the saving grace of God. Thus human understanding of good is relative indeed, for we think and convince ourselves we are good, when in fact we are not. And we are especially not good once we reject and persuade others to reject the descriptive, absolute good that communicated his goodness upon the cross! He acted out his love by crossing this veil of separation. It is now our duty to respond with our love and come to God, and not simply call our actions good as if they deserve merit from the side of goodness.

Non-Christian religions only speculate as to the nature of God. They say God is composed of justice and love, along with other divine attributes. What these religions fail to see is that there is no room for speculations and prescriptive truths within the nature of God, since God, the Natural Artist, revealed his abstract essence of love, mercy, justice, and good in concrete form, empirically and descriptively.

Simply by the use of reason, Socrates and Plato, 400 years before Christ, remarkably described God's abstract transcended nature, reality, and truth with amazing accuracy. The accuracy of these philosophers was verified when the abstract transcendent reality of truth, which Socrates simply prescribed and maintained that it must exist, became incarnate, descriptive, and concrete upon planet earth in the form of Jesus. Not only did the prophecies of the Old Testament prophets become fulfilled when Jesus arrived, but the Philosophy of Socrates and Plato became verified as the true philosophy. Since the incarnation, crucifixion, resurrection, and tearing of the veil, everyone, regardless of sex, age, intellect, or status can become philosophers possessing knowledge and understanding of absolute, eternal and universal truth. It is explained by our present-day scholars in the second volume of the nine volume collection *A History of Philosophy*...

> *[Plato] did not himself enter into the promised land of truth, though he approached near to it: it is Christianity alone which is the true philosophy. Moreover, Plato's philosophy was highly intellectualist, caviar for the multitude, whereas Christianity is for all, so that men and women, rich and poor, learned and unlearned, can be philosophers.* [6]

Plato's philosophy continues to remain unattainable for the masses, which "A History of Philosophy" portrays as, "caviar for the multitude." But God made himself descriptive and simple to understand and thus became not caviar, but bread for the multitude of the world. Thus everyone is able to understand and partake of his divine essence. He became not a decaying loaf of bread made with human hands that simply tantalizes the taste buds and temporarily satisfies the stomach, but the living bread whose justice satisfies the mind, and freedom liberates the soul.

Where else but in God's justice have women found equality to men in thousands of years of male-controlled and dominated societies? Where else may the poor find wealth and equality to the rich, except in the wealth of possessing divine love which the crucified Savior offers, which no amount of money can buy? Where else have the uneducated found equality of knowledge concerning the good, that education, even in our best universities, remains ignorant of as they have removed the scriptures from their curriculum? Where else has the sting of death, the natural enemy of humanity, been conquered, revealing and assuring humanity of an afterlife? Greek philosophy might very well speak in the language of caviar to a Washington diplomat such as William Bennet, or a Vice Presidential candidate such as James Stockdale, who spent many years in solitary confinement in Vietnam, but in the language of bread the Bible speaks to all.

Socrates: Maybe all of what you are saying is true, Philo, but I refuse to accept that modern philosophers are ignorant of all this. Is it possible to call one "philosopher" today who remains ignorant of the world's most reproduced book? Is it possible to be ignorant of the fact that what is written in this book is also acted out and dramatized in many churches worldwide? Do you not find it odd, that modern philosophers would be ignorant of the incarnate Logos, who seems to have single-handedly brought Greece to its knees, and transformed the landscape of world history more than anyone else?

Philo: The philosophers of Greece remained open-minded as they were in pursuit of identifying the absolute good, hundreds of years before the absolute good was made manifest and descriptive. This is contrary to most modern philosophers, who have concluded that the absolute good does not exist even after God became revealed as the descriptive good. Mortimer Adler, one of our most prominent American philosophers, views modern philosophy in dire need of restoration; for Adler believes that a true philosopher must return to the masters in Greece and their teachings. Likewise, Albert Einstein, our greatest scientist, who single-handedly transformed the landscape of twentieth century science, identified that "the ancients knew something which we seem to have forgotten."

Modern philosophy states that it is irrational for supernatural phenomena to occur. Thus, when they read the scriptures, they eliminate all miracles, because miracles, they say, defy the laws of physics. When modern philosophers read the scriptures they discount the virgin birth, for such an act, they claim, would be contrary to the laws of biology. They will not accept the supernatural resurrection of Christ due to their modern-day humanistic rational perspective that states "dead people remain dead." Therefore, a supernatural resurrection could not have happened, and did not happen, according to these modern philosophers.

Socrates: And how does one identify the word "supernatural," Philo?

Philo: To these people, supernatural means to defy the laws of physics and biology, which they say is impossible.

Socrates: But why limit the meaning of this word? Does not supernatural mean "more natural," and does not "more natural" describe living in a more exalted state of existence, which is closer to the right side, which we all desire? A more natural existence entails possession of the essence of justice, as opposed to injustice. Would not a person become more natural if he behaved more justly, and supernatural if everything he did was just and good? Would not more natural include acting in a more loving way and possessing more freedom? Supernatural, then, would be to possess undeviating love, eternal goodness, and everlasting freedom. Does not one become more natural when one ceases to lie and begins to tell the truth, and supernatural if everything one does and says is true every time?

If this is indeed God incarnate as you claim, then the more natural or supernatural essence of the Logos must be identified in his more natural or supernatural essence of love, justice, good, freedom, and truth. For neither the physical nor biological laws can contain or impose their force upon such a supernatural being. If this is indeed the Logos incarnate, then he is the author of all laws, including laws of freedom, love, justice, goodness, biological, and physical laws.

Philo: How right you are, Socrates. By limiting the word "supernatural," modern philosophers only apply this meaning to the physical and biological laws as they pertain to Christ and the scriptures. They fail to acknowledge that even the law of death cannot conquer ideal love which is supernatural, for ideal love is eternal and conquers all including death. God has ordained the law of death but also the law of love, life, and forgiveness. Constant and undeviating justice lives eternally; relative justice dies prematurely. That which is true remains forever. That which is false decays and perishes.

The human physical body that seeks for false, relative, physical pleasures will die. The spirit within, that seeks for eternal truths, which the Logos offers, will live. Human nature, as is observed, describes life as temporary and death eternal, but the supernatural essence of God reveals that death is temporary and that life is eternal. This eternal, constant, unchanging, and supernatural essence of God, the incarnate Logos, is described in word and deed. For he is, indeed, author of all of the laws, and thus transcends all of the laws. He is therefore truly free from any physical or biological coercion, far above all laws, including the laws of death and of the grave.

Within the incarnate Logos reside love, justice, mercy and good. Only in him does humanity attain freedom. For he revealed that freedom does indeed necessitate pain, bloodshed and death in our chaotic reality. He offered us freedom from the left by the tearing of the partition of separation, thus obtaining mercy, pardon and forgiveness for a rebellious humanity. This is freedom from eternal death. Freedom from ignorance concerns the very existence of God, as the lamb liberates from the lion.

We must begin to break down the walls of separation and forgive one another as we are forgiven, since God has torn down his justified wall of separation and is willing to forgive us. But although he paid a heavy price for this bridging of the chasm between himself and his beloved humanity, humans continue to shore up the walls, not only between each other, husband and wife, brothers and sisters, but most tragically between themselves and God; walls against Christ the Logos, against his word, against his deeds, against his justice and love, against his church, his freedom, and truth.

Since the incarnation of the Logos, Greece would appear to have ceased in its producing world-renowned philosophers such as Socrates, Plato, and Aristotle. However, distinguished and prominent Christian philosophers or theologians such as Origen, Athanasius, Clement of Alexandria, and many others made their appearance and taken the place of the ancient philosophers. The writings of these philosopher-theologians are not only to be found in our American churches, but are also in our universities.

Likewise, world-renowned tragic and epic poets such as Aeschylus, Euripides, Pindar, and other acclaimed poets who came before Christ would also appear to have vanished from the world's stage. But in reality, such men are still being studied in our universities today. Only now we know them by names such as Basil the Great and John Chrysostom. They are the philosopher-poets of the Church. Poetic masterpieces of men such as Basil the Great and John Chrysostom are not only found in our universities but can also be heard throughout the world today, in most Christian churches.

The ancient poets, Jewish and Greek, were themselves eventually replaced after the incarnation of God by Christian poets who followed the early Jewish and Greek traditions to write the New Testament in poetic form. Christian philosopher-poets wrote about the one archetypal epic, which revealed the incarnate Logos. Their poetry describes the tragedy of a fallen humanity, and the tragic death of the Logos who died in our place, only to resurrect.

The incarnate Logos affected the Greeks so profoundly that his nature continues to be communicated not only in the Church, but in the state of Greece as well. For his banner of divine love, identified in the symbol of the cross, is incorporated into the design of the Greek flag. Here in the States, in the name of human justice, our courts are removing the sign of the cross, God's communicated love, from our public buildings.

The representative of justice, divine justice, continues to be communicated beyond the church-walls in Greece, witnessed in all of their courtrooms, which possess a painting of Jesus Christ. In our courtrooms we find justice represented by a picture of our current president of the United States. In one country the picture symbolizing justice will change every four or eight years, as new elections dictate; in the other country it will remain the same.

Even in our school system, we have raised an intellectual wall between ourselves and God, as we have removed the Ten Commandments from the classrooms and his book from our schools, while in Greece the Bible continues to be taught and studied in their school system.

It was the timeless questions of Socrates and Plato, 400 years before Christ, that produced a fertile ground in Greece, where knowledge of the incarnate Logos was philosophically understood. It was Socrates, who envisioned that humans are in a cave of illusion, and concluded that if one entered our cave from the reality of truth, he would be misunderstood, misidentified, misinterpreted, scorned, and would probably be killed. Well it happened, friend, 400 years after this famous statement. Humanity laughed at the one from true reality, mocked him, spit on him, crucified him. I have seen many college professors continue to laugh and belittle some of their students who place their faith and trust in him, even today. He expressed his nature of absolute compassion, love, justice, good, and truth, while simultaneously exposing our nature of relative justice, unattainable good, distorted love, and unfounded truth.

Greek philosophy, and in particular Platonic philosophy, based on the dialogues of Socrates, have been identified in much more than art, literature, and the Star Trek series on television. For Platonic philosophy is the discovery of transcendent truth by means of reason alone. Most Americans are ignorant of the fact that the philosophers of Greece are viewed as the equivalent of the Hebrew prophets of Israel. For both prophets of Israel and philosophers of Greece paved the way and made humanity open to acknowledge God's incarnation. As Clement of Alexandria, third century philosopher-theologian states...

> *The divine Logos has always illuminated souls; but whereas the Jews were enlightened by Moses and the Prophets, the Greeks had their wise men, their phi-*

losophers, so that philosophy was to the Greeks what the Law was to the Hebrews. [7]

And for Socrates, a just and righteous man, to willingly die in the name of truth for his love of justice, describes our painful and misconstrued nature of relative justice and obscure truth in our cave of illusion. For in his act of sacrifice, Socrates prescribed how truth ought to be, which paved the way for the incarnate and righteous Logos to willingly and painfully die upon the cross for the sake of freedom, love, truth, and justice describing how it is to be.

Christ is not simply a wise man as was Socrates, whose free acceptance of death in the name of truth nevertheless has a similarity with the sacrifice of the Cross.... He is the eternal witness to the Father and to the love that the Father has had for His creatures from the beginning. [8]

Christ is absolutely original and absolutely unique. If He were only a wise man like Socrates, if He were a 'prophet' like Muhammad, if He were 'enlightened' like Buddha, without any doubt He would not be what He is. He is the one mediator between God and humanity. He is mediator because He is both God and man.

—His Holiness, John Paul II
Roman Catholic Pontiff [9]

12

The Natural Artist

The recurrent mythological event of the death and resurrection of a God, which had been for millenniums the central mystery of all of the great religions of the nuclear Near East, became in Christian thought an event in time, which had occurred but once, and marked the moment of the transfiguration of history
—Joseph Campbell [1]

Philo: It'll be dark pretty soon, Socrates. The stars will be coming out. Maybe we should call it a day.

Socrates: The arena is yours, Philo. You have riveted us into our seats with this descriptive truth of yours.

Philo: Your curiosity remains intact, however. I'm not certain that I have fully convinced you about the incarnation of the Logos.

Socrates: There are many unanswered questions that need to be addressed. Allow me to agree with you that this was, indeed, God in descriptive form. You do realize that the ancient Egyptians believed that Horus was the true son of God, who was born of the virgin Isis, and who died and resurrected from the dead three days later?

Philo: I am aware of the virgin-born savior of ancient Egypt, along with his Goddess-mother, Isis!

Socrates: Then you must know that this belief dates back to at least three thousand years before the birth of Jesus.

Philo: Yes, I am familiar with the ancient date of this belief.

Socrates: I am also curious to know if you considered the fact that 3,500 years before Jesus, the Babylonians worshipped the son of God, Tammuz, born of the virgin, Astaroth. [2]

Philo: Indeed I have. In fact Tamuz was supposedly crucified on a cross, similar to Jesus, and resurrected three days later.

Socrates: Being born and raised in Greece, you must be aware of the Son of Zeus, Hercules, born of his virgin mother, who entered the underworld of Hades for three days and three nights, in order to bring his friends out. You must also be familiar with the other Greek gods born of virgin mothers such as Asklepious and Perseus. [3] They all predate this Jesus by thousands of years. What do we make of this, Philo? If this Jesus was the divine incarnation, or communicated word of God, then how was such communication divulged to these pre-Christ civilizations?

Philo: A timeless question indeed, Socrates. These are but mythological saviors predating Christ and his life. As a matter of fact, I have spent years of research concerning this question, and this book which I have written documents my research pertaining to these mythological saviors which predate the incarnation of Christ.

Socrates: So what is it that separates myth from reality? Is it by faith that you have drawn your conclusions that the previous virgin-born saviors are myths and only the incarnation of Jesus a reality? Or are your convictions based on facts, evidence, and reason?

Philo: I draw my conclusions by the same means which humanity discerns between truth and falsehood, distinguishes right from wrong, identifies justice and injustice. By this same means humankind discerns between myth and reality. Since the Logos is reason and discourse, and reason was in the beginning with God, is the same as God, and reason became flesh, I draw my conclusions based on the reasonable and communicated means offered by the Logos and not by faith.

Speculative philosophy or natural theology focuses on humanity's search for God through general revelation, such as observing nature or examining the precise conditions upon this planet which have produced and continue to sustain life. Practical philosophy or revealed theology focuses on God's search for his creation through special and personal revelation of his being.[4] When humans communicate with God, through prayer, they do so in a manner of faith. God, however, communicates via reasonable means; thus faith and reason are compatible within divine communication. Faith between humanity and God, reason between God and humanity.

Socrates: You are speaking as if the Logos-the Spirit-of-Reason, lives within you. How is it that you seem so convinced that you possess this Spirit of Truth? Does the rest of the company present here lack this Spirit?

Philo: The eternal Spirit of Yaweh God, was encased in the corporal, empirical manifestation identified in Yawh-Shua, or Jesus for 33 years. This same Spirit continues to be dynamically alive and active as it continues to guide, communicate with, and save those that place their trust in him. Therefore the means of discernment between myth and reality comes from the Holy Spirit.

Socrates: What new doctrine is this? A Holy Spirit? Suppose you define your terms.

Philo: It is the Spirit which communicates truth, Socrates. It identifies ideal attributes of divine essence. It offers verification of the incarnate Logos.

Socrates: And how does this Spirit communicate to you? In particular, communicate that the previous virgin-born saviors were myth, but that this Christ is a reality? How do we attain your means of discernment?

Philo: You must first understand, Socrates, that for 2,000 years there has been an invisible separation within all people of this world. There was a division that became initiated upon the cross that has become the archetypal division ever since. The criminal who was crucified on the one side of Jesus acknowledged the true nature of Christ. The criminal on the other side rejected him. If you walk the streets today and ask, "Who is this Christ?" you will see that humanity continues to be divided. The one side will say he was the son of, and the same as God, the other will say he was not. One will identify his divinity and say he is the Savior born of a virgin, the other side will say he was a product of fornication born out of wedlock.

One will identify his special, communicated revelation of love and justice by that descriptive act upon the cross; the other side allows him only human qualities. The one side identifies his divine nature documented in written form in the scriptures, while the other side, unable or unwilling to accept the scriptures as divine truth, will accept many undocumented fables such as Jesus having gone to India and being taught by human gurus. These two types of people, one which identifies with his divine nature and the other side that grants him only a human nature, continue to exist even today.

Socrates: Am I correct in assessing that humanity is divided into two groups? The one group identifies with and beholds the Spirit of Truth, while the other group rejects it or simply ignores it?

Philo: Those that have not experienced the Spirit of Truth read and interpret the Bible along with its laws and God's incarnation subjectively. To them the Bible is literature. Those, however, that behold the Spirit know that it is not the scriptures being interpreted by humankind, but it is humankind that is being interpreted by the scriptures.

Socrates: Am I right in assessing that Dr. Lattison and Professor Thomas lack this Spirit of Truth? They seem rather puzzled as you are describing this invisible entity.

Philo: Invisible yet powerful. Is it not the case that substances possessing the most powerful properties are made of invisible stuff. X-rays and gamma rays are invisible to the naked eye, but possess a most powerful source of energy. Gravity is invisible, yet its powerful substance still has scientists puzzled as to what it is. Likewise, the invisible Spirit of God is the powerful means of communicating the nature of God to humanity.

The nature of God, and his reality, could be compared to our reality consisting of space, matter, and gravity. Space, for example, is vast. Everything in our known universe is contained within it. Its grandeur is revealed in the fact that space has no verifiable center, for we have yet to determine an identifiable edge.

Moreover, while we know that matter is the substance which exists within space, science reveals that the primary substance of matter is composed of space itself. Matter is the physical manifestation that becomes empirically known, thus identified and recognized by the senses. We can see, hear, smell, feel, and taste matter. Then there is the third component, gravity, which is that unknown, invisible force that moves things. It moves the earth, planets, and stars. Gravitational power is the only known substance that is capable of producing black holes. It is the force by which we perceive time as it moves matter, causing change, within space. Between these three: space, matter, and gravity we are somehow offered our reality.

Likewise, God is analogous to space, for it is God that is the invisible substance whose grandeur has no verifiable center, for he has no identifiable edge. Analogous to matter, the physical manifestation and empirically identifiable substance of God, is contained within Jesus. He is the incarnate, physical, empirically identifiable reality, of God. As the primary substance of matter is space, the primary substance of Jesus is God.

Going further in this analogy, gravity, the invisible and unknown force that causes change as it moves things, corresponds to the Holy Spirit, which is that invisible force that moves us and changes us. By the force of gravity the sun continues to shine, while it keeps us grounded upon planet earth. Likewise, the force of the Spirit illuminates the nature of God as it keeps us grounded in his word. It is this Spirit of Truth that causes a fallen humanity to repent and change. Once the Spirit takes root within a person it is not that individual any longer interpreting the laws of God, but the laws are interpreting the fallen individual.

Due to its nature of purity, justice, good, and holiness, once the Spirit awakens our consciousness, its particular nature of truth authenticates the laws, thereby convicting the adulterer, the liar, the thief. It reveals divine doctrine as it illuminates ignorance, arrogance, and self-righteousness. The Spirit of Truth rebukes the one holding false doctrine. Similar to space, matter and gravity that produces our earthly reality, God, Jesus, and the Spirit produce the reality of divinity, the nature of God.

Once the Spirit penetrates our mind and soul it corrects our perception of human, relative justice as it reveals the absolute, whose nature is just. It reveals our true nature, which is on the left side of injustice, as we identify with God's right side of justice. It communicates God's nature and attributes within our invisible mind and soul, that we may identify Jesus as the one archetypal revelation of mercy and grace in its ideal state of being. It moves us from physical, eros love, from the left, which is to take and possess, to agape love, on the right, which is to give, as we identify with the one who gave himself, and offered salvation for all.

Therefore, those who have received this Spirit of Truth will connect with the life-giving Spirit originating from the divine reality on the right. It is analogous to the spring water on top of the mountain that penetrates the dirty puddle. By this means of purification the puddle becomes cleansed, making it possible to come in contact with the pure and natural spring above. This, Socrates, is the teleology and refined state of being for the soul. First to identify our wrongdoings, followed by purification and cleansing delivered by forgiveness that we may come into unity with God.

Socrates: Then the absolute and constant nature of God....

Philo: What is absolute and constant, Socrates? When science finally discovered an absolute substance, they simultaneously recognized that it must remain absolute. This fact reveals that all else must modify its reality and bow to the absolute that will remain absolute and constant.

Socrates: Is this a possibility? Are you telling us that scientists have identified a substance that remains absolute in the physical universe?

Philo: Indeed they have! It is the speed of light. Dr. Lattison will verify its absolute nature, as it travels at a constant 186,000 miles a second. What makes it absolute is that it is irrelevant how fast one is moving towards the speed of light or away from it. Their own perception of time, space, and speed, will be adjusted and become modified as the physical laws dictate. Thus, the speed of light which is absolute and constant will remain so at 186,000 miles per second. All else becomes modified.

Thus, if the reality of absolute justice, love and goodness has been revealed and made descriptive, what is left for humanity to do but modify their relative reality of unjustifiable goodness, love, opinions, and beliefs?

Likewise God's laws, nature, and reality of truth, will remain absolute. This dictates that it is humankind who must change. This unchanging reality of God, in particular, is also a lesson for the hundreds upon hundreds of religions, especially found in this country, that are not Christ-centered. These belief systems attempt to modify the nature of God. They want to dictate the nature of God to conform to their ideas without acknowledging his incarnation, without identifying his personal revelation in Christ. As they expect God to bow to the passions and desires of humanity, they remain ignorant that it is they who need modification, and that they are the ones that must bow to the one whose justice is absolute, whose goodness remains constant, and whose love is eternal.

Socrates: You have failed to address the question, Philo. Scholars of humanistic studies have historically known, plain and simple, that an array of sons-of-god, resurrected saviors, born of virgin mothers, were worshipped in practically every civilization predating the birth of

Jesus. They pre-date this incarnation of Jesus by thousands of years. Are they simply myth and fiction?

Philo: It is amusing that we should arrive at such a discussion, since it was you, Socrates, who battled against such beliefs of the Athenians. It was you who challenged these virgin- born savior myths, drawing the conclusion that they were simply idols of worship! Your disputation of the religion of the masses, and the status quo, brought upon yourself the condemnation of death. Although you did not bow to these images and mythological gods, you did maintain that traces of truth are to be found within the myths.

Socrates: It seems that you possess some form of special revelation, as if you have been given reasons of discernment. What reasons do you provide for this discernment? If the nature of truth has dismissed all previous saviors into molten images and revealed this Christ as truth, reality, and the true Savior, I do wonder about modern scholars of humanistic studies who have analyzed these savior myths. Have they also arrived at the conclusion that all the pre-Jesus saviors were myths and only this incarnation of Jesus was a reality?

Philo: Bill Moyers, an acclaimed journalist for PBS and CBS News, interviewed our most famous American scholar on mythology, Joseph Campbell. Writes Moyers;

> *The images of God are many, he [Joseph Campbell] said, calling them 'the masks of eternity...' He [Campbell] wanted to know what it means that God assumes such different masks in different cultures, yet how it is that comparable stories can be found in these divergent traditions-stories of creation, of virgin births, incarnations, deaths and resurrections, second comings, and judgment.* [5]

Evidently Joseph Campbell seems to lack the Spirit of Truth since he has not discerned between myth and reality.

Socrates: Then how is it that the Spirit of Truth reveals to you, Philo, that all other saviors are myths, but this Jesus is a reality? They all seem to possess threads of commonality: a virgin mother, God as a Father, a three day burial, followed by a miraculous resurrection.

Philo: This is not revealed to me but to all who sincerely repent, desire to know, and to follow the Spirit of Truth.

Socrates: Then let us also follow this Spirit of Truth that we may be guided to discernment between myth and reality. Between idol saviors and the true living Savior.

Philo: Then imagine, Socrates, a dozen children living in the museum across the street. They have been there since birth and have a skewed understanding of reality concerning the nature of justice, good, freedom, love and truth. Their natural father, who possesses these supernatural attributes, in the meantime, is planning to visit them in the museum. As we agreed, it would be wise for the father to send some letters of arrival to the children in order that he may be known when he arrives.

Socrates: We did discuss this issue.

Philo: Then you do remember, that this written revelation of the father coming to the museum is analogous to the Old Testament written letters of the coming Father to planet earth.

Socrates: Yes, you did make this connection.

Philo: Suppose that the father, outside the museum, not only communicated his coming by letters, but also sent some pictures of himself. Pictures are the simplest and most universal means of communication. Would you not say that the father conducts himself in a wise manner by offering more than one method of communication? Is he not attempting to sincerely communicate to the children by also utilizing pictures, the simplest and most universal means of communication?

Socrates: The pictures would certainly validate the letters concerning the arrival of the father, as the letters would in turn authenticate the pictures.

Philo: But in their skewed understanding of reality calling bad-good and injustice-justice, what if some of the children discovered a manner of distorting the meaning of the father's pictures, thus desecrating the intention of the pictures? As the pictures of the father are hanging on the museum walls, what if the children began producing inanimate statues, lifeless idols, and started telling each other stories about mythological fathers from the pictures? Would you not say that the pictorial images of the natural father have been corrupted into myths, idols and lifeless statues by the artificial artists within the muscum?

Socrates: Unquestionably. The pictures have fallen victim to misrepresentation and abuse in such a scenario.

Philo: Imagine the children believing that many fathers exist in the lifeless idols copied from the pictures. In this case, it would not be the pictures that have fallen victim to abuse, but the father has been grossly misrepresented and maligned. Now would this be justice or injustice done to the father along with his pictures, and his simple means of communication?

Socrates: Injustice, of course. But the true victims in this case Philo, are neither the pictures nor the father; the true victims are the children who have embraced myth instead of reality, falsehood instead of truth, and lifeless idols instead of identifying with their one and only living father.

Philo: Then we agree, Socrates, that prior to the living father's arrival in the museum, many inanimate statues, lifeless idols, and mythological fathers, are found with a strikingly similar resemblance with the father?

Socrates: As you have described it, yes.

Philo: Then we can conclude that prior to the arrival of the living father in the museum, all of the idols and mythological fathers were but a fabrication, a distortion, and misrepresentation. But when the real father arrived, he appeared precisely as his letters had informed the children, and as his pictures has instructed them.

Socrates: A double revelation this would be.

Philo: All of the inanimate, fictitious fathers predating the living father are lifeless idols and myths, but the living father who finally arrived is alive and true. Therefore, with knowledge of the pictures that were copied into idols, we may discern myth from reality. We may separate idols and their myths from the authentic, living father who physically appeared though it be after the appearance of the counterfeit idols and myths.

Socrates: Why, yes.

Philo: In addition, when the father finally appeared in the museum, what if four separate individuals documented the life of the real and authentic father? Would there not be a definite correspondence between the prophetic pictures the father had sent and the four individuals who documented his appearance, after he arrived?

Socrates: Indeed! As the pictures were communicating the nature of the coming father prior to his arrival, we would expect the documentation of his life, by the four individuals, following his presence, to correspond with the prophetic pictures.

Philo: Then in the same manner, Socrates, what if the coming of God in the incarnation of Jesus, was indeed communicated by pictures? Images of himself would establish simple communication and knowledge of his coming and of his nature.

Socrates: Then you are stating that Father God not only disclosed his coming in written form of the Old Testament, but also communicated through the universal language of pictures as well. Is this what you are divulging here, Philo?

Philo: Indeed.

Socrates: If you can direct us to these divine pictures, Philo, then you might very well have a valid argument. All of the virgin-born saviors, in every civilization, predating Christ and his appearance, would be but lifeless idols; mythological saviors reproduced from the pictures. This Jesus, therefore, would be the authentic, living Savior. But pictures, Philo? Are we not stretching the imagination a bit?

Philo: Pictures indeed, Socrates!

Socrates: Well, where are they Philo? I would like to examine them myself. And what does God's nature of justice, as a prophetic picture, look like?

Philo: What else but the scales; the scales of justice.

Socrates: I was anticipating that you would have stated a picture of the cross, for as you stated earlier, it single-handedly seems to be the symbol of divine love and justice combined. Presuming that what you are saying is true.

Philo: Within these heavenly images, which total 48 in number,[6] we do find the sign of the cross. In fact the cross is located below the scales of justice. God revealed his virgin birth by an image of a woman which he distinguished as a "virgin." Next to this image he placed an image of the scales revealing that it is he, the one born of a virgin, that will offer divine justice. The ancient civilizations fabricated idols of these signs calling the virgin by various names; Isis in Egypt, Astraea in Babylon, Ceres in other places, etc.[7] Many times the virgin is erroneously depicted in the idols as holding the scales of justice. All of God's divine signs communicating the nature, being, and incarnation of the living Father, were reproduced as statues, idols, and myths. This includes the virgin woman who continues to hold the scales as a symbol of justice in our courts. Another corruption of idolatry copied from the signs.

Socrates: In heaven's name, Philo! You cannot possibly suggest that these are the divine signs in the stars of the heavens. In the name of Zeus, even a shepherd in ancient Greece was able to identify these divine images. You cannot possibly be telling me that modern scholars, including Lattison and Thomas here, are ignorant of this universal, divine means of communication?

Philo: Then we agree that these prophetic signs begin with the image of the virgin and end with the picture of the lion.

Socrates: Without doubt!

Philo: Then it will be of interest to you to know that these prophetic pictures which Father God sent to the world thousands of years before his incarnation, correspond in every detail with the four separate individuals who documented the life of Jesus after the incarnation. These four being Matthew, Mark, Luke and John of the New Testament.

In the first of these prophetic pictures, it was foretold prior to the incarnation that Virgo the virgin was to give birth to the Holy Child. We see the correspondence in the incarnation of Jesus as the first page of the New Testament begins with the virgin giving birth to Christ.[8] It was foretold in the last of these prophetic pictures that human history will terminate with the coming of Leo the lion. Likewise in the last book of the Bible, the book of Revelation, it is written that the apocalypse is opened by Jesus returning as the omnipotent lion.[9] Between the first prophetic picture of the virgin and the concluding sign which is the lion, we find a picture of, Aries, the male lamb. Likewise, in the New Testament, between the virgin birth of Christ and his return as a lion, it is written that he is the lamb.

Socrates: In the name of truth, Philo. These divine images have been fulfilled in their specific, chronological order. I cannot imagine that Lattison and Thomas are ignorant of these images. What about the remaining signs between the virgin and the lion? Are Scorpio, Sagittarius, Aquarius, Pisces and the rest communicating the divine nature and incarnation of the one God?

Philo: All twelve signs proclaim various aspects of the nature, birth, death, life, and second coming of Jesus. The Natural Artist who produced living art, which we see in his trees, flowers, and animals, has not only utilized planet earth as a canvas for his artistry but the universe is his magnificent tapestry, as he has sketched images of himself in the stars of the heavens.

This unrivaled masterpiece of universal proportions in the heavens has been a sign to the ancients as well as to modern peoples. The same story which was told to the ancient by the stars continues to be told even today. The scientist Dr. Lloyd Motz has further classified this pictorial revelation in the heavens as "stellar imaging" [which] "was well known to primitive peoples." [10]

As William Tyler Olcott stated, "There is little doubt that the constellations were the result of a deliberate plan." [11]

The Natural Artist who produced the living lamb upon planet earth is the same Natural Artist who deliberately drew his loving nature of a lamb upon the heavens in the stellar image of Aries, the male lamb. He is the Master Artist that produced the powerful lion upon planet earth and revealed his omnipotence and artistic nature in his stellar image of Leo the lion.

The sign of Virgo depicts his virgin birth. Next to Virgo the sign of Libra, the stellar image of "The scales" as God depicts that it is he, the virgin-born savior, who balances the scales of justice. The image of Aquarius, "The water-pourer" is his image of divine cleansing. Similar to the spring above that cleanses the dirty puddle water, Aquarius is his nature of cleansing a filthy humanity, baptizing his followers with the Holy Spirit and waters of salvation.

As Jesus, the true Aquarius, stated to the woman at the well...

Whosoever drinketh of this water shall thirst again: But Whosoever drinketh of the water that I shall give him shall never thirst; but the water that I shall give him shall be in him a well of water springing up into everlasting life. [12]

Socrates: Am I to accept this bitter truth, that this universally acknowledged drama in the heavens which was a theater of divine status, for all of the ancients, is lost knowledge to modern humanity? What in heaven's name has happened to wisdom Philo?

Philo: Wisdom, Socrates? In today's world? And without the Spirit of Truth? H.A. Ray has written a book titled "The Stars" whose cover boasts high acclamations by prominent scientists and scientific journals. Ray identifies that the ancients did indeed know something which we seem to have forgotten today.

Ray concludes...

A plain Chaldean shepherd, more than three thousand years ago, probably knew the sky better than most of our college graduates today.... [13]

If modern people, including college graduates, usually cannot locate even one of the twelve signs along the ecliptic of the heavens; how will they ever identify the total number of 48 signs that have been a shining witness revealing the coming Messiah since ancient times?

Go to our universities, Socrates. Visit our college graduates and question the historian concerning the Jewish Encyclopedia which reveals that each of the twelve Tribes of Israel carried one of the twelve Zodiac signs upon their banner or standard. [14] Then inquire of the professors if this is simply trivia, or is there a deeper meaning to be found?

Visit our universities and question the Archaeologist as to why excavations in the ancient Jewish temples, such as Beth Alpha and Hammas, contain the twelve signs of the Zodiac inscribed upon the floor of these temples? [15] Summon them and ask if there is a relationship and significance between the twelve signs above with the twelve tribes below?

The average person, when receiving an envelope from Australia mailed with a stamp depicting the Australian flag sees nothing but the four dominant stars. Few know that these stars depict the sign of Crux, the Southern Cross, which is located at - 60 degrees declination and 12 hours right ascension in the tropic skies below the scales of justice.

Are our modern day college graduates capable of identifying with the true meaning of this sign in the heavens, and its prophetic relationship to the physical cross on which Jesus was crucified outside of Jerusalem?

Are the professors of humanistic studies capable of distinguishing the stars that make up the constellation of the cross and comprehend the poet John Greenleaf Whittier who wrote "The Cry of a Lost Soul:"

The traveler...

Lifts to the starry calm of heaven his eyes;

And lo! rebuking all earth's ominous cries,

The Cross of pardon lights the tropic skies! [16]

Visit the science department and carry with you the *Journal of the History of Ideas*, a journal that boasts affiliation with our most prestigious universities. In the October-December 1991 Issue we find a chapter titled "Augustine and Galileo on Reading the Heavens." Galileo, founder of modern science, is cited,

Would the censorship of all science be anything other than the condemnation of those many passages of Scripture in which we are taught that the glory and grandeur of the Creator can be seen in all of his works, and divinely read in the open book of the heavens? [17]

Ask our modern scientists why the author of this article seems rather confused as to what Galileo actually meant.

Socrates: Truly, departments of theological studies, whose specialization is to study the nature of God, must not have remained ignorant of such revelations?

Philo: In this young country we specialize in technology and scientific advancements, both dominated by the physical universe. We do not emphasize history, philosophy, and other humanistic studies. Similar to modern philosophy that is dragging itself through the muddle of prejudice and quicksand of ignorance, likewise many of our liberal modern theology schools here in America, have run amok. They are divided into two groups. One group of universities teaches sound Spirit-filled theological doctrine identifying the divine nature of Jesus as they associate with the historical church. Most liberal universities deny this doctrine.

Visit our liberal theology departments at our prestigious universities, and inquire of Albert the Great Magnus, who was teacher and mentor of one of our most famous theologians, Thomas Aquinas. In the book "the meaning of the Zodiac," Magnus is cited,

The Mysteries of the Incarnation, from the Conception on to the Ascension into heaven, are shown us on the face of the sky, and are signified by the stars. [18]

Socrates: What tragedy, Philo. Has the modern philosopher not taken such evidence into consideration?

Philo: Suppose you lived in the museum, Socrates, and were one of the children there. As a philosopher in the museum, you would be well versed concerning the father's pictures hanging on the wall. As a seeker of truth you would also dispute with the other children in the museum, whose religion was simply idols and myths copied from these pictures. Once the father arrived, as the pictures proclaimed, all one would need to do to convince you of his appearance would be to first point to the idols copied from the pictures, and second, point to the pictures themselves. Once the father's physical appearance and life is described to you, his life would correspond with all of his pictures; thus all of the idols revealing many fathers would be fabrications verified as myths.

In similar fashion, following the death and resurrection of Jesus, the Apostle Paul delivered this good news to the Greeks. Paul met with the top Philosopher of Athens who was Dionysius the Aeropagite. Although the New Testament, which describes the life of Christ, was not yet written, Dionysius was familiar with the Old Testament. It was translated into the Greek language in 250 B.C. As an astronomer, [19] Dionysius was well versed in the signs of the heavens. He thus recognized the mythological saviors in the religion of the lay people, copied from these stellar images from above.

We read in the Bible that Paul the Apostle converted Dionysius by simply pointing to the idols and then reciting from the Greek poets, [20] who described each one of the signs in the heavens above. Consequently the Bible tells us that Dionysius became a believer and converted to Christianity. History tells us that Dionysius became the first Christian Bishop of Athens. [21]

In Greece today, Dionysius is as well known as George Washington is in the U.S.A. I am saddened to say that none of my philosophy professors here in America, even at the graduate level, have ever heard of him. Plato demanded that to become a philosopher one must study geometry as well as astronomy. [22] Plato would not allow any student into his academy without first becoming an expert geometrician capable of calculating the heavens mathematically. Dyonisius the Aeropagite, following the advice of Plato, traveled to the distant city of Alexandria in order to receive the best possible education in astronomy. Today one can receive a Ph.D. in philosophy without one course in astronomy. What is worse, one can receive a doctorate in philosophy, here in the States, without having read one book of the Bible.

It is a historical and archaeological fact that the two greatest impacts upon world history are the signs above and the Bible. The universal legacy, which the signs above have left upon world history, is second to none. For two thousand years the influence of the Bible, which records the life of Jesus precisely as the signs had revealed him to be, has surpassed any other writings upon our planet.

How, I ask, in the name of truth, does one receive the title of philosopher today by remaining ignorant of the two greatest influences upon our planet?

Visit the science department at any local university and inquire of the astrophysicist, in particular, as to who named the image of Orion, depicting the return of Jesus in the heavens, and they will agree with Dr. Chartrand, Vice President of the National Space Society that, Orion was named by ancient man.[23] But ancient man disagrees with the modern scientist. We are told by the prophet Amos, and by Job of the Old Testament, that "Orion was made by the Lord."[24]

Not only do the signs trace their origins to antiquity, but also so do the names of their individual stars. Which brings upon us a curious dilemma as to who named the stars? Their names reach back to "ancient times" according to the Encyclopedia of Astronomy.[25]

Socrates: Since you mentioned it, Philo, who did name the stars? It was a peculiar notion in ancient Greece that each star possessed a name corresponding to the name of its allotted sign thereby further identifying the particular sign to which a star belonged.

Philo: Who was responsible for this phenomenon that named the stars to correspond each with an allotted sign, Socrates? In the sign of Leo the lion the star in the tail of the lion is called Denebola, meaning, "tail of the lion."[26] Algieba in the heart of the lion means "the lion's mane."[27] In Aries the lamb the star Hamal means the [lamb].[28] No one questions the fact that the names of each sign correspond with the names of the stars to which they belong.

Socrates: Are you making the claim that God named particular stars within each designated sign, thus further identifying each one of the signs? Are you stating that God established yet another means of communication?

Philo: This is the claim of Plato. For it was your pupil who stated that it is soul that orders the motion of the stars and that mind or reason guides the cosmos.[29] Which I must agree is an accurate and true statement. For it is proclaimed in Psalm 147 of the Bible that God "numbers the stars he calls them all by their names." Not only did the prophetic utterance of the Old Testament prophets become fulfilled with the arrival of the Messiah, but their cry of the coming Savior corresponded with the same outburst declared by each one of the signs above. Both of these means of communication were also in unison with his prophetic voice in the stars themselves.

As the earth spins on its axis all of humanity, throughout the Four Corners of our planet, is able to view these signs and attain knowledge of God from this universal means of communication.

As the Bible states...

The heavens declare the glory of God; and the firmament showeth his handiwork. Day unto day uttereth speech, and night unto night showeth knowledge. There is no speech nor language, where their voice is not heard. Their line is gone out through all the earth, and their words to the end of the world. In them he has set a tabernacle for the sun.[30]

Socrates: Then your belief is that the Logos, the infinite reason, communicated his coming within the unlimited and unrestricted space in order that the whole world may come to know?

Philo: Indeed, Socrates. God did not solely utilize the Old Testament scriptures in Israel to divulge his coming but also utilized the vast expanse of the heavens. The Persian Magi, commonly known to the lay-people as "wise men," had not been communicated to by the Old Testament scripture but were waiting for the coming Messiah as his images in the stars proclaimed his coming, his nature, and his glory.[31] And how did God validate that the one, true, authentic and living Savior, foretold in the stars, was at hand? By none other than a new star, the star of Bethlehem, leading the Magi to the living Savior.

Such an impact have these divine signs promulgated upon the inhabitants of planet earth that most, if not all, newspapers and many magazines, continue to display these twelve signs as a prophetic medium, on a daily basis.

Socrates: Are you not giving us a confusing message here, Philo? You have been describing articles of ignorance for the populace, as it concerns the signs, all of this time. But now you claim that practically every newspaper communicates God's revelation every day?

Philo: The message that they proclaim is inaccurate and fallacious. Go visit some of these newspapers, Socrates, any newspapers throughout the world and ask them, "What exactly are you proclaiming in the Horoscope also known as the astrology column, strange fellows? Is the future of each human written in the stars, as your newspaper claims, or was the future of the life of God written in the stars, whose fulfillment you have failed to identify?"

Socrates: Before we proceed any further, Philo, you need to distinguish between an astronomer, whose skill is indeed the greatest of all sciences, and the astrologer. For they seem to be bipolar opposites.

Philo: Indeed, many people fail to identify such a massive difference between these two. The astronomer is a scientist, and a scholar of mathematics and physics, who usually spends well over 10 years in college. The astrologer, however, needs no education, not even a high school diploma. Astronomers should never be confused with astrologers. To be an astrologer one simply needs to predict the future by using these signs. The only commonality astronomers and astrologers have is that they both utilize this Zodiac map of the heavens. To the astronomer the Zodiac is a map helping in locating positions of stars upon the heavens as a geographical map helps in identifying physical locations. It is the astrologer who utilizes this map in a deceptive manner.

Socrates: If the astrologers' craft is to predict the future by utilizing these signs while these signs have been fulfilled in the incarnation of God, then the predictions of the astrologers concerning future events must consistently turn out to be false. Their erroneous predictions should be obvious and easy to identify.

Philo: Many of the astrologers' predictions are stated ambiguously. They abuse language in order that they might justify their craft. But when they attempt to predict future events that offer verifiable results, their statements have consistently been proven false. After examining astrologers' predictions, both astronomers and philosophers alike have confirmed that the astrologers' prophetic statements are fallacious.

Such was the case with Mason Sexton's "Harmonic Research," a financial newsletter that attempts to predict the Stock Market by astrology. At a subscription price of $960 dollars a year, Forbes Magazine, a financial publication, identified "Harmonic Research" as "the most expensive newsletter" [32] which they monitor. Only 1,000 subscribers will produce almost 1 million dollars annual income for the astrologer Saxton. We can reason then, that with this much money at stake Saxton must hire the most expensive astrologers. As fate would have it, in the January 15, 1988 issue, "The Long term 12-24 months" forecast by Harmonic Research was that "The U.S. stock market continues to be in the early stages of a major bear market with an ultimate downside target of Dow 577 by 1992." [33]

Harmonic Research's astrological prediction was that the Dow Jones Industrials, which were at 1916 [34] when this prediction was made, would go down to the 577 level in four years, when in fact the Stock Market did the exact opposite. It rose to 2226 January 15, 1989. Then rose the second year to 2689. Thus beyond a shadow of a doubt the astrologers forecast was proven wrong. Instead of falling more than one thousand points, the market closed in 1992 at 3,301, [35] more than 2,600 points higher than Harmonic Research's dire prediction.

We agreed that once the human father sent pictures to the children in the museum there is an injustice committed against the father and his pictures in having produced lifeless idols and mythological fathers. The future, however, is written in the pictures as it concerns the coming father. Now, what if some children began to foretell the future by using the father's pictures? Would that be injustice done to the father and his pictures?

Socrates: If the pictures are foretelling the nature and personality of the coming father, then justice would be served if this is what is being proclaimed by the children.

Philo: But the children are not foretelling the future as it concerns the coming father, Socrates. They are extracting money from the gullible masses as they foretell and make promises of fame, wealth, power, sex and a great love life. By pointing to the father's pictures they are promising physical love, monetary gains and success. They are defiling the message of the images, violating the nature of the father and his simple means of communication.

Socrates: This would indeed be a legitimate claim for injustice.

Philo: Then you see, Socrates, Father God placed his birth, personality, and nature, in the heavens above, but astrologers have misrepresented the true meaning of the pictures. For the astrologers claim that it is our birth, nature and personality, which are foretold and depicted in the stars. Father God reveals the future as it concerns his life upon planet earth in the stars but astrologers mislead the foolish people by telling them it is their life written in the stars. Father God reveals his nature of love, glorified, sacrificial love; yet, it is the astrologers who desecrate God's revelation and his glory, as they desire glorification and monetary gain for themselves. The Natural Artist, whose nature is Ideal Justice, revealed this particular attribute in many signs, such as Libra the scales and Crux the cross, but astrologers have unjustly profaned these images, proclaiming their own wicked and skewed misunderstanding, as they divert people away from God's simple means of communicating justice.

The artificial artist borrows from the cow or living art of the Natural Artist and produces lifeless, imitation art in the leather jacket or leather shoe. In similar fashion, the artificial artist borrows from the living, descriptive means of communication from the Natural Artist in the heavens and offers prescriptive, lifeless, distorted communication instead.

Astrologers claim that success for their clients is written in the stars, violating the true message of the Natural Artist who successfully fulfilled all of these signs in their precise order. These sorcerers offer fame for the masses, attempting to become famous themselves while remaining unable to recognize the one Natural Artist whose fame even planet earth cannot contain. For the images and fame of the Natural Artist are displayed in the expanse of the heavens, whose life is recorded in the world's most published book. These soothsayers offer wealth and power for the populace while amassing spiritual poverty for themselves concerning the nature of truth, justice, freedom, divine love and the Natural Artist. I now ask, Socrates, when their earthly journey is finished do you think astrologers will meet with the lamb or lion?

Socrates: You give the analogy that similar to the living father who sent a two-fold revelation via pictures and letters to the children in the museum, likewise God revealed his coming by the two-fold revelation of pictures in the heavens and written letters through the prophets of the Old Testament.

Philo: Truly, he has.

Socrates: This, then, would be a multitude of letters spanning different epochs, or periods of time.

Philo: For over 1,000 years before the incarnation of the Natural Artist, Father God had a continuous line of communication via a multitude of prophets in Israel.

Socrates: Would you not think, then, that the human father who sent pictures of himself to the museum was informed that the intentions of the pictures had become desecrated? Would he not know that his pictures were fabricated into idols of worship, and that soothsayers were utilizing his pictures to predict the future for profit? In his wisdom, the father should caution the children against such defilement of his pictures. In particular, such caution should be made clear in the letters, which the father sends the children.

Philo: In this case, Socrates, you are stating that if God revealed his coming via the two-fold revelation of pictures in the heavens and the written word of the Old Testament, then he should warn his people against worship of idols copied from his pictures and caution his people against predicting the future. Such direction, then, should be made evident in his letters of the Old Testament.

Socrates: It does seem the reasonable thing to do.

Philo: Indeed, it does Socrates! In the first book of the Bible, the book of Genesis, it is stated on the first page that *"God said, Let there be lights in the firmament of the heavens to divide the day from the night; and let them be for signs, and for seasons."* [36]

The word "Signs" in the Hebrew is "something or someone to come" and the word seasons, in Hebrew, means in its "appointed time." [37] What followed from the revelation of the signs in the heavens were idols made with human hands, copied from these divine images. Mythological saviors were produced. Graven images were fabricated, instilling fear and terror within the people of the world.

God, however, denounces such customs, as he thunders against these practices:

Hear ye the word which the Lord speaketh unto you, O house of Israel, Thus saith the Lord, Learn not the way of the heathen, and be not dismayed at the signs of heaven; for the heathen are dismayed at them. For the customs of the people are vain: for one cutteth a tree out of the forest, the work of the hands of the workman, with the axe. They deck it with silver and with gold; they fasten it with nails and with hammers, that it move not.... But they are all together brutish and foolish: the stock is a doctrine of vanities... Thus shall ye say unto them, The Gods that have not made the heavens and the earth, even they shall perish from the earth, and from under these heavens. He hath made the earth by his power, he hath established the world by his wisdom, and hath stretched out the heavens by his discretion. [38]

The message is clearly stated throughout the scriptures that "all the Gods of the nations are idols: but the Lord made the heavens." [39] This is the message our modern-day scholars fail to receive. They insist that since previous virgin-born saviors pre-date Jesus, Christianity cannot be true. When in fact, all of these saviors were but idols, molten images, and counterfeits of God's revelation in the heavens.

These modern scholars fail to identify what the Bible makes plain...

> *The heavens declare his righteousness, and all the people see his glory. Confounded be all they that serve graven images, that boast themselves of idols: worship Him all ye gods.* [40]

Socrates: In this case, Philo, God must have condemned as well the perverse art of the astrologer in his letters of the Old Testament.

Philo: The living Father's voice of disapproval towards this manipulation and distortion of his truth is well documented:

> *Let now the astrologers, the stargazers, the monthly prognosticators, stand up and save thee from these things that shall come upon thee. Behold, they shall be as stubble; the fire shall burn them; they shall not deliver themselves from the power of the flame.* [41]

As we agreed, Socrates, good is a relative term, within human reality. We think we are good, when in fact we are not. By human standards someone might very well be perceived as good, but by God's standard nobody is good. As it was stated earlier, on a scale of 1 to 10, one being good and ten being evil, Adolph Hitler would place himself much closer towards the one on the side of good. Will not the astrologer also place himself much closer to the one? In their hearts astrologers surely believe that they are good. Many of them even believe that, in their practice, they are doing the work of the Lord!

You stated that justice is one with good and pleasure, located on the right. But an act producing good and pleasure that is without justice is a distorted good that is attained from the left, which is the side of injustice. In this case the inequitable monetary gains of an astrologer, his endeavor to achieve fame and glory, are unjustified in the face of ideal justice. In his devious craft the astrologer obscures ideal justice and clouds the communicated good. Therefore, the astrologer is attaining a good that is without justice, which is but a false, decayed-good, a spoiled temporary pleasure, that has dire consequences when the astrologer comes face to face with the omnipotent lion, whose nature is justice; justice by force.

Now suppose that the astrologer drives his neighbor to chemotherapy treatment every week, and expects nothing in return. Is this a good act that must be deemed good by God, as professor Thomas likes to believe?

It is stated throughout the Bible that the two worst offenses against God are idol worship and astrology. Both happen to be distortions of God's divine revelation in the signs. Therefore only the ideal, communicated good, which is one with justice and truth, is capable of passing judgment on what good truly is. God's goodness, the essence of which is immense and unconditional love, is revealed in the sacrificial lamb. This nature of God, symbolic of the lamb, is willing to pardon and forgive all sinners, all trespasses. This even includes the trespasses of the astrologers. Forgive, that is, if they repent, ask for forgiveness, cease their evil, misconstrued craft, and be baptized by the Spirit of Truth. In case they do not repent, and do not change their ways, he is also a God of immense and unconditional power and vengeance symbolized by the lion.

Socrates: Then it seems that there is one-and only-one meaning to each of these signs, which proclaim the nature of the "one good," the "one God." But astrologers erroneously offer many meanings for each one of these signs.

Philo: This morning alone astrologers working for one thousand newspapers will offer one thousand different meanings concerning the sign of Virgo the virgin. One thousand more interpretations pertaining to Aquarius, Aries, Leo and the rest of the signs. One day alone, 1,000 astrology columns will total twelve thousand interpretations. Tomorrow, those same thousand newspapers will offer twelve thousand more different meanings for each one of the twelve divine signs. In the course of one year these same newspapers will produce millions of interpretations.

Socrates: An interesting piece of information divulged here, Philo, for this seems to be part of the philosophers' dilemma which we have faced since ancient times–the dilemma between the one and the many. There is but one correct answer to a mathematical equation, but a multitude or an infinite number of wrong ones. There is but one bullseye by which the archer may hit the target, but a multitude of ways of missing it.

Philo: Indeed. As Aristotle has stated "There are many ways of going wrong, but only one of going right, which is why it is easier to fail than to succeed. There are many ways of missing the target but only one way to hit it." [42] Likewise, there is but one true meaning to the signs above, but astrologers have fallen for the corruption of the many.

They therefore divide, separate, and defile the "One" who delivers "one meaning," one corresponding revelation, between divine pictures of his future coming above and the Bible, which records his divine arrival and life on earth. For the one that is true and eternal remains "one." He is the ideal communicated good that remains constant, whose justice is absolute. He is the same yesterday, today and forever.

In similar fashion, as it concerns the one and the many, we see that there are a multitude of religions that miss the mark, leading to failure, but only one that is right that leads to truth. As the fourteenth chapter of John cites Jesus: "I am the way, the truth, and the life, none may come to the Father but by me."

The Bible is not open to personal interpretation, thus left vulnerable to human abuse, as many like to believe. But the pictures above, along with the star names, correspond with the written word of the Old Testament, which further correspond with the symbols, rituals, and traditions of Israel. The one true God of the New Testament fulfilled all these means of communication in the incarnation. His life is recorded in the New Testament, which continues to be supported and corroborated by rituals, traditions, and symbols, in the Christian church. Those that believe each one is free to interpret the scripture as they wish remain ignorant of God's multi-faceted means of communication, and God's formula for freedom.

Socrates: Then such information concerning the true meaning of the signs, and condemnation against astrology, should be divulged to the masses, Philo. Is it only the trained theologian that possesses this Spirit of Truth, and is thus aware of these facts? Are the masses left in the darkness? Are the people becoming informed?

Philo: Such information is well known for those that abide with the Spirit of Truth. These multi-faceted means of communication have been disclosed in the churches and Christian universities. God's revelation of himself in the heavens has even been disclosed on national television to the general public. From Florida in the east, Dr. James Kennedy has strongly criticized astrology from his pulpit on his national television show. Kennedy also proclaimed to the public that the twelve signs above plus the remaining thirty six, making for forty eight in all, detail and reveal the birth, death, and life of Jesus Christ.[43]

In Los Angeles, in the west, Dr. Gene Scott, a philosopher, theologian, and pastor has also been teaching on television on a regular basis for 20 years. Dr. Scott denounces astrology as have all legitimate Christian churches, be it Catholic, Orthodox, or conservative Protestant. Likewise, Dr. Scott has also narrated in detail the 48 signs in the heavens as they correspond with the written scriptures, both revealing Jesus, his birth, life, and nature.[44]

As it is stated, those that possess the Spirit of Truth hear and understand truth, and those that do not remain in darkness, chained in Socrates' cave of illusion. They see only shadows of reality, calling justice-injustice and evil-good. In this case, the horoscopes and astrology columns are but a pale shadow, a false doctrine, and a distortion of truth. They misrepresent the true reality which is communicated to humanity from above.

Socrates: Is this, then, what your book describes, Philo?

Philo: An ageless means of communication in the heavens above, common knowledge to the ancients, is news to modern scholars. A two thousand-year-old book that is the world's best seller remains foreign to many in our modern times. Humankind draws conclusions on opinions and beliefs, rather than facts and evidence. I believe that my convictions are justified beliefs, in the face of the facts and evidence. Anyone who desires to challenge my assertions and who chooses to dispute my conclusions should first read my book, *Children of the Zodiac*.[45]

Socrates: Then all the gods in the heavens or "children of the zodiac" are but a part of God's multi-faceted means of communication, which has been distorted into myth and idol worship.

Philo: We have yet to fully exhaust all of God's means of communication, Socrates. There remain many more.

For God has indeed utilized other means of revealing his nature. One way is by means of numbers. In abstract form, they communicate concrete units in the physical universe. Unfortunately, similar to the astrologer, numerologists have distorted God's numerical means of communication.

The number 7, for example, is the number of God's perfection. We easily identify this number in the Old Testament as the high priest would enter the veil of separation into the Holy of Holies, once a year, and spill the blood of the sacrificed animal 7 times upon the mercy seat and upon the laws. We identify this number of perfection in the words of Jesus, who counsels us to forgive seven times seventy. This number of perfection is also established in the Natural Artist's perfect week consisting of seven days. The number twelve communicates his perfect government.[46] It informs us that he governs not only planet earth, but the whole universe. He established his perfect government upon planet earth in the concrete units of the twelve tribes of Israel, which communicated his coming in the Old Testament. In the New Testament, God established his perfect government in the concrete units of the twelve Apostles, whose responsibility was to communicate his incarnate message to the world. His perfect government is revealed throughout the universe for the world to know his nature, which is declared and communicated in the twelve signs of the Zodiac. There are twelve months in a year twelve chapter....

"Ring" "Ring"

Dr. Lattison:... Ugh?..... Philo? Where did he go? Socrates? Huh? Hello!

Margaret: Good morning Dr. Lattison, this is your secretary, Margaret. What are you doing at home? Your class started at 9:30 and it is now well past ten. Where have you been?

Dr. Lattison: What? Oh my God!... No!... No! It can't be. Margaret. I ah...I was just starting to watch the 8 o'clock...ah "Wake up New York" morning show on TV. But I must have... eh fallen. Wait-wait... Ron Jensen was planning an interview at the museum....but... but...

Margaret: Dr. Lattison why are you shouting? Are you O.K.? Your 9:30 class was dismissed. You have a lunch appointment with Dr. Thomas from the philosophy department in less than an hour.

Dr. Lattison: Yeah, yeah, Dr. Thomas, yes. What is it? What is it? It's all illusion, Margaret. What is true? Do you attend church Margaret?

Margaret: What kind of question is this Dr. Lattison? One month ago you forced Dr. Wesley to remove the Ten Commandments from his theology classroom, by authority of the state. Last week, at the University, you attempted to enforce a state law that has yet to be implemented, of having all the Christians take their crosses off their necks while on campus, including myself. Now you ask me if I attend church?

Dr. Lattison: Yeah... Laws. Who is it..."who is this Christ" anyway? Who am...? Margaret! Do you... did you watch this morning's "Wake up New York" show?

Margaret: Dr. Lattison, why are you shouting? I only saw the first twenty minutes. They were discussing issues concerning religion and attributes of God. They interviewed two Christian professors; one from Florida and one from California. Real deep stuff. It was all Greek to me.

Dr. Lattison: Socrates and Philo... No! It can't be!... ...or is it...

Margaret: Who is Philo?

Dr. Lattison: Margaret!

Margaret: Dr. Lattison?

Dr. Lattison: My God!

For the scientist who has lived by his faith in the power of reason, the story ends like a bad dream. He has scaled the mountains of ignorance; he is about to conquer the highest peak; as he pulls himself over the final rock, he is greeted by a band of theologians who have been sitting there for centuries.
—Dr. Robert Jastrow[47]
Founder and former director of NASA's Goddard Institute for Space Studies

Science without religion is lame, religion without science is blind.
—Albert Einstein[48]

Search and you shall find. Knock and it will open for you.
—The Apostle Matthew

Socrates: (469 BC—399 BC) Ancient Greek philosopher. Spent his whole life in pursuit of truth.

Philo: (c.20 BC—c. AD 50) A Hellenistic [Greek] Jew and a leading citizen of the Jewish community in Alexandria.... [Philo] was able to find the doctrines of Plato and the Stoics already present in the words of Moses.... Philo is important not only for his use of allegorical interpretation of the [Old Testament], but also because of his attempt to synthesize Greek philosophy with the world of Hebrew Thought. [49]

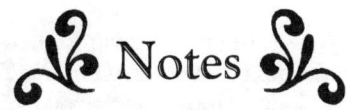 Notes

Chapter 1
Wake Up New York!

1. Douglas J. Soccio, *Archetypes of Wisdom: An Introduction to Philosophy, 2nd ed.,* (New York: Wadsworth Publishing Co., 1995) 4.

2. T. Z. Lavine, *From Socrates to Sartre: The Philosophic Quest* (New York: Bantam, 1984) 60.

3. Peter Rhode ed., *The Diary of Soren Kierkegaard* (New York: Carol, 1993) 25.

4. William J. Bennett, *The De-Valuing of America: The Fight for Our Culture and Our Children* (New York: Summit, 1992) 159-160.

5. T. Z. Lavine, *From Socrates to Sartre: The Philosophic Quest* (New York: Bantam, 1984) 52-53.

6. Haig A. Bosmajian and Hamida Bosmajian, *The Rhetoric of the Civil-Rights Movement* (New York: Random House, 1969) 40-41.

7. James Stockdale, "The World of Epictetus," Atlantic April 1978: 104-105.

8. Harold North Fowler, *Plato: With an English Translation* (London: Harvard University Press, 1966)

400, 402. Translation in this text by John Kotselas *Phaedo 117C - 118E*.

9. Emma J. Edlestein and Ludwig Edelstein, *Asclepius: A Collection and Interpretation of the Testimonies* (Baltimore: Johns Hopkins Press, 1945) 136.

10. Bantam, *The Dialogs of Plato: With an Introduction by Eric Segal* (New York: Bantam, 1986) vii.

11. Peter Rhode ed., *The Diary of Soren Kierkegaard.* (New York: Carol, 1993) 120.

Chapter 2
The Artificial Artist

1. Irving M. Copi and Carl Cohen, *Introduction to Logic*, 9th ed. (New York: Macmillan, 1994) 454.

2. Christof Koch, "What is Consciousness?" *Discover* 13.2 (1992): 95.

3. Peter Radetsky, "How Did Life Start?" *Discover* 13.2 (1992): 74.

4. "10 Great Unanswered Questions of Science?" *Discover* 13.2 (1992): 47.

5. Paul Davies, *God and the New Physics* (New York: Simon & Schuster, 1983) 62.

6. Gerald L. Schroeder Ph.D., *Genesis and the Big Bang: The Discovery of Harmony Between Modern Science and the Bible* (New York: Bantam, 1990) 8.

Chapter 3
The Two Horses

1. Bantam, *The Dialogs of Plato: With an Introduction by Eric Segal* (New York: Bantam, 1986) 91.

2. Gil Elliot, *Twentieth Century Book of the Dead* (New York: Charles Scribner's Sons, 1972) 1.

3. William S. Anderson, *Ovids' Metamorphoses* (Norman: University of Oklahoma Press, 1972) 59. Translation in this text by John Kotselas from Book 7, Lines 21-22.

4. Pomegranate Artbooks, *Einstein a Portrait: With an Introduction by Mark Winokur* (Corte Madera: Pomegranate, 1984) 30.

Chapter 4
Justice

1. A.E. Wardman and J. L. Creed trans., *The Philosophy of Aristotle*, (New York: New American Library, 1963) 286.

2. A.E. Wardman and J. L. Creed trans., *The Philosophy of Aristotle*, (New York: New American Library, 1963) 291.

3. Francis Crick, *The Astonishing Hypothesis: The Scientific Search for the Soul* (New York: Macmillan, 1994) 261.

4. Stephen Priest, *Theories of the Mind* (Boston: Houghton Mifflin, 1991) 2.

5. Bantam, *The Dialogs of Plato: With an Introduction by Eric Segal* (New York: Bantam, 1986) 67-68.

6. Benjamin Jowett trans., *The Republic: Plato* (New York: Vintage, 1991) 44.

7. *ibid.*

8. R. J. Hollingdale trans., *A Nietzsche Reader*, (New York: Penguin, 1977) 40.

Chapter 5
Freedom

1. Eknath Easwaran trans., *The Dhammapada* (Tomales: Nilgiri, 1985) 104.

2. David Ray Griffin et al., *How are God and Evil Related?* (Claremont: The Center for Process Studies, 1988) 2.

3. A. E. Wardman and J. L. Creed trans., *The Philosophy of Aristotle* (New York: New American, 1963) 126.

4. The Presidency of Islamic Researches, IFTA, Call and Guidance, *The Holy Qur-an: English Translation of the Meanings and Commentary* (AL-Madinah AL-Munawarah: The Presidency of Islamic Researches, IFTA, Call and Guidance, 27/10/1405 AH) Surah 4 A 157-159.

5. G. Lee Bowie, et al, *Twenty Questions: An Introduction to Philosophy* (New York: Harcourt Brace Jovanovich, 1992) 49.

6. John W. Bashore Ph.D., *Seneca: Moral Essays* vol. 2 (Cambridge: Harvard, 1928) 251.

7. Friedrich Nietzsche, *Human All Too Human: A Book for Free Spirits,* R. J. Hollingdale trans. (New York: Cambridge, 1986) 305-306.

Chapter 6
Illusion

1. James R. Ware trans., *The Sayings of Chuang Chou*, (New York: New American Library, 1963) 28-29.

2. Paul Shorey, Ph.D., *Plato the Republic: With an English Translation by Paul Shorey* (Cambridge: Harvard University Press, 1963) 118, 120, 122, 124, 128. Paraphrase in this text by John Kotselas 514A - 517A.

3. Pomegranate Artbooks, *Einstein a Portrait: With an Introduction by Mark Winokur* (Corte Madera: Pomegranate, 1984) 94.

4. Friedrich Nietzsche, *Human All Too Human: A Book for Free Spirits,* R. J. Hollingdale trans. (New York: Cambridge, 1986) 215.

Chapter 7
Love

1. Alvin Plantinga ed., *The Ontological Argument: From St. Anslem to Contemporary Philosophers* (Garden: Anchor, 1965) 4-5.

2. Benjamin Jowett trans., *The Republic: Plato* (New York: Vintage, 1991) 281.

3. Douglas J. Soccio, *Archetypes of Wisdom: An Introduction to Philosophy, 2nd ed.,* (New York: Wadsworth Publishing Co., 1995) 487.

4. A. E. Wardman and J. L. Creed trans., *The Philosophy of Aristotle,* (New York: New American Library, 1963) 291.

5. Douglas J. Soccio, *Archetypes of Wisdom: An Introduction to Philosophy* 2nd ed. (Belmont: Wadsworth, 1995) 552.

6. T. Z. Lavine, *From Socrates to Sartre: The Philosophic Quest* (New York: Bantam, 1984) 322.

7. Douglas J. Soccio, *Archetypes of Wisdom: An Introduction to Philosophy* 2nd ed. (Belmont: Wadsworth, 1995) 493.

8. Douglas J. Soccio, *Archetypes of Wisdom: An Introduction to Philosophy* 2nd ed. (Belmont: Wadsworth, 1995) 8-9.

9. *ibid.*, 584.

10. *ibid.*, 583.

11. Peter Pauper, *Francis Bacon: The Essays or Counsels, Civil and Moral, of Francis Ld. Verulam* (New York: Peter Pauper, ND) 65-66.

12. I. Bywater, *Aristotelis: Ethica Nicomachea* (London: Oxford University Press, 1962) 32. Translation in this book by John Kotselas.

Chapter 8
The Veil

1. Robert Wright, "What Does Science Tell Us About God?" *Time* 28 December 1992: 44.

2. George H. Smith, *Atheism: The Case Against God* (Buffalo: Promethous Books, 1979) 76-77.

3. B. B. Kirkbride Bible Co. Inc., *The Thompson Chain-Reference Bible* 5th ed. (Indianapolis: Kirkbride Bible Co. Inc. 1988) Exodus 26:33.

4. B. B. Kirkbride Bible Co. Inc., *The Thompson Chain-Reference Bible* 5th ed. (Indianapolis: Kirkbride Bible Co. Inc. 1988) Hebrews 6:19.

Chapter 9
The Modern Philosopher

1. Wayne Martindale and Jerry Root, eds., *The Quotable Lewis* (Wheaton: Tyndale, 1989) 474.

2. G. Lee Bowie, et al, *Twenty Questions: An Introduction to Philosophy* (New York: Harcourt Brace Jovanovich, 1992) 44.

3. Mortimer Adler, *Ten Philosophical Mistakes* (New York: Macmillan, 1985) 200.

4. Pomegranate Artbooks, *Einstein a Portrait: With an Introduction by Mark Winokur* (Corte Madera: Pomegranate, 1984) 58.

Chapter 10
Divine Love

1. Kenneth J. Gergen, *The Saturated Self: Dilemmas of Identity in Contemporary Life* (New York: HarperCollins, 1991) 122.

2. Sinclair B. Ferguson et al., *New Dictionary of Theology.* (Downers Grove: Inter-Varsity, 1988) 395.

3. B. B. Kirkbride Bible Co. Inc., *The Thompson Chain-Reference Bible* 5th ed. (Indianapolis: Kirkbride Bible Co. Inc. 1988) John 1.

4. A. R. Mowbray & Co., *St. Anthanasius on the Incarnation: The Treatise De Incarnatione Verbi Dei* (London: A. R. Mowbray & Co., 1953)

5. B. B. Kirkbride Bible Co. Inc., *The Thompson Chain-Reference Bible* 5th ed. (Indianapolis: Kirkbride Bible Co. Inc. 1988) John 10:30.

6. B. B. Kirkbride Bible Co. Inc., *The Thompson Chain-Reference Bible* 5th ed. (Indianapolis: Kirkbride Bible Co. Inc. 1988) John 14:9

7. W. R. M. Lamb, MA, *Plato: With an English Translation* (Cambridge: Harvard University Press, 1961) 102.

8. B. B. Kirkbride Bible Co. Inc., *The Thompson Chain-Reference Bible* 5th ed. (Indianapolis: Kirkbride Bible Co. Inc. 1988) John 10:18.

9. Nancy Wilson Ross, *Buddhism: A Way of Life and Thought* (New York: Alfred A. Knopf, 1980) 32.

10. John C. H. Wu trans. Paul K. T. Sih, ed. *Lao Tzu / Tao Teh Ching: Asian Institute Translations, No. 1,* (New York: St. John's, 1961) 17.

11. B. B. Kirkbride Bible Co. Inc., *The Thompson Chain-Reference Bible* 5th ed. (Indianapolis: Kirkbride Bible Co. Inc. 1988) John 15:13.

12. Paul Davies, *God and the New Physics* (New York: Simon & Schuster, 1983) 143.

13. Douglas J. Soccio, *Archetypes of Wisdom: An Introduction to Philosophy* 2nd ed. (Belmont: Wadsworth, 1995) 86.

14. J. A. K. Thomson trans., *The Ethics of Aristotle: The Nicomachean Ethics Translated* (London: George Allen & Unwin Ltd, 1953) 248.

15. B. B. Kirkbride Bible Co. Inc., *The Thompson Chain-Reference Bible* 5th ed. (Indianapolis: Kirkbride Bible Co. Inc. 1988) Romans 5:8.

Chapter 11
Divine Justice

1. T. Z. Lavine, *From Socrates to Sartre: The Philosophic Quest* (New York: Bantam, 1984) 42.

2. Mortimer Adler, *Aristotle for Everybody: Difficult Thought Made Easy* (New York: Bantam, 1980) 109.

3. Benjamin Jowett trans., *The Republic: Plato* (New York: Vintage, 1991) 33.

4. Kenneth J. Gergen, *The Saturated Self: Dilemmas of Identity in Contemporary Life* (New York: HarperCollins, 1991) 124.

5. Wayne A. Meeks, *The First Urban Christians* (New Haven: Yale, 1983) 141.

6. Frederick Copleston, S.J., *A History of Philosophy*, vol. II (New York: Image 1993) 30.

7. Frederick Copleston, S.J., *A History of Philosophy*, vol. II (New York: Image 1993) 26.

8. John Paul II, *Crossing the Threshold of Hope* (New York: Alfred A. Knopf, 1994) 43-44.

9. *ibid.* 42-44.

Chapter 12
The Natural Artist

1. Joseph Campbell, *Occidental Mythology: The Masks of God New York:* Penguin, 1976) 334.

2. Joseph Campbell, *Occidental Mythology: The Masks of God New York:* Penguin, 1976) 362.

3. *ibid* 129.

4. Thomas C. Oden, *John Wesley's Scriptural Christianity* (Grand Rapids: Zondervan, 1994) 79.

5. Joseph Campbell, *The Power of Myth* (New York: Doubleday, 1991) xviii.

6. John Charles Duncan Ph.D., *Astronomy: a Textbook,* 5th ed. (New York: Harper & Brothers, 1955) 2.

7. Mark R. Chartrand, *Skyguide: A Field Guide to the Heavens* (New York: Golden, 1990) 196.

8. B. B. Kirkbride Bible Co. Inc., *The Thompson Chain-Reference Bible* 5th ed. (Indianapolis: Kirkbride Bible Co. Inc. 1988) Matthew 1:23.

9. *ibid* Revelation 5:5

10. Lloyd Motz and Carol Nathanson, *The Constellations* (New York: Doubleday, 1988) xv.

11. William Tyler Olcott, *Star Lore of All Ages* (New York: Putnam, 1911) 3.

12. B. B. Kirkbride Bible Co. Inc., *The Thompson Chain-Reference Bible* 5th ed. (Indianapolis: Kirkbride Bible Co. Inc. 1988) John 4:13.

13. H.A. Rey, *The Stars: A New Way to See Them* (Boston: Houghton Mifflin, 1980) 17.

14. Isidore Singer Ph.D., *The Jewish Encyclopedia* (New York: Funk and Wagnall, 1905) 688.

15. Rachel Hachlili, *Ancient Jewish Art and Archaeology in the Land of Israel* (New York: E. J. Brill, 1988) 356-357.

16. John Greenleaf Whittier, *Poems of Nature: Poems Subjective and Reminiscent: Religious Poems* (Boston and New York: Houghton, Mifflin and Co., 1892) 257.

17. Eileen Reeves, "Augustine and Galileo on Reading the Heavens" *Journal of the History of Ideas* 52.4 (1991): 572.

18. Francis J. Mott, *The Meaning of the Zodiac* (Boston: A. A. Beauchamp, 1941) 96.

19. William Byron Forbush, *Fox's Book of Martyrs* (Grand Rapids: Clarion Classics, 1967) 6-7.

20. B. B. Kirkbride Bible Co. Inc., *The Thompson Chain-Reference Bible* 5th ed. (Indianapolis: Kirkbride Bible Co. Inc. 1988) Acts 17.

21. F. L. Cross and E.A. Livingstone eds., *The Oxford Dictionary of the Christian Church* (New York: Oxford UP, 1990) 405.

22. Benjamin Jowett trans., *The Republic: Plato* (New York: Vintage, 1991) 271-272.

23. Mark R. Chartrand, *Skyguide: A Field Guide to the Heavens* (New York: Golden, 1990) 69.

24. B. B. Kirkbride Bible Co. Inc., *The Thompson Chain-Reference Bible* 5th ed. (Indianapolis: Kirkbride Bible Co. Inc. 1988) Amos 5:8, Job 9:9.

25. Gilbert E. Satterthwaite, *Encyclopedia of Astronomy* (New York: Hamlyn Publishing Group Ltd., 1970) 428.

26. Mark R. Chartrand, *Skyguide: A Field Guide to the Heavens* (New York: Golden, 1990) 156.

27. *ibid*

28. Mark R. Chartrand, *Skyguide: A Field Guide to the Heavens* (New York: Golden, 1990) 118.

29. R. G. Bury, Litt.D., *Plato with an English Translation: IX Laws* (Cambridge: Harvard University Press, 1961) page 561/966 E.

30. B. B. Kirkbride Bible Co. Inc., *The Thompson Chain-Reference Bible* 5th ed. (Indianapolis: Kirkbride Bible Co. Inc. 1988) Psalms 19:1-4.

31. B. B. Kirkbride Bible Co. Inc., *The Thompson Chain-Reference Bible* 5th ed. (Indianapolis: Kirkbride Bible Co. Inc. 1988) Matthew 2:1-12.

32. Mark Hulbert, "How Much is Astrology Worth?," *Forbes* October 1989: 259.

33. Mason Sexton, "Forecast" *Harmonic Research* 4.1 (1988): 1.

34. "The Dow Jones Averages," *Wall Street Journal* 15 January 1988: 44.

35. "Markets Diary," *Wall Street Journal* 4 January 1993: C1.

36. B. B. Kirkbride Bible Co. Inc., *The Thompson Chain-Reference Bible* 5th ed. (Indianapolis: Kirkbride Bible Co. Inc. 1988) Genesis 1:14.

37. Ethebert William Bullinger, *The Witness of the Stars* (Grand Rapids: Kregel, 1967) 177-178.

38. B. B. Kirkbride Bible Co. Inc., *The Thompson Chain-Reference Bible* 5th ed. (Indianapolis: Kirkbride Bible Co. Inc. 1988) Jeremiah 10.

39. *ibid* Psalm 96:5.

40. *ibid* Psalm 97:6-7.

41. *ibid* Isaiah 47:13-14.

42. I. Bywater, *Aristotelis: Ethica Nicomachea* (London: Oxford University Press, 1962) 32. Translation in this book by John Kotselas

43. "The Real Meaning of the Zodiac," with Dr. James Kennedy, *Coral Ridge Ministries,* XETV, San Diego, 8 Dec. 1985.

44. Dr. Gene Scott, *God's Message in the Stars* Delores Press Inc., ND. Delores Press may be reached for further inquiry by calling 1 (800) 338-3030 or by writing to Delores Press Inc. at 1501 South Glendale, Glendale California 91205. You may tune into Dr Scott's program by tuning to Satellite Galaxy 6 Transponder 19 74.2

45. John Kotselas, *Children of the Zodiac* (San Diego: Athena Publishing, 1998). Not yet released.

46. Robert D. Johnston, *Numbers in the Bible: God's Unique Design in Biblical Numbers* (Grand Rapids: Kregel, 1990) 83.

47. Robert Jastrow, *God and the Astronomer* (New York: W.W. Norton & Co. Inc., 1978) 116.

48. Paul Arthur Schilpp ed., *Albert Einstein: Philosopher–Scientist* (Cambridge: Cambridge University Press, 1970) 285.

49. Sinclair B. Ferguson et al., *New Dictionary of Theology.* (Downers Grove: Inter-Varsity, 1988) 509-510.

Order Form

Additional copies of **Socrates In New York** may be ordered directly from Athena Publishing.

To order by telephone please call Toll Free:
1(888)473-3503 24 hours a day 7 days a week. Please have your AMEX, Discover, Visa or MasterCard ready.

To order by Fax: Complete this form and fax to **1(888)473-3502**

To order by mail, write to: Athena Publishing
P.O.box 34424-356
San Diego, CA. 92163-4424

❏ Check ❏ Money Order ❏ Charge
Card # _____
Exp. Date _____

❏ AMEX   ❏ Discover   ❏ Visa   ❏ MasterCard

Name on Card: _____

Signature ✗ _____
(Required for Credit Card orders only)

Name: _____
Address: _____
City: _____ State ____ Zip _____

Shipping:
Please send **$4.00 for** first book **&**
$2.00 for each additional book.

California Residents please add **7.75%** sales tax to your order.

Order Form

Additional copies of **Socrates In New York** may be ordered directly from Athena Publishing.

To order by telephone please call Toll Free:
1(888)473-3503 24 hours a day 7 days a week. Please have your AMEX, Discover, Visa or MasterCard ready.

To order by Fax: Complete this form and fax to **1(888)473-3502**

To order by mail, write to: Athena Publishing
P.O.box 34424-356
San Diego, CA. 92163-4424

❑ Check ❑ Money Order ❑ Charge
Card # _____
Exp. Date _____

❑ AMEX ❑ Discover ❑ Visa ❑ MasterCard

Name on Card: _____

Signature ✘ _____
(Required for Credit Card orders only)

Name: _____
Address: _____
City: _____ State ____ Zip _____

Shipping:
Please send **$4.00 for** first book **&**
$2.00 for each additional book.

California Residents please add **7.75%** sales tax to your order.

MIA GARCIA
888-263-7287
Ex. 22697 96
CAPA-02039509